TODAY in HISTORY

MUSICALS

Joe Stollenwerk

emmis

books

For further information, contact the publisher at:

Emmis Books
1700 Madison Road
Cincinnati, OH 45206
www.emmisbooks.com

Library of Congress Cataloging-in-Publication Data
Stollenwerk, Joe, 1973-
  Today in history : musicals / by Joe Stollenwerk.
     p. cm. -- (Today in history series)
  ISBN-13: 978-1-57860-265-0
  ISBN-10: 1-57860-265-3
  1. Musicals--United States--History and criticism. 2.
Musicals--Chronology. 3. Musicals--Miscellanea. I. Title. II. Series.
  ML2054.S86T63 2006
  782.1'4097471--dc22

                              2006002510

Designed by Carie Adams
Edited by Jessica Yerega

Distributed by Publishers Group West

INTRODUCTION

If you're reading this, you probably like musicals. A lot. Maybe you find yourself humming show tunes while you're at your desk, or you collect recordings of *Gypsy*, or you fall asleep wondering, "Who won the Best Actor in a Musical Tony Award in 1976?" Whatever your particular quirks are, musicals are in your blood.

If you can even believe it, I know some people who don't like musicals. Personally, I feel sorry for them. Yes, musicals *can* be cheesy and cardboard, but so can anything. (And sometimes cheesy is just what you're looking for.) But the thing I love about musicals is that the genre is so vast. In the "musicals" section of my CD shelf I have Rodgers & Hart and Rodgers & Hammerstein; Sondheim and *South Park*; Jerry Herman and Kurt Weill; *Show Boat* and *Avenue Q*; Mary Martin and Marianne Faithfull. No matter what my mood is that day, I've got a musical to fit it.

I will never forget coming to school one day in the fall of 1979; I was in the first grade at Country Parkway Elementary in Buffalo, New York. I could not believe that my classmates weren't buzzing about the incredible television event I had watched the night before: *The Sound of Music*. I had no idea that it was a movie and not a TV show, nor that it was fourteen years old, but that didn't matter. A fan of musicals was born. (My lifelong infatuation with nuns also began at this time, especially when Portia Nelson and Anna Lee stole the Nazis' spark plugs so the von Trapps could escape!)

Perhaps this love of musicals has to be carefully taught. Through my parents, especially my mother, I was exposed to musicals in various forms. I grew up on cast albums of movies like *Grease* and *Hello, Dolly!* and, I hesitate to report, *The Jazz Singer* with Neil Diamond. When I finally saw *Dolly!* on TV, I was simply enthralled by how Barbra

Streisand could whip up an entire town into a production number and get them to board a train for New York City—all just by singing a show tune. Same thing with *The Music Man*—Robert Preston could razzle-dazzle the "River City citizens" to do whatever he wanted them to, and to do it in 4/4 time.

I wore out my parents' Broadway cast record of *A Chorus Line*—but not before it withstood years of scratching and abuse whenever I would put it on and dance around the family room. Dance: 3. Enthusiasm: 10. Listening to people singing about wanting to be in a Broadway musical made me want to do the same. Even though I couldn't really sing as a kid, I loved participating in school and musical choruses.

Finally, in high school I got to play actual *parts* in shows, and thanks to my voice teacher Anne Moss and chorus director Chuck Peery, I did learn to sing a little. It was a thrill to be in some of the shows I'd loved for so long, like *The Music Man* and even *A Chorus Line* (I couldn't—and still can't—dance, but when you're a boy, they are willing to take what they can get).

In high school, I also got to see the national company of *A Chorus Line*, and had a life-altering experience when I saw a local production of *A Little Night Music*. It was my first taste of Sondheim, and I went out and listened to every cast album of his I could get my hands on. Years later, I had the great fortune of working with the director of that show, Dennis Murphy, on a number of musicals.

As an adult, I've been lucky to see some great performances in great musicals—Betty Buckley in *Triumph of Love*; Tommy Tune in *Bye Bye Birdie*; *Elaine Stritch: At Liberty*; Faith Prince in *The King and I*; Stehanie D'Abruzzo in *Avenue Q*. Each one has been what Lily Tomlin would call "a peak experience." When you see a great musical, you carry part of it with you, and on days when everything just seems crappy, you can pull out your program and remember the electric feeling of high notes, story told in song, the audience laughing and applauding together, and the rush that always comes when you realize the show is almost over and you start wishing it would last a little bit longer. And as Yente the Matchmaker might have said, a bad musical, God forbid, is better than no musical, God forbid.

In putting this book together, I'm sure that I've left someone out, and some reader somewhere is going to say, "How could you leave ___ out of a book about musicals?" My apologies in advance: with maybe one exception, I've tried to include everyone. If I missed a few along the way, perhaps it's because there are *so* many people and shows and events that I contemplated including.

A note on setup: This book takes you day by day through a year's worth of the ups and downs in the history of musicals. Each page starts off with a musical-related event that happened on that day. Then, there's a bit of "Broadway Banter," my favorite quotations regarding musicals. And as a daily bonus, you'll find one last factoid or question or item of food for thought: "Casting Couch" tells of the often odd world of casting decisions; "Backstage" dishes about what goes on behind the scenes; "Star Power" puts the spotlight on the leading men and ladies; "It Takes a Village" focuses on the creators of musicals— writers, directors, and producers; "By the Numbers" lists the cold hard facts; "Also on This Day" and "Pop Quiz" expand your knowledge of musicals trivia.

In addition to all the people I named above, I want to thank my friends and relatives who encouraged me during the writing of this book—keeping me excited about it, suggesting bits of trivia, making me feel far more important than I really am, or helpfully saying, "Don't you think you should be farther along now?" Also, special thanks to my friend Jon Vater, who introduced me to many of the camp classics I've written about here. Finally, my biggest thanks to Jack Heffron and especially Jessica Yerega for the opportunity to write this book.

I hope you enjoy this book as much as I've enjoyed researching and writing it. I thought I knew a lot about musicals before embarking on this endeavor, but the genre is so vast that I ended up adding a lot to my personal repertoire of cocktail party trivia! I hope you do too, and that it influences you to buy some new CDs or explore a new singer or composer. I welcome your comments or questions: Feel free to e-mail me at todayinmusicals@yahoo.com. And—most important—after you read this, go see a musical. See you at the theater!

JANUARY

Ginger Rogers and Warner Baxter in the 1933 film *42nd Street*.

1

January

(1937) All Talking! All Singing! All Skating? Before *Starlight Express*, the musical sensation on skates was Sonja Henie, who made her debut on this day on movie screens across America in *One in a Million*. Henie, a Norwegian skater who had won three Olympic gold medals in figure skating, chose to stretch her acting chops by playing a Swiss Olympic figure skater. Henie was a hit, and went on to make numerous similar ice musicals.

broadway banter

"The musical blows the dust off your soul."
—Mel Brooks

STAR POWER

Elizabeth Swados wrote an adaptation of *Alice in Wonderland* called *Alice at the Palace*. The bizarre 1981 off-Broadway musical starred Meryl Streep as Alice, as well as Debbie Allen, Mark Linn-Baker, Michael Jeter, and Deborah Rush.

January

(1972) Taye Diggs, born today, may have risen to fame by playing Winston in *How Stella Got Her Groove Back*, but he's really just a Broadway Baby at heart. He made his Broadway debut in the 1994 revival of *Carousel*, then went on to play Benjamin "Benny" Coffin III in the original production of *Rent*, a role he reprised in the 2005 film. Along the way, he married his *Rent* costar, Idina Menzel, whom he would also appear opposite in *The Wild Party* and *Wicked*. He also appeared in the stage and screen versions of *Chicago*, playing the Bandleader in the latter.

broadway banter

"God bless the theater. And please let there be a way for it to thrive ... forever."

–Carol Burnett

CASTING COUCH

Barbra Streisand auditioned to take over the role of Liesl in the original Broadway production of *The Sound of Music.* She didn't get it.

(1952) Wild again, beguiled again: Jule Styne revived a production of Rodgers and Hart's *Pal Joey* that opened today on Broadway. The show was only twelve years old, having bowed in 1940 with Gene Kelly in the title role; the dark and cynical show was better appreciated by the critics this time around. Helen Gallagher won a Tony for playing the chorus girl Gladys Bumps; she would later be replaced by Nancy Walker. Vivienne Segal was bewitched, bothered, and bewildered for the second time as Vera, and singing the scene-stealing striptease number "Zip" was the young Elaine Stritch.

January

broadway banter

"I had a role–I didn't come in until the second act, supposedly–it wasn't much of a part. By the time Pal Joey *opened in Philadelphia, I had five numbers of my own–I had a great role!"*

–June Havoc, the original 1940 Gladys Bumps

STAR POWER

Gloria Swanson, the silent film star who would later play Norma Desmond in *Sunset Boulevard*, sang in a number of early talkies, including the musical *Music on the Air.*

4

January

(1962) When your parents are Shirley Jones and Tony-winner Jack Cassidy, you're destined for a musical life: Patrick Cassidy was born today. In early life, he was overshadowed by his *Partridge Family/Hardy Boys* brothers, Shaun and David. But Patrick came into his own on the stage. He played the Balladeer in the original off-Broadway production of *Assassins,* and went on to appear in *Aida, Annie Get Your Gun,* and— playing opposite his mother—*42nd Street.*

broadway banter

"I'm telling you, the only times I really feel the presence of God are when I'm having sex, and during a great Broadway musical!"

–Father Dan, in Paul Rudnick's Jeffrey

BACKSTAGE

Oklahoma! was filmed on location in ... Arizona, because Oklahoma itself was too developed to give the feel of the turn of the century.

January

(1975) *The Wiz* eased on down the road for the first time today. This updated, downtown retelling of *The Wizard of Oz* would run for more than four years on Broadway, featuring the talents of Stephanie Mills, Andre De Shields, Hinton Battle, Dee Dee Bridgewater, and, making her Broadway debut as a munchkin, *The Cosby Show*'s Phylicia Rashad (then Phylicia Ayers-Allen).

In 1978, a turgid film version would be released, starring Diana Ross as the world's oldest Dorothy, with supporting performances from Lena Horne, Richard Pryor, Nipsey Russell, and the then-black Michael Jackson.

broadway banter

Connie: We gotta go ... somewhere where they'd never look for us because there's no theatre, no musical theatre, no dinner theatre, no culture at all.

Carla: Los Angeles.

–Connie and Carla, *written by Nia Vardalos*

STAR POWER

Deborah Kerr lost twelve pounds while filming *The King and I* because of the weight of the period costumes.

6

January

(1963) Starving orphans, thieves, a woman who gets murdered by the man she loves ... a recipe for a musical comedy hit? Apparently. *Oliver!* opened on Broadway, adapted from Charles Dickens's novel and paving the way for such starving-orphan-and-thieves shows as *Annie* and *Les Miserables*. The hit song "As Long as He Needs Me" provided many a female singer with a torch song for her cabaret act, and feminist scholars with fodder for studies on women and violence in musical theater.

broadway banter

"Why did they have to screw up a perfectly serviceable wagon story with all that fruity singing?"

—Homer Simpson, *after renting* Paint Your Wagon
on an episode of The Simpsons

CASTING COUCH

The first choice for the role of Peggy Sawyer in *42ⁿᵈ Street* was Loretta Young.

(1943) In the midst of war, the patriotic *Something for the Boys* opened today. Despite the suggestive wit of Cole Porter, the voice of Ethel Merman, and an upbeat World War II score featuring the lyric, "By the Miss-iss-iss-iss-iss-iss-iss-innewah," *Boys* would become only a modest success, running for one year and one day.

January

broadway banter

"You do an eclectic celebration of the dance! You do Fosse, Fosse, Fosse! You do Martha Graham, Martha Graham, Martha Graham! Or Twyla, Twyla, Twyla! Or Michael Kidd, Michael Kidd, Michael Kidd, Michael Kidd! Or Madonna, Madonna, Madonna! ... but you keep it all inside."

—Armand in The Birdcage, by Elaine May

BACKSTAGE

In its original showings in Austria and Germany, the final third of *The Sound of Music* was cut completely, giving the film a Nazi-free and far less dramatic ending.

8
January

(1935) Some say that *Hair* ushered in the era of the rock musical, but they forget that Elvis Presley, born today, sang in numerous fifties' and sixties' film rock-and-roll musicals like *Love Me Tender*, *Viva Las Vegas*, and *Girls! Girls! Girls!* If mothers were afraid of their children seeing Elvis shake his pelvis on a tiny black-and-white TV set, they would have fainted seeing it on the big screen in Technicolor. If you look closely at Elvis in his break out role in *Jailhouse Rock*, you'll see that the number on his prison uniform changes from 6239 to 6240.

Nearly thirty years after his death, Elvis even spawned his own musical: *All Shook Up*, which flopped on Broadway in a big way in 2005.

broadway banter

"There are no tricks. It's just sheer honesty."

–Ann Reinking

STAR POWER

Before he made it big with a string of hits of Frank Capra, James Stewart warbled the Cole Porter tune "Easy to Love" in *Born to Dance*.

9

January

(2006) Shakespeare once wrote "it out-Herods Herod," and today, Andrew Lloyd Webber "out-Webbered" himself. *The Phantom of the Opera* played its 7,486th performance, becoming the longest-running show in Broadway history, breaking the record held by *Cats. Phantom* also launched more popular tunes than perhaps any other musical of its generation, including "Music of the Night" and "All I Ask of You."

broadway banter

"*See* Jekyll & Hyde: *perfect for people who find Andrew Lloyd Webber's music too challenging.*"
—*Announcer in* Forbidden Broadway Cleans Up Its Act,
by Gerard Alessandrini

BY THE NUMBERS

The longest-running Broadway Musical as of:

Year	Show	# of performances
1945	*Irene*	670
1955	*Oklahoma!*	2,212
1965	*My Fair Lady*	2,717
1975	*Hello, Dolly!*	2,844
1985	*A Chorus Line*	4,738
1995	*A Chorus Line*	6,137
2005	*Cats*	7,485

10

January

(1904) Ray Bolger, born today, readily admitted that his main legacy was his performance as the Scarecrow in *The Wizard of Oz*. But Bolger turned in a slew of other stellar musical performances, primarily on stage, as the lead dancer in *On Your Toes*, creating George Balanchine's "Slaughter on Tenth Avenue" ballet, *Life Begins at 8:40*, *By Jupiter*, and his Tony Award-winning *Where's Charley?*

broadway banter

"When was the last time Barbra Streisand cleaned out your garage? And when it's time to do the dishes, where's Ray Bolger? I'll tell you. Ray Bolger is looking after Ray Bolger."

—Homer Simpson on The Simpsons

IT TAKES A VILLAGE

The original lyricist for *Man of La Mancha* was poet W. H. Auden.

11
January

(2000) A Christmas musical that opened in January? Only with a title like *James Joyce's The Dead*. The show actually takes place on the Epiphany, which is January 6, but nonetheless, the story concerns an Irish Christmas party given by three spinster sisters. The result was better than it might sound, and even won a Tony for Best Book of a Musical.

The cast included faded musical performers of yesteryear Marni Nixon, Sally Ann Howes, and Daisy Eagan; one-time Siamese twins Alice Ripley and Emily Skinner; and unlikely singers Blair Brown, Stephen Spinella, and Christopher Walken. Walken, before he became a *Saturday Night Live* spoof, was actually an accomplished musical performer, and can be seen tapping up a storm in the 1981 film *Pennies from Heaven*.

broadway banter

> "The darndest things can happen on stage and people think it's part of the show."
>
> —Carol Channing

STAR POWER

Bing Crosby starred in both the 1936 and 1956 film versions of *Anything Goes*, neither of which was terribly faithful to the original stage production.

12
January

(1946) Perennial song and dance man Andre De Shields was born today. His first big Broadway break came with the title role in the original production of *The Wiz*, and from there he went on to *Ain't Misbehavin'*, *Stardust*, and *Play On!* In 2000, he scored a huge hit playing Noah "Horse" Simmons in the stage musical adaptation of *The Full Monty*, copping his second Tony nomination.

More than a mere performer, in 1984 he also wrote, choreographed, directed, starred in (and probably handed out programs for) *André de Shield's Haarlem Nocturne*.

broadway banter

"You know what Kate Smith used to say about a bad rehearsal. Usually means a bad performance."

—Jeanette in The Full Monty, *lyrics by David Yazbek*

POP QUIZ

Q: What was the first musical to win the New York Drama Critics' Circle Award?

A: *Carousel*

(1925) Gwen Verdon was born today, and in the era of Merman and Martin, she managed to snag four Tony Awards, including three for Best Leading Actress between 1956 and 1959. As she approached middle age, her partner in crime and sometimes husband Bob Fosse created two star vehicles for her: *Sweet Charity* and *Chicago*.

Unfortunately, Verdon had only one shot at a big movie musical: recreating the role of Lola in *Damn Yankees*. She would get the chance, however, to entrance moviegoers in later life with *Marvin's Room* and the *Cocoon* movies.

13
January

broadway banter

"*Sing out, Louise! Sing out!*"

—*Rose in* Gypsy, *by Arthur Laurents*

STAR POWER

Prior to her breakout role in *Can-Can*, Gwen Verdon trained Marilyn Monroe and Jane Russell for their dance numbers in *Gentlemen Prefer Blondes*.

14
January

(1904) Cecil Beaton was born, and had he done nothing else, he would be remembered today for his sumptuous costume designs for the stage and film versions of *My Fair Lady*, also serving as complete production designer for the latter. All told, his work on *My Fair Lady* netted him a Tony and two Oscars.

Beaton's career was long on quality but low on quantity. He designed only a dozen or so other films and stage productions, including the film *Gigi* (another Oscar) and Broadway's *Saratoga* and *Tenderloin*. His last original work for the stage was *Coco*, the musical biography of Coco Chanel, for which he designed dozens of "Chanel" gowns.

broadway banter

"We've been doing this for years. We even dubbed Rin-Tin-Tin."

—*Studio head Jack Warner on casting Audrey Hepburn in* My Fair Lady, *then dubbing her singing with Marni Nixon*

BACKSTAGE ————————————

Jack Warner gave away tickets to the New York premier of *Yankee Doodle Dandy* in exchange for the purchase of bonds to support the war effort. Many seats were bought for as much as $25,000 in war bonds a piece, and Warner raised almost $6 million for the U.S. Treasury during World War II.

15
January

(1911) If you were to describe Cy Feuer, born today, in just one word, it would have to be "prolific." He began his career in Hollywood, serving as a composer, songwriter, and/or musical director for nearly two hundred movies between 1938 and 1947. Then, he took off for Broadway, where he would win four Tony Awards for producing such musical hits as *Where's Charley?*, *Guys and Dolls*, *Can-Can*, *Silk Stockings*, and *How to Succeed in Business Without Really Trying*.

Sadly, Feuer's last two outings as producer were his two biggest flops: 1979's Broadway musicalization of *I Remember Mama* (starring Liv Ullman and featuring Richard Rodgers's final score), and 1985's misguided film version of *A Chorus Line*.

broadway banter

"As Joan Crawford once said, 'I'll show ya a pair of Golden Globes!'"

—Bette Midler, after winning two Globes for The Rose

CASTING COUCH

Richard Beymer couldn't sing or dance and could barely act, but other original choices for the role of Tony in *West Side Story* were even odder: Marlon Brando, Elvis Presley, Paul Anka, Frankie Avalon, and Fabian.

16
January

(1964) *Hello, Dolly!* opened on Broadway today, and though the show became one of the biggest smash hits of all time, its road to Broadway was bumpy. With its original title of *A Damned Exasperating Woman*, it's not hard to believe. Jerry Herman wrote the score for Ethel Merman, but she didn't want to take on another long-running show right after *Gypsy*. When Ethel turned him down, he dropped two of the show's songs. Enter Carol Channing, who would play the role the rest of her life. Herman ended up cutting more numbers, getting a few uncredited assists, and writing "Before the Parade Passes By" at practically the last minute.

Merman would ultimately become the final Dolly Levi in the show's original Broadway run.

broadway banter

"Too Commercial? What is that? ... I love the word commercial."

—*Jerry Herman*

BACKSTAGE

Kiss Me, Kate played on Broadway with a comma in the title, but when made into a film, it became *Kiss Me Kate,* sans comma.

17

January

(1908) If the Broadway musical had to be reduced to one icon, it might very well be this one: Ethel Merman, who was born today. "Merm" didn't achieve legend status just by starring in numerous hits spanning some forty years, including *Annie Get Your Gun, Anything Goes, Call Me Madam, Gypsy,* and *Hello, Dolly!,* though that didn't hurt. More important, Ethel changed the way Broadway singers sang: With her performance of "I Got Rhythm" in *Girl Crazy,* she all but invented "belting." She introduced the sound that Broadway divas for generations following would emulate.

broadway banter

"Ethel did not just sing loudly ... Ethel Merman sang incisively, hitting her notes like a gong. The sound then reverberated all through the theater."

–Geoffrey Mark

STAR POWER

In the original production of *Show Boat,* the black role of Queenie was played by Tess Gardella, a white actress whose blackface stage name was "Aunt Jemima."

18
January

(1998) *Ragtime* opened on Broadway at producer Garth Drabinsky's new theater, the Ford Center for the Performing Arts. The show was a critical and box office hit, but shortly after opening, Drabinsky's company Livent filed for bankruptcy amidst various rumors of scandals.

Ragtime, however, endured on Broadway for two more years, netting Tonys for its writers, orchestrator, and perennial Best Featured Actress winner, Audra McDonald.

broadway banter

"Floatation devices have been placed under your seats, should the actors appear to be in over their heads."

–Stewardess in Forbidden Broadway 2001: A Spoof Odyssey, *by*
Gerard Alessandrini

BACKSTAGE

On the Town, partially filmed on location in New York City, was the first movie musical to shoot musical numbers on location.

19

January

(1917) If you've ever seen anything about musicals on television, you've seen John Raitt, born today, in *Carousel*. Before he became a clip in a montage, Raitt blew the roof off the Majestic Theater, making his Broadway debut at age twenty-six with one of the quintessential musical theater songs, Billy Bigelow's "Soliloquy."

Raitt's career post-*Carousel*, though, was marked by a string of flops—*Three Wishes for Jamie* (92 performances), *Magdalena* (88 performances), and worst yet, *Carnival in Flanders* (6 performances). In 1954, however, Raitt finally received a worthy if lightweight vehicle for his talents, *The Pajama Game*, which he got to reprise in the film version. Oh—and along the way he fathered a singer by the name of Bonnie.

broadway banter

"Carousel *seemed to us a rather long evening. The* Oklahoma! *format is becoming a bit monotonous, and so are Miss de Mille's ballets.*"

—Wilella Waldorf

IT TAKES A VILLAGE

Tony Walton was hired as costume designer for his first film, *Mary Poppins*, largely because he was married to its star, Julie Andrews.

20

January

(2002) The movie musical is reborn: *Moulin Rouge* won three Golden Globe awards today. An unlikely summer hit, the film showed the world what Ewan McGregor, Nicole Kidman, and Jim Broadbent can do with a handful of twentieth-century pop tunes. The night of the Globes, it won Best Musical/Comedy, Best Actress for Kidman, and—in an odd twist given that most of its music was not original—Best Original Score. Amazingly, one of the film's only original tunes, "Come What May," lost Best Song to *Kate and Leopold*'s "Until."

When Oscar nominations were announced a few weeks later, the film got eight nods, but nothing for "Come What May." Since it was originally written for another Baz Luhrmann film, *William Shakespeare's Romeo + Juliet*, the Academy ruled it ineligible, even though it had been cut from the film and never released.

broadway banter

"I have four notes, two of them good."

—Cyril Ritchard

CASTING COUCH

Chicago stars Renee Zellweger and Catherine Zeta-Jones were both considered for Nicole Kidman's role in *Moulin Rouge!*.

(2003) *Camp* premiered today at the Sundance Film Festival. Director Todd Graff based the screenplay on his own experiences as a kid going to musical theater camp. The movie features memorable performances of teens tackling decidedly adult material ranging from *Follies* to *Company* and *Dreamgirls* to *Promises, Promises.*

21
January

broadway banter

"My major memory of my teens is when Oscar took me to New Haven to see the first night of Carousel. *I was so moved at the end of the first act that I cried into Dorothy Hammerstein's fur—she had this good-luck fur she always wore—and you know tears can stain fur, and I think she was never able to use it again because I was bawling so heavily. But I remember the way the stage looked at the end of the first act and I was just awash."*

—Stephen Sondheim

POP QUIZ

Q: What was the first Oscar-winning song from an animated Disney film?

A: "When You Wish Upon a Star," *Pinocchio,* 1940

22
January

(1904) Everything was beautiful at the ballet: George Balanchine was born today. Born Georgy Melitonovich Balanchivadze, Balanchine made his first major contribution to Broadway with *Ziegfeld Follies of 1936*, directing its ballets. He then teamed up with Rodgers and Hart, choreographing their shows *Babes in Arms*, *The Boys from Syracuse*, and *On Your Toes*, including the groundbreaking "Slaughter on Tenth Avenue" ballet.

He also married two of his dancing stars from *Toes*—Tamara Geva and Vera Zorina—who played the female lead Vera Barnova in the 1936 and 1954 productions, respectively. Interestingly, he directed both women after he had been divorced from them for a number of years.

broadway banter

"Oh, please—I don't want to hear about how Broadway's dying. 'Cause I just got here."

—Bebe in A Chorus Line, by James Kirkwood and Nicholas Dante

BACKSTAGE

Meet Me in St. Louis was based on the reminiscences of Sally Benson; the film even kept the same names of the Benson family members and their same address.

(1941) *Show Boat* and *Oklahoma!* get most of the credit for advancing the musical form, but sharing some of that credit should also be *Lady in the Dark*, which opened on Broadway today. With music by Kurt Weill, lyrics by Ira Gershwin, and book and direction by Moss Hart, *Lady* centered on the psychoanalysis of career woman Liza Elliott, played by Gertrude Lawrence. Created as a star vehicle for Lawrence, she was nearly upstaged by relative newcomer Danny Kaye, who tongue-twisted his way through some fifty Russian composers' names in the showstopper "Tschaikowsky."

23
January

When it was filmed in 1944 with Ginger Rogers, only one song from the stage show was kept: "The Saga of Jenny."

broadway banter

"Offstage, she was one of the least good-looking stars there was ... [but] onstage, with the lighting and costumes, Gertrude Lawrence was a presence."

—Morton Gottlieb

STAR POWER

Muhammad Ali starred in the musical *Buck White* in 1969; it lasted all of seven performances.

24

January

(1936) The film version of the smash stage hit *Anything Goes* premiered, though you might not have recognized it as such. As was often the case back in the day, the studio paid for the rights to the production, then threw out much of the score. Studio execs built up Bing Crosby's role by replacing or altering most of Cole Porter's classic, witty tunes with songs by a variety of other songwriters. And Ethel Merman got to reprise a few of her big hits, including "I Get a Kick out of You" and the title number.

broadway banter

"Don't you get rather depressed by films about drug addicts? I do. If we have to have films about drug addicts, why can't they be musicals, I mean it would be so much more cheerful?"

—Hermione Gingold *in* Sticks and Stones

IT TAKES A VILLAGE

"Say a Prayer for Me Tonight," sung by Leslie Caron in the film *Gigi*, was actually written for another Lerner and Loewe musical: *My Fair Lady*. It was cut during tryouts.

(1996) The musical *Rent* played its first preview performance off-Broadway today, and, tragically, its creator Jonathan Larson died suddenly of an undiagnosed aortic aneurysm at the age of thirty-five. Larson's legacy, a topical, visceral rock opera, opened a few weeks later to universal acclaim, and quickly transferred to Broadway, becoming the biggest hit of the 1990s and winning numerous Tony Awards, including two for its late creator.

January

Its successful nine-year-plus run on Broadway, several national tours, and film version have not made this Pulitzer Prize-winning hit immune from satire. Gerard Alessandrini spoofed it in his off-Broadway revue *Forbidden Broadway*, retitling it *Rant* and revising its song titles to "Too Gay for You, Too Hetero for Me," "Seasons of Hype," and "This Ain't Boheme."

broadway banter

"It took Johnny fifteen years of really hard work to become an overnight sensation."

—Julie Larson, accepting the Tony Award for
Rent *for her deceased brother, Jonathan Larson*

CASTING COUCH

The first choice for Gene Kelly's animated dance partner in *Anchors Aweigh* was Mickey Mouse, but Walt Disney wouldn't release his number-one "actor" to do an MGM picture.

26

January

(1988) The music of the night began: *The Phantom of the Opera* opened on Broadway. And as of this writing, it shows no signs of closing: With more than 7,500 performances, it is now the longest-running show in Broadway history. Michael Crawford and Sarah Brightman (then Mrs. Lloyd Webber) made their Broadway musical debuts with this show, and to date, each has returned to the Great White Way only once: Crawford in the laughably terrible *Dance of the Vampires*, and Brightman as a replacement cast member in Lloyd Webber's *Aspects of Love*.

broadway banter

"*Andrew Lloyd Webber's new musical is, he says, 'about a man who is hideously ugly who falls hopelessly in love with this girl and is only able to express himself through his music.' Only those of a very cruel frame of mind would suggest the musical was at all autobiographical.*"

—David Shannon

STAR POWER

Vivien Leigh, best known for her Oscar-winning portrayals of Southern belles, won a Tony for Best Actress in a Musical for *Tovarich*.

27

January

(1885) Just the way you look tonight: Jerome Kern was born today. He made his Broadway debut at nineteen, contributing songs to *Mr. Wix of Wickham*, and went on to write songs for some fifty Broadway productions, including *Sally, Very Good Eddie, Roberta, The Ziegfeld Follies*, and most famously, *Show Boat*. Kern then made his mark in Hollywood, contributing songs to numerous movies, including *Swing Time, Lady Be Good*, and *Cover Girl*.

MGM paid him tribute by filming a highly fictionalized musical biopic, *Till the Clouds Roll By*. Robert Walker starred as Kern, and many of MGM's top musical stars did specialty numbers, including Judy Garland, Lena Horne, Frank Sinatra, and Cyd Charisse. Kern himself, however, died of a stroke before filming began, and the script had to be rewritten.

broadway banter

"If this Peter Bogdanovich fiasco were any more of a dog, it would shed."

–John Barbour, on At Long Last Love

BACKSTAGE

One of the dancing orphans in the film *Annie* was Sabrina Mar, who went on to become a U.S. gymnastics champion and, later, an animator for *South Park*.

28

January

(1988) *Sarafina!* opened on Broadway, another musical with an unlikely topic: Apartheid and the Soweto riots of 1976. Written and directed by Mbongeni Ngema, the unconventional musical featured a cast of unknown South African students. The political show became a surprise hit, running for a year and a half and winning five Tony nominations. In 1992, *Sarafina!* became a film, losing much of its score and changing the plot in order to become more of a vehicle for Whoopi Goldberg.

broadway banter

"All of you kids on the Upper West Side watching this on television: Stick with it, it could happen to you!"

—Gary Beach, *accepting his Tony for* The Producers

IT TAKES A VILLAGE

After losing fifteen times, Randy Newman finally won an Oscar for his song "If I Didn't Have You" from *Monsters, Inc.*

January

(1959) It's considered a lesser work, but it was Walt Disney's favorite of his animated films: *Sleeping Beauty* premiered today. Personally, I think you'd have to look far and wide to find a better villain than Maleficent, the evil fairy queen who ultimately transforms herself into a dragon.

Sleeping Beauty's classical score, which was largely adapted from Tchaikovsky's ballet of the same name, and painstaking animation—far more detailed than most other cartoons of the time—make the film a fitting companion for Disney's other misunderstood labor of love, *Fantasia*.

broadway banter

"I do wish Alfred Drake could have one big song number with a lot of sock to it–for instance, something titled 'My Heart Belongs to Baghdaddy.'"

–John Chapman on Kismet

CASTING COUCH

When *Porgy and Bess* was being written, Al Jolson campaigned hard to play Porgy.

30
January

(1928) If Hal Prince, born today, lined up all his Tonys, they would stretch to the moon. Well, not literally. But he holds a record twenty Tony Awards for directing and producing shows throughout a Broadway career that's lasted some fifty years. His track record includes many of the classics of musical theater, including *West Side Story*, *Fiddler on the Roof*, *Cabaret*, *Company*, *Sweeney Todd*, *Evita*, and *The Phantom of the Opera*.

But, as with Babe Ruth, when you hit the most home runs, you also end up with the most strikeouts. Among Prince's fabulous flops were *Grind* (seventy-one performances), *Merrily We Roll Along* (sixteen), *Roza* (twelve), and *A Doll's Life* (the musical sequel to *A Doll's House*, if you can believe it, five performances).

broadway banter

"I can't believe I just shook Hal Prince's hand!"

—John Rando, *accepting his Tony for Best Director for* Urinetown

IT TAKES A VILLAGE

When Hal Prince took on the task of directing *Evita,* he originally wanted to have three different actresses play the title role.

(1921) Hello, Carol! Carol Channing, whose name was selected by her father for maximum impact in newspaper headlines, was born today.

Channing has the rare distinction of having not one but two career-making roles: Lorelei Lee in *Gentlemen Prefer Blondes* and Dolly Levi in *Hello, Dolly!* She would return to both roles throughout her long career. However, she also has the unenviable distinction of having had both those roles in the film versions given to more bankable stars, both of whom were as different as could be from the wide-eyed baritone Channing: Marilyn Monroe in *Gentlemen* and Barbra Streisand in *Dolly.*

31
January

broadway banter

"I am not making an ass out of myself alone. If I do this number, we all do this number!"

—*Stella Deems in* Follies, *by James Goldman*

STAR POWER

Carol Channing once appeared on Nixon's enemies list.

FEBRUARY

Liza Minnelli as Sally Bowles in the 1972 film *Cabaret*.

February

(1860) Bridging the era of Viennese operettas and early American musical comedies, Victor Herbert was born today. Although he wrote dozens of operettas and light operas in the first two decades of the twentieth century, he's best known by modern audiences for Madeline Kahn's hilarious rendition of his "Ah! Sweet Mystery of Life" in the Mel Brooks film *Young Frankenstein*. The operetta for which the song was originally written, *Naughty Marietta*, also became a smash film success for Jeanette MacDonald and Nelson Eddy.

broadway banter

"The Broadway musical is America's cultural gift to the performing arts. The Viennese may have given us the form, but we have taken the musical and made it an international art."

—Lawrence Kasha

ALSO ON THIS DAY

Hildegarde Loretta Sill was born in 1906. Known as "The Incomparable Hildegarde," this singer is credited with starting the trend of star "mononyms," which later gave us Cher, Madonna, etc. A star throughout the 1930s and '40s, she later appeared in Sondheim's *Follies* and performed into her nineties.

2 February

(1925) The mother of the ladies who lunch was born today: Elaine Stritch. She may not have become a household name of the magnitude of Merman or Martin, but she has stritched her way through some sixty years of Broadway musicals, working with legends like Richard Rodgers, Noel Coward, and Stephen Sondheim.

Stritch, or Stritchie, as Coward called her, has had her share of flops (*Goldilocks*), failures (getting fired from a stock production of *The Women*), and missed opportunities (losing the role of Dorothy on *The Golden Girls*), all of which she frankly discussed in her Tony-winning one-woman show, *Elaine Stritch: At Liberty*.

broadway banter

"I was having a musical comedy nightmare. They were going to revive West Side Story *with Robert Goulet and Cher. We've got to stop them!"*

–Buzz in Terrence McNally's Love! Valour! Compassion!

POP QUIZ

Q: What is a "sitzprobe"?

A: An unstaged sing-through of a show putting actors and orchestra together for the first time, a.k.a. a "sitting rehearsal."

(1956) From Pseudolus to Max Bialystock, Starina the drag queen to Timon the meerkat ... Nathan Lane was born today. Actually, Joseph Lane was born today, but since another actor in Equity already had that name, Lane was forced to choose another when he joined the union. Having just played Nathan Detroit in *Guys and Dolls,* he picked Nathan, and it must have been a good choice: His first Tony nomination would come a few years later for playing that same role on Broadway.

February

broadway banter

"This means a lot to me because, as you know, I'm an enormously unstable, desperately needy little man."

—Nathan Lane, accepting his first Tony Award

CASTING COUCH

Frank Sinatra was the film producer's original choice to play Harold Hill in *The Music Man.*

4
February

(1982) *Pump Boys and Dinettes* opened on Broadway, and all across America, a cheer went up from community theaters and summer stock companies, as they would now have a guaranteed money-making show to run every few years. This entertaining yet innocuous revue was set in a filling station and diner off "Highway 57" and is quite possibly the original white trash musical, featuring such catchy songs as "Fisherman's Prayer," "Drinkin' Shoes," "Farmer Tan," and "The Night Dolly Parton Was Almost Mine."

Original cast member and co-author Debra Monk later went on to become the busiest supporting actress on Broadway in the 1990s (*Steel Pier, Company*) and played a few dozen party-favor-sized roles in movies (*Jeffrey, The Producers*).

broadway banter

"You have to find the right agent. Signing with an agent is like a marriage. It's a relationship."

—Jeffrey Dunn

ALSO ON THIS DAY

Eddie Foy Jr. was born, one of "the Seven Little Foys" as a child. He went on to star on Broadway in *The Red Mill, Rumple,* and most notably, *The Pajama Game* (also on film).

5

February

(1959) When a group of top musical theater talent gets together, the result is almost always either a huge hit or a memorable flop. But on this day, Bob Fosse, Dorothy Fields, Gwen Verdon, and Richard Kiley got together and opened *Redhead* on Broadway: a modest "whodunit" musical that became a modest hit. The show won seven Tonys, but mostly because this was the weakest season for musicals in "the golden age." The show was most notable for bringing Verdon her fourth Tony in five years, and for the directorial debut of choreographer Fosse.

The show's co-author, Sidney Sheldon, later achieved some small fame as a novelist, and its composer, Albert Hague, went on to play music teacher Mr. Shorofsky in the film and TV show *Fame*.

broadway banter

"What I love most about song writing is when I overhear a truck driver humming a song of Johnnie's and mine."

—Fred Ebb

CASTING COUCH

In the film *Tommy*, the original choice to play the Acid Queen was David Bowie.

6

February

(1969) *Dear World*, an adaptation of Jean Giraudoux's French fantasy *The Madwoman of Chaillot*, opened on Broadway. The delicacy and magic of Giraudoux's original were not terribly well suited to the brassy musical comedy songwriting style of Jerry Herman. Moreover, audiences who had just seen Angela Lansbury in *Mame* had difficulty accepting her as an eighty-year-old madwoman. Despite a few nice moments and a knockout, Tony-winning performance from Lansbury, the show flopped.

broadway banter

"With its eye-shattering cobalt blue fiberglass set and nauseating poster, Footloose *has the look of a winner of minus three Tony Awards."*

–Mary Dennin, *"phony theater critic," in*
Forbidden Broadway Cleans Up Its Act, *by Gerard Alessandrini*

IT TAKES A VILLAGE

Andrew Lloyd Webber's first choice for the lyricist for *The Phantom of the Opera* was the sixty-six-year-old Alan Jay Lerner. After beginning work on the show, he had to withdraw because of health issues.

February

(1940) When You Wish Upon a Star ... *Pinocchio* premiered. Though it won two Oscars for its music, it was a box-office flop. Ned Washington, who co-wrote the songs with Leigh Harline and Paul J. Smith, later went on to write the theme to TV's *Rawhide*.

In her first farewell concert, Barbra Streisand said this was one of her favorite Disney movies ... perhaps because of the nasal similarities between the diva and the film's title character?

broadway banter

"Three of the most talented people our theater possesses—Lillian Hellman, Leonard Bernstein, Tyrone Guthrie—have joined hands to transform Voltaire's Candide *into a really spectacular disaster."*

—Walter Kerr

BACKSTAGE

After the forgettable "Sweet Leilani" from *Waikiki Wedding* won Best Song, the Academy changed the voting rules so that the thousands of screen extras were no longer eligible to vote in that category.

8

February

(1965) Two of the last movie musicals of the golden era went head to head for the first time at the Golden Globe Awards. In one corner, weighing in with four nominations, but none for any of its original songs, *Mary Poppins*. And in the other corner, weighing in with five nominations, including one for Audrey Hepburn, *My Fair Lady*. *MFL* would triumph for Best Musical/Comedy, Director, and Actor for Rex Harrison, a feat it would duplicate at the Oscars two months later, while Julie Andrews was the only winner for *Poppins*.

broadway banter

"There's something so honest and down to earth with somebody who will stand on a stage and sing 'I love you,' and then dance 'I love you'; that's so honest, and innocent in a way."

—Bebe Neuwirth

BACKSTAGE————————————

André Previn, music director of **My Fair Lady**, had no idea they were not using Audrey Hepburn's own vocals until he heard they were hiring her vocal replacement. Marni Nixon, who sang most of Eliza's music, was sworn to secrecy when she was ultimately hired.

9

February

(1984) *The Rink* opened on Broadway. In addition to showcasing Broadway legends Chita Rivera and Liza Minnelli, the show launched the career of *Seinfeld*'s Jason Alexander and Scott Ellis, who would later receive four (so far) Tony nominations for directing.

The show brought Chita her first long-awaited Tony Award, but not much else: It ranks among Kander and Ebb's least-distinguished scores, and though the show ran less than eight months, Liza left the company, due in part to her various battles with substance abuse. Her replacement: Stockard Channing, who a few years earlier replaced another daughter of Hollywood royalty, Lucie Arnaz, in *They're Playing Our Song*.

broadway banter

"All right, I'm gonna be blatant now. When a musical wins Best Musical ... and it has no words in it, it has canned music, I don't think anybody sings ... something is different, very different."

–Chita Rivera, on Contact

POP QUIZ

Q: Who was the only replacement cast member to receive a Tony nomination?

10

February

(1898) Bertolt Brecht, a triple threat in his own right as an influential dramatist, stage director, and poet, was born today in Augsburg, Bavaria. He made his first mark on musical history thirty years later when he and Kurt Weill premiered *Die Dreigroschenoper*, later known in English as *The Threepenny Opera*, in Berlin. Various productions have featured a diverse range of Macheaths, from Jerry Orbach to Raul Julia, from Sting to Jesse Martin to Alan Cumming.

In the United States, two of his songs were popularized by unlikely performers: Bobby Darin made "Mack the Knife" a huge hit, and The Doors recorded "Alabama Song."

broadway banter

"What's the Polish word for fiasco? Whatever it is, I'm not sure even it is adequate to describe the unique experience that is Metro, *the hit Warsaw musical that arrived on Broadway last night."*

—Frank Rich

STAR POWER

Meryl Streep starred in the first Broadway production of the Brecht/Weill musical *Happy End* in 1977.

11
February

(1979) Weren't we just talking about *They're Playing Our Song*? Well, it opened on Broadway today. Lucie Arnaz and Robert Klein starred in—and in fact were the only cast members in—the fictionalized romance between Marvin Hamlisch and Carole Bayer Sager. With a book by Neil Simon, the show became a hit, though none of the show's pop tunes ever caught on outside the theater.

broadway banter

"[One] day I came in while he was working and I had this gigantic lollipop. My father took one look at it and said, 'Margaret, get away from me with all that sticky stuff! You're going to get it all over the piano!' I started to leave and I heard him say, 'No—that's it! The lollipop!' So I guess you can say I inspired 'On the Good Ship Lollipop.'"

—Margaret Whiting

IT TAKES A VILLAGE

Richard Rodgers almost gave up songwriting to become an underwear salesman.

12
February

(**1903**) Baritone Todd Duncan, the original Porgy, was born today. When performing *Porgy and Bess*, he and composer George Gershwin made the National Theatre drop its policy of segregating its audiences.

He appeared with Ethel Waters in another all-black musical, *Cabin in the Sky*, as well as *Lost in the Stars*, the Kurt Weill/Maxwell Anderson musical adaptation of *Cry, the Beloved Country*, the searing tale of race in South Africa. He continued to pass on his knowledge to voice students into his nineties.

broadway banter

"My mother took me to Radio City every Saturday morning when I was a kid and she used to say to me, 'One day you'll be up there'; I always thought she meant a Rockette."

—*Scott Wittman, accepting his Tony for writing lyrics to* Hairspray

STAR POWER

The 1983 Broadway revival of *Show Boat* starred Lonette McKee, the first non-white actress to play the role of Julie, a mulatto.

(1957) Before she was dubbed in *My Fair Lady*, Audrey Hepburn had the chance to show off her pleasant if not powerful singing voice in *Funny Face*, which opened the day before Valentine's Day.

Hepburn oozes charm and sincerity as an intellectual who is whisked away to Paris to become a fashion model by a photographer, played by Fred Astaire. Hepburn more than acquits herself in the romantic Gershwin music and the comic numbers by Roger Edens and Leonard Gershe. She even gets to show off her first love—dance—with a modern jazz dance in a smoky French café.

13
February

broadway banter

"The play is laid in two mythical countries. One is called Lichtenburg, the other is the United States."

—Howard Lindsay and Russel Crouse, *describing their* Call Me Madam

BACKSTAGE

In the British release of 1933's *Hallelujah, I'm a Bum,* the title and Al Jolson's lyrics had to be changed to *Hallelujah, I'm a Tramp* since "bum" meant only "butt" in that country.

14
February

(1934) Here's a story of a lovely lady... Long before she played the most wholesome mom in TV history, Florence Henderson sang up a storm on Broadway, playing wholesome ingénues in shows like *Fanny, Wish You Were Here,* and *The Girl Who Came to Supper,* as well as the national tour of *Oklahoma!* In her spare time, she has sold Wesson Oil, appeared in numerous Brady-related sequels and specials, and become a licensed hypnotherapist.

broadway banter

"The sound is something between a bark, a croak, and a quaver, and it doesn't quite match the movement of the lips. Did Lucille Ball sync her own singing in Mame, *or did Dick Cavett dub it for her?"*

—Pauline Kael

IT TAKES A VILLAGE

Dorothy and Herbert Fields's original title for their Ethel Merman vehicle *Something for the Boys* was *Jenny Get Your Gun.* A few years later, this title was, of course, recycled into *Annie Get Your Gun,* another Fields/Merman project.

15

February

(1950) *Cinderella* opened today, and all of Walt Disney Studios held its breath. The studio had not had an animated hit since 1937's *Snow White and the Seven Dwarfs*, and if *Cinderella* didn't succeed, it could have meant the end of the studio. The film, however, was a smash success, an "instant classic" despite the oxymoronic nature of that phrase, and its songs by Mack David, Jerry Livingston, and Al Hoffman are among the most beloved today.

Verna Felton, who voiced the Fairy Godmother, was one of the busiest actors at Disney Studios; her next role would be quite different, though: the Queen of Hearts in *Alice in Wonderland*.

broadway banter

"Nothing can kill a show like too much exposition."

—Officer Lockstock in Urinetown, by Mark Hollmann and Greg Kotis

CASTING COUCH

Among the ensemble of the original Broadway company of *The Lion King* were the show's co-creator Lebo M and his wife, Nandi Morake.

16
February

(1956) June was busting out all over ... in February. Following the success of the film version of *Oklahoma!*, the movie *Carousel* premiered today, reuniting stars Shirley Jones and Gordon MacRae. The soaring score—which Richard Rodgers claimed was his favorite of all his works—couldn't quite overcome the downbeat storyline of spousal abuse and murder, and the film was not a success at the box office.

broadway banter

"If somebody wants to sing my songs after I'm gone, nobody will be happier than my dead body."

—*Richard Rodgers*

ALSO ON THIS DAY

Two dancing dames were born: perpetual Broadway replacement Gretchen Wyler (1932) and movie cutie Vera-Ellen (1921).

(1976) *Rockabye Hamlet* opened on Broadway. Four days later—and to no one's surprise, with the possible exception of creator Cliff Jones, who wrote the book, music, and lyrics—the show closed. The only surprise might have been who directed this seven-performance bomb: Gower Champion. Jones's song titles included the title number, "He Got It in the Ear," "The Rosencrantz and Guildenstern Boogie," and in a fit of originality, "Shall We Dance."

Amazingly, a number of the cast managed to live down this fiasco, including Meat Loaf (the Priest) and Beverly D'Angelo (Ophelia, in her sole Broadway endeavor to date).

17
February

broadway banter

"Is it the real Hamlet, *or is it a musical?"*

—*Felicia Dantine in Paul Rudnick's* I Hate Hamlet

BACKSTAGE

Pippin was the first show to play in the Kennedy Center Opera House in Washington, D.C.

18

February

(1970) Susan Egan was born—one year exactly before her *Triumph of Love* costar Christopher Sieber. Egan made her Broadway debut by originating the role of Belle in *Beauty and the Beast*, garnering a Tony nomination. She was then a replacement for leads in *State Fair*, *Cabaret*, and *Thoroughly Modern Millie*. Her big shot at stardom came in 1997 with *Triumph of Love*, but despite her winning performance, the show fizzled on Broadway. Seiber went on to snag a Tony nod for *Monty Python's Spamalot*.

broadway banter

"For starters, this production might have spent a little less time searching for the perfect Asta and a lot more time trying to find the right Nick and Nora."

—*Frank Rich on the flop* Nick and Nora

POP QUIZ

Q: Can you name all five Marx Brothers?

A: Groucho, Harpo, Chico, Zeppo, and Gummo

19
February

(1978) In the burgeoning era of rock musicals, the composer of the hip *Sweet Charity* and the lyricists of pop standards like "Make Someone Happy" teamed up to write ... a comic operetta? *On the Twentieth Century* opened on Broadway, and though it never became a mega-hit, it holds a special place in the hearts of many fans. The show was pure frothy entertainment, from the fresh-sounding 1930s-ish music of Cy Coleman, to the witty book and lyrics of Comden and Green, to the art deco designs of Robin Wagner and Florence Klotz, to the dazzling soprano vocalizations of Madeline Kahn (she really could sing!), to the breakout role of a little-known comic actor and Juliard graduate named Kevin Kline.

broadway banter

"Now we've all heard of the Schubert Brothers: J.J., O.O., and Uh-Uh. Over the years, they've been sending out road companies of great shows like No, No Nanette, Yes, Yes, Yvette, *and* If, If, Iphigenia.*"*

–Betty Comden

STAR POWER

Alexis Smith starred opposite Robert Alda in the George Gershwin biopic *Rhapsody in Blue* and opposite Cary Grant as Cole Porter in *Night and Day.*

February

(1946) She likes to sing, she likes to dance, she likes Wheat Thins ... Sandy Duncan was born today. Between Mary Martin and Cathy Rigby, Sandy owned the role of *Peter Pan*, nabbing her third Tony nomination for her performance in 1980.

In addition to the boy who never grew up, Sandy also played the puppet boy who turned into a human girl in the made-for-television musical *Pinocchio*, costarring Danny Kaye and Clive Revill.

broadway banter

"George [Gershwin] and I, with great trepidation, walked into Mr. Belcher's ... office, and I demonstrated [the song]. 'Well, boys, it sounds pretty good,' he says, 'what about $300?' And we were silent. And he said, 'All right, $500. That'll be $250 for each of you.' I thought when he said $300, he wanted us to give him $300 to publish it!"

—*Irving Caesar, on getting "You, Just You" published*

CASTING COUCH

Among the actors considered for the role of Captain von Trapp in the film *The Sound of Music* were Sean Connery, Richard Burton, and Yul Brynner.

21

February

(1953) Christine Ebersole, an actress who personifies the Little Engine That Could, was born today. Never a star, Ebersole has toiled in the trenches for more than twenty-five years, first gaining notice as Ado Annie in the 1979 revival of *Oklahoma!* The next twenty years brought mostly small movie roles (*Tootsie, Amadeus*), missed opportunities (one season on *Saturday Night Live*), and Broadway flops (the 1980 revival of *Camelot* with an aging Richard Burton, the seventeen-performance *Getting Away with Murder*, and the four-performance *Harrigan 'n Hart*).

But in 2001, Ebersole landed the plum role of Dorothy Brock in the lauded revival of *42nd Street*, and she even managed to win a Tony—primarily because the steamroller that was *The Producers* did not having a Leading Actress contender.

broadway banter

"*Broadway's one of the only places that you instantly get surrounded by the best and learn from the best.*"

—*Brooke Shields*

ALSO ON THIS DAY

Unlikely Broadway belter Tyne Daly was born in 1946. In addition to winning a Tony for playing Mama Rose in *Gypsy*, Daly played Jason Alexander's nagging mama in the TV *Bye, Bye Birdie*, and sang leading roles on CD recordings of *On the Town* and *Call Me Madam*.

22

February

(1971) Lea Salonga was born today, and just over twenty years later, she would become one of the youngest Tony-winners ever for her leading role as Kim in *Miss Saigon*. The following year, she joined the cast of *Les Miserables* as Eponine, and in 1995 she reprised the role in the televised Tenth Anniversary Concert, dubbed "The Dream Cast."

In between stage assignments, Salonga provided the singing voices for Jasmine in *Aladdin* and the title role in *Mulan*, and on November 7, 2005, she made her Carnegie Hall debut with a stunning three-hour concert, joined by friends Andrea McArdle, Liz Callaway, and Paolo Montalban for duets.

broadway banter

"If anyone doubts that the contemporary musical theater can flex its atrophied muscles and yank an audience right out of its seats, he need look no further than the Act I finale of Les Miserables.*"*

—*Frank Rich*

BACKSTAGE

The cockroaches used in *Victor/Victoria* had to be kept frozen, then heated up with a hairdryer right before their scene was shot.

23

February

(1938)

"Thanks for the Medicare,
For Blue Cross and Blue Shield,
For a hip that finally healed,
Remember on prescriptions:
Generic's a steal!"

Before Estelle Getty sang this parody on *The Golden Girls*, Bob Hope's slightly more famous performance of "Thanks for the Memories," from the film *The Big Broadcast of 1938*, won an Oscar today for Best Song. Also picking up an Oscar that night was Walt Disney. Actually, he took home a total of eight Oscars: He was awarded a special Oscar for the pioneering *Snow White and the Seven Dwarfs* that had one regular-sized statue and seven miniature statuettes.

broadway banter

"She had no clear idea of how he sounded. But it was not a pretty sound. Dubbing was essential."

—Alan Jay Lerner, on Leslie Caron in Gigi

ALSO ON THIS DAY

Wonderful Town, starring Rosalind Russell and Edie Adams, opened on Broadway in 1953.

24
February

(1946) We may associate *Grease*'s Danny Zuko with John Travolta, but the role was originated on Broadway in 1972 by prolific Lifetime Television Movie actor Barry Bostwick, born today. He won a Tony for the short-lived *The Robber Bridegroom* in 1977, and returned to Broadway in 1991 to star in the even-shorter-lived *Nick and Nora*.

Bostwick may be best known today for his portrayal of Brad in the camp classic *The Rocky Horror Picture Show*, which he and costar Susan Sarandon have spent more than thirty years celebrating and trying to live down.

broadway banter

"I'd like to thank my Armenian family for my roots and my hairdresser Gary for restoring them to their natural color."

—Andrea Martin, accepting her Tony for My Favorite Year

CASTING COUCH

Elia Kazan, legendary director of such gritty dramas as *A Streetcar Named Desire* and *On the Waterfront*, played a jazz clarinetist in *Blues in the Night*.

25

February

(1973) *A Little Night Music* opened on Broadway. Based on an obscure Ingmar Bergman film, Stephen Sondheim, Hugh Wheeler, and Harold Prince adapted the story of intertwining lovers into a funny and romantic *adult* musical.

The show's best-known song, "Send in the Clowns," became Sondheim's number-one hit thanks to recordings by everyone from Frank Sinatra to Judy Collins to Barbra Streisand. But the song almost wasn't even written: At the last minute, director Prince asked Sondheim to write a song for the leading lady late in the show. Sondheim didn't want to, feeling the scene belonged to her ex-lover, who was returning to his wife. Sondheim wrote it overnight, it went into the show, and the rest ... is history.

broadway banter

"*Broadway is the light that never grows dim, the fire that never burns low—the heart that always palpitates.*"

—*Walter Winchell*

STAR POWER

Matthew Garber, who played young Michael Banks in *Mary Poppins*, died at the age of twenty-one, having made just three films.

26
February

(1921) The endearingly over-the-top Betty Hutton was born today. Love her or hate her, Hutton's career burned brightly for a few short years in Hollywood musicals. Today, she's best known for the title role in *Annie Get Your Gun*, a role she was given after MGM fired Judy Garland shortly into filming. Hutton won plenty of fans, but personally, I find her hammy comedy stylings unwatchable and her "energetic" singing unlistenable. Truth be told, trying to fill the shoes of Garland, not to mention Merman and Martin, would have been a tall order for anyone.

Not long after *Gun*, Hutton's career hit the skids, and she ultimately wound up washing floors in a rectory for a time. Finally, in 1980, Hutton stepped into the role of Miss Hannigan for a month in the long-running Broadway production of *Annie*.

broadway banter

"Hey, he's not happy at all. He lied to us through song. I hate when people do that!"

—Homer Simpson *on* The Simpsons

IT TAKES A VILLAGE

Aside from being the composer of *Once upon a Mattress* and *The Mad Show*, Mary Rodgers also authored the young adult novel *Freaky Friday*.

(1935) "The Continental" became the first Oscar-winner for Best Song. The song, a seventeen-minute song and extended dance sequence, was featured in the second Fred Astaire/Ginger Rogers pairing, *The Gay Divorcee*. The movie, based on Astaire's stage success *Gay Divorce*, dropped all of the Cole Porter tunes from the original except for "Night and Day."

February

broadway banter

"She gave him sex. He gave her class."

–Katharine Hepburn, on Ginger Rogers and Fred Astaire

BY THE NUMBERS

Year	Show	Ticket Price	Increase
1943	Oklahoma!	$4.30	
1953	Wonderful Town	$6.60	50%
1964	The Sound of Music	$9.90	50%
1977	Annie	$20.00	100%
1980	42nd Street	$40.00	100%
1989	Jerome Robbins' Broadway	$60.00	50%
1994	Show Boat	$75.00	25%
2005	Monty Python's Spamalot	$111.00	50%

28
February

(1948) The eternally young Bernadette Peters was born today. Bernadette made a huge splash in 1968, first in *Dames at Sea* off-Broadway, then in *George M!* on Broadway. In the next decade, "B.P." couldn't quite live up to her initial promise, appearing in Broadway flops *La Strada*, *On the Town*, and *Mack and Mabel*, then the uneven musical films *Pennies from Heaven* and *Annie*.

Finally, she hit her stride when she paired up with Stephen Sondheim, becoming the quintessential interpreter of his music and starring in *Sunday in the Park with George*, *Into the Woods*, and *Gypsy* on Broadway. Ironically, she would win her two Tonys for non-Sondheim shows: *Song and Dance* and *Annie Get Your Gun*. In between, Peters found time to camp it up as the wicked stepmother in the version of *Cinderella* starring Brandy.

broadway banter

"What it means is—we may be going to Broadway!"

—Corky St. Clair in *Waiting for Guffman*,
by Christopher Guest and Eugene Levy

CASTING COUCH

Seventeen years in the making, the much-anticipated film version of *Evita* was rumored to star, at various points, Liza Minnelli, Barbra Streisand, Olivia Newton-John, Bette Midler, Ann-Margret, Meryl Streep, Michelle Pfeiffer, and Pia Zadora.

February

(2004) They weren't quite musicals, but almost: *A Mighty Wind* and *The Triplets of Belleville* went head to head at the Oscars tonight. Both films featured numerous songs that were integral to the storytelling, and each one received an Oscar nomination—a rarity in the days of nominating songs that are featured only as the final credits roll.

Neither song emerged victorious, though, as the steamroller that was *The Lord of the Rings: The Return of the King* copped the Oscar for "Into the West."

broadway banter

Miss Piggy: Can you stand there in your rented tuxedo and honestly say that I am not Oscar material?

Johnny Carson: Oscar Meyer, maybe.

STAR POWER

Diane Keaton was a featured player in the original production of *Hair* in 1968.

MARCH

Catherine Zeta-Jones in her Oscar-winning performance as
Velma Kelly in the 2002 film *Chicago*.

(1979) Attend the tale: *Sweeney Todd* opened on Broadway today, sparking the question, "Just what is it?" Some critics called it an opera, some stood by musical theater. I think the disco remix of the title tune pretty much settles that vote (check out *A Collector's Sondheim* if you don't believe me).

The show was a culmination for many of the key people involved: the last great show for the Sondheim/Prince collaboration, the last of Angela Lansbury's four Tony Awards, and the only Tony for Len Cariou after a decade of playing musical leading men.

1
March

broadway banter

"Sweeney Todd *is one giant step for vegetarianism.*"

—*T. E. Kalem*

POP QUIZ

Q: What lush Gershwin ballad was originally written as a fast dance chorus?

A: "Someone to Watch Over Me"

March

(1965) The hills were alive with the sound of music. Julie Andrews spun on a mountaintop near Salzburg, Austria, and an iconic film image was born. Few filmgoers realized that the difficult helicopter shot almost didn't happen: Because of bad weather and the wind the helicopter itself created as it flew perilously close to Andrews, the shot was delayed and took numerous retakes. The final version, of course, succeeds because it *looks* effortless.

If the film wasn't a smash success with critics, it was with audiences. *The Sound of Music,* which premiered today, saved the nearly bankrupt Twentieth Century Fox studio, and it was near the top of the list of all-time top-grossing movies for some twenty years.

broadway banter

*"No I never hear from Sheldon, but I read what he is up to.
He's working on a musical 'bout Rommel as a boy."*

—Emma *in* Song and Dance, *lyrics by Don Black*

BACKSTAGE ————————————

When *The Sound of Music* was dubbed into other languages, the song "Do, Re, Mi" provided a unique challenge: The musical scale of do, re, mi, etc., exists in all languages, but the words do not correspond to words meaning "doe," "ray," "me," etc. in any other language. Ultimately, the filmmakers were able to find suitable translations.

(1975) Over the years, legendary actresses have sunk their teeth into the character of Joan of Arc in various plays about her: Ingrid Bergman, Julie Harris, Lynn Redgrave, and ... Ann Reinking? Today, *Goodtime Charley* opened, and playing opposite Joel Grey as the Charles, the Dauphin of France, Reinking attempted to play Joan. The 104-performance flop lost $1.1 million.

March

broadway banter

"*Good grief! Don't you know* anything? Chicago *was a thirties musical, starring little Miss Alice* Faye. *Don't you know* anything?"

—*Martha in Edward Albee's* Who's Afraid of Virginia Woolf?

IT TAKES A VILLAGE———————

Harold Prince was parodied in the musical *Say, Darling,* which told how a book is made into a musical. Robert Morse played the Hal Prince character, Ted Snow.

4
March

(1937) Luise Rainer became the first person to win an Oscar for acting in a musical, the epic (i.e., long) *The Great Ziegfeld*. Rainer got to show off her sweet singing voice and her somewhat melodramatic acting abilities playing Anna Held, the Austrian singing sensation whom Florenz Ziegfeld (played by William Powell) discovers, marries, then leaves for Billie Burke (later of Glinda the Good Witch fame).

Rainer also won an Oscar the next year for Pearl Buck's epic (i.e., long) tale of Chinese peasants, *The Good Earth*. After that, she would rarely make another film appearance.

broadway banter

"Ziegfeld was a man who had no equal when it came to taste in the theater."

—Oscar Hammerstein II

STAR POWER

As *Panama Hattie* neared its Broadway opening, star Ethel Merman ordered that rising starlet Betty Hutton's one big song be cut from the show, as it was getting too much attention. The event found its way into Jacqueline Susann's risqué showbiz roman à clef, *Valley of the Dolls*. Hutton got the last laugh, though, when she played Merman's role in the film version of *Annie Get Your Gun*.

5

March

(1908) Rex Harrison's speak-singing of Henry Higgins's songs in *My Fair Lady* in 1956 paved the way for Robert Preston and others to rise to musical theater fame without being able to sing. Harrison, born today, later spoke the Oscar-winning "Talk to the Animals" in *Doctor Dolittle*, and revisited *My Fair Lady* on Broadway in 1981.

Harrison also probably gets the award for creating the most film roles that would later become musicalized: Charles in *Blithe Spirit* (1945, later the musical *High Spirits*), the King of Siam in *Anna and the King* (1946), and John in *The Fourposter* (1952, later *I Do! I Do!*), among others.

broadway banter

"That was the only time I've ever rooted for the Nazis."

—Rex Harrison, *after viewing* The Sound of Music

STAR POWER

During the filming of *My Fair Lady*, Rex Harrison refused to lip-synch to his own pre-recorded tracks, as was the custom. He performed all his numbers live on the set.

6

March

(1948) When you need a biblical musical on stage or animated, Stephen Schwartz is your man. Schwartz, born today, first hit the scene when he contributed lyrics to Leonard Bernstein's *Mass*, the pro-peace theater event that opened the Kennedy Center for the Performing Arts in 1971. That same year, his folk/rock/hippie musical *Godspell*, a retelling of the Gospel according to Saint Matthew, opened off-Broadway.

Later, he returned to biblical themes with the stage musical *Children of Eden* and animated cartoon *The Prince of Egypt*. Along the way, he found time to write the scores to *Pippin*, *Working*, *Pocahontas*, and *The Hunchback of Notre Dame*, among others. More recently, he wrote the score for a little show named *Wicked*.

broadway banter

Sarah Jessica Parker: "*We love musicals. We see every one and sing showtunes all day long.*"

Matthew Broderick: "*In other words, we're geeks.*"

POP QUIZ

Q: How many Tony nominations does Clint Black have?

A: One, for contributing songs to the flop *Urban Cowboy*, a nomination shared by a total of thirty songwriters.

March

(1946) Following the success of *Oklahoma!* onstage, Rodgers and Hammerstein jumped to the silver screen with another charmingly hokey Great Plains musical: *State Fair*. On this day, their song "It Might as Well Be Spring" won them their only Oscar together. (Hammerstein received four other nominations, winning for "The Last Time I Saw Paris" with Jerome Kern, but this was Rodgers's one and only Oscar nomination.)

broadway banter

"If you read all the fine print in the Playbill for Marilyn: An American Fable, you'll discover that the new musical at the Minskoff has sixteen producers and ten songwriters. If you mistakenly look up from the Playbill to watch the show itself, you may wonder whether those twenty-six persons were ever in the same rehearsal room—or even the same city—at the same time."

—*Frank Rich*

IT TAKES A VILLAGE

Frank Loesser's Oscar for Best Original Song for "Baby, It's Cold Outside" was a controversial one: Many Academy members claimed to have heard Frank and his wife perform the number at parties for years before its inclusion in *Neptune's Daughter*.

8

March

(1921) Her voice was almost always dubbed, but virtually no one could outdance Cyd Charisse, born today. She began her career as a ballerina, then toiled in film for ten years in bit parts and "dance specialties" before achieving stardom as Gene Kelly's dance partner in *Singin' in the Rain*. The other highlights of her relatively brief career included *The Bandwagon, Brigadoon, It's Always Fair Weather,* and *Silk Stockings*.

At the age of sixty-eight, Charisse made her Broadway debut as Elizaveta Grushinskaya, the aging Russian ballerina in *Grand Hotel*.

broadway banter

"Deborah Kerr and Cyd Charisse and Natalie and me:
We can lip-synch right on key!"

—*"Audrey Hepburn" in* Forbidden Hollywood, *by Gerard Alessandrini*

STAR POWER

The female leads in the film *Victor/Victoria* both played *Cinderella* on TV: Julie Andrews in 1957, and Lesley Ann Warren in 1965.

9

March

(1940) You wouldn't know it from his film career alone, but Raul Julia, born today, was a prolific Broadway singer/actor, and what's more, he could actually sing—well! Julia made his Broadway musical debut as Proteus in the rock/soul version of *Two Gentlemen of Verona*, copping a Tony nomination in the process. Unfortunately, he next signed on for another Galt MacDermot musical: *Via Galactica*, one of the biggest flops of the 1970s.

He would get better projects in the revivals of *Where's Charley?* and *The Threepenny Opera*, giving a delectable portrayal of Mack the Knife opposite Ellen Greene. In 1982, he created the role of Guido Contini in Tommy Tune and Maury Yeston's *Nine*. For the fourth time, he lost the Tony Award. His final musical outing before his untimely death in 1995 was a revival of *Man of La Mancha*, starring opposite Sheena Easton.

broadway banter

"Streisand will return to Broadway when Hollywood comes to Dunsinane."

—William Goldman

CASTING COUCH

In the early workshops of **A Chorus Line**, the role of choreographer Zach was played by Barry Bostwick. He was replaced with Robert LuPone, brother of Patti, though the creative team nearly went with Chris Sarandon instead.

10

March

(1954) *The Threepenny Opera* opened at the Theater de Lys off-Broadway; it was the first major American production of the jazz- and opera-infused musical by Kurt Weill and Bertolt Brecht. The actors, working for just five dollars a week during rehearsals and twenty-five dollars for performances, included such future stars as Charlotte Rae, Bea Arthur, Jo Sullivan, John Astin, and Paul Dooley, as well as the legendary Lotte Lenya, Weill's widow and chief interpreter of his music.

The show was perhaps the most unexpected hit of all time, running for seven years (breaking *Oklahoma*'s record), making three million dollars on a ten-thousand-dollar investment, and becoming the only off-Broadway production to be honored with a Tony nomination.

broadway banter

"When did despair becoming enjoyable? ... Even Brecht wrote musicals."

—*Father Dan in Paul Rudnick's* Jeffrey

IT TAKES A VILLAGE

It may have seemed Mel Brooks came out of nowhere to win several Tonys for *The Producers* in 2001, but he actually wrote the book for 1962's *All American*, a flop vehicle for Ray Bolger.

(2001) Here's to Ed Kleban: *A Class Act* opened on Broadway. Who's Ed Kleban? you well may ask. His one claim to fame was writing lyrics for *A Chorus Line*. In the ensuing years, Kleban wrote lyrics and music to a number of musicals, none of which ever got produced, but among which were *Gallery*, a show based on various famous works of art, and musicalizations of *The Americanization of Emily*, *A Thousand Clowns*, and *The Heartbreak Kid*.

11
March

Linda Kline and Lonny Price fashioned a book musical fictionalizing Kleban's life and using nearly two dozen of his songs, winning Kleban a posthumous Tony nomination for his songs. Kleban, who died in 1988 at the age of forty-eight, left the proceeds of his earnings on *A Chorus Line* to start a foundation to support young theater songwriters.

broadway banter

"Now kiddies, a Charm song is the Southern belle of musicals—it don't have to do a lick of work—it just has to make the audience smile."

—Lehman Engel in A Class Act

BACKSTAGE

Kiss Me Kate was originally shot in 3-D—the only full-length musical so filmed. However, the short-lived fad died out before the film was released, so it was rarely seen in this format.

12
March

(1946) A sequin was born. I mean, a star was born: Liza Minnelli, daughter of movie musical royalty Judy Garland and Vincente Minnelli. Liza made her first on-screen appearance at age one, in her parents' film *In the Good Old Summertime*, and she never looked back. At sixteen, she landed her first major role in New York in the minor hit *Best Foot Forward*. She then won a Tony for *Flora the Red Menace* (setting the record for the youngest Best Actress in a Musical winner) followed by an Oscar for her definitive performance of Sally Bowles in *Cabaret* and an Emmy for *Liza with a "Z."*

After that, Liza spent much of the next thirty-plus years making various comeback attempts, each time recovering from various illnesses, addictions, and broken marriages to rebound and capture the hearts of millions of fans.

broadway banter

"When I was a little girl, my father took me to see The King and I. *And since I thought my father was the king, I thought the story was about us. That turned out not to be true."*

–Liza Minnelli

STAR POWER

After spelling her name in the song "Liza with a 'Z,'" Liza Minnelli was upset to find her last name spelled "Minelli" on publicity posters when *New York, New York* was reissued.

(1973) A revised revival of the 1919 musical comedy *Irene* opened on Broadway as a vehicle for film songstress Debbie Reynolds. The show was originally directed by, of course, Sir John Gielgud—not exactly a natural choice for a dated, faded musical. (He was ultimately replaced by Gower Champion, who still couldn't make the show a success.)

13
March

Miss Debbie, best known for having sung in the rain and having been jilted by hubby Eddie Fisher for Liz Taylor, sang her heart out, and ultimately, her voice out as well: At one performance, faced with laryngitis, she acted her performance with her lines read by, of course, Sir John Gielgud. The audience heckled her, to which she replied, "I don't have to be here. I could be home with my seven maids."

broadway banter

"Debbie Reynolds was indeed the girl next door. But only if you lived next door to a self-centered, totally driven, insecure, untruthful phony."

—Eddie Fisher

CASTING COUCH

Debbie Reynolds's replacement in *Irene* was former MGM musical star Jane Powell.

14

March

(1947) "No wonder Meryl Streep calls her Glenn Close but no cigar." So said "Patti LuPone" in *Forbidden Broadway.*

Close, born today, appeared in three quickly closing Broadway plays before making her singing debut as Princess Mary in Richard Rodgers's Henry VIII bio-musical, *Rex,* which became her longest-running show at forty-eight performances. She then enjoyed a longer run as P.T. Barnum's wife in the hit *Barnum,* but it would then be almost fifteen years before she was singing on Broadway again, this time in the role of a lifetime: Norma Desmond in *Sunset Boulevard.* Close copped her third Tony Award for her over-the-top performance. Her most recent musical endeavor, though—ingénue Nellie Forbush in the TV version of *South Pacific*—may prove to be her last, after those reviews ...

broadway banter

"She can't act. She can't sing, and she can't dance. A triple threat!"

—Cosmo on Lina Lamont in Singin' in the Rain,
by Betty Comden and Adolph Green

ALSO ON THIS DAY

Before she hunted Doctor Lecter, young Jodie Foster sang in the musical film *Tom Sawyer,* released today in 1973.

(1987) Roller-skating trains? Only from Andrew Lloyd Webber. *Starlight Express*, the choo-choo train musical, opened on Broadway today. The creative team made a go at recreating the smash success of *Cats*, and the results were, well, mixed. Among the original cast were future Broadway choreographer Joey McKneely, future *Ally McBeal* secretary Jane Krakowski, and the original "Annie," Andrea McArdle.

15

March

broadway banter

"Don't hate me because I'm beautiful; hate me because I'm Zeus, Jupiter, and Oprah combined!"

—Matthew Broderick, hosting the Tonys

POP QUIZ

Q: What are the only three Broadway songs to win the Song of the Year Grammy?

A: "Send in the Clowns," "What Kind of Fool Am I," and "Hello, Dolly!"

16
March

(1969) At a time when the United States faced war, domestic unrest, and social upheaval, a staunchly pro-American show opened on Broadway: *1776*. Librettist Peter Stone proved that you could musicalize even the creation of the Declaration of Independence, as the traditional-style show beat the tribal love rock musical *Hair* and pop musical *Promises, Promises* for the Best Musical Tony.

Perhaps due in part to the fact that Sherman Edwards, *1776*'s composer/lyricist, was a former history teacher, the show didn't whitewash history: The song "Molasses to Rum" illustrated how the Founding Fathers were culpable in the legalization of slavery in America.

broadway banter

"*The kind of show that teaches one to be grateful for small mercies. Such as the final curtain.*"

—*Clive Barnes, on the ill-fated sequel* Bring Back Birdie

IT TAKES A VILLAGE

One man's trash is ... later that same man's treasure. While writing *Gypsy*, Jule Styne recycled melodies from songs he'd written for several previous shows, all having been cut prior to opening. This included "Everything's Coming up Roses," originally written for *High Button Shoes* in 1947.

17

March

(2005) Original *Monty Python* creator Eric Idle teamed up with prolific and versatile director Mike Nichols to bring *Spamalot* to the stage, opening on Broadway today. The schtick-filled show starred *Frasier*'s David Hyde Pierce, *The Simpsons*' "Apu," Hank Azaria, and—thirty years after *The Rocky Horror Picture Show*—Tim Curry. But almost stealing the show in the breakout role of a lifetime was Sara Ramirez as the Lady of the Lake, singing the show-stopping "Diva's Lament" and, sending up contemporary Broadway pop ballads, duetting with Christopher Sieber on "The Song That Goes Like This."

broadway banter

"I'll never understand what people see in musicals. I mean, why settle for The Sound of Music *when you can have* Dialogue of the Carmelites?"*

—Mendy in *Terrence McNally's* The Lisbon Traviata

BACKSTAGE

Andrew Lloyd Webber first began working on *Sunset Boulevard* long before it was actually staged. In fact, he wrote a song for *Sunset* called "One Star" that found its way into *Cats* as a little ditty called "Memory."

18
March

(1927) Give 'em the old razzle dazzle ... John Kander was born today. He's best known for his brassy, show-biz tunes from shows like *Cabaret*, *Chicago*, and *New York, New York*, written with long-time writing partner Fred Ebb. But he was a more diverse composer that that, writing the unique score to *Zorba* and beautiful ballads like "A Quiet Thing," "I Don't Remember You," and "If You Leave Me Now."

After 1997's short-lived *Steel Pier*, Kander and Ebb were not able to bring a new show to Broadway, after many attempts to get their adaptations of *The Visit* (first for Angela Lansbury, then Chita Rivera) and *The Skin of Our Teeth* off the ground.

broadway banter

"All my life I wanted to be a dancer in vaudeville. Oh yeah. Have my own act. But, no. No. No. No. It was one big world full of 'No.'"

—Roxie Hart in Chicago, by Fred Ebb and Bob Fosse

STAR POWER

Eleanor Audley provided the voice for two of Disney's greatest villains: *Cinderella*'s Wicked Stepmother and *Sleeping Beauty*'s Maleficent.

(1982) *Victor/Victoria*, the first good musical comedy film to come along in years, opened in New York City. To tell the story of homosexuals, female impersonators, and the battle of the sexes, director Blake Edwards paired stars of two of the most family-friendly musicals of the 1960s: wife Julie Andrews and Robert Preston. The film's risqué nature may seem tame today, but it broke new ground when it debuted in the Reagan years.

Thirteen years later, Edwards and Andrews brought *Victor/Victoria* to the Broadway stage, with somewhat disappointing results all around.

19
March

broadway banter

"Oh my God!"

—*Donna Murphy, winning a Tony for* The King and I
over Julie Andrews for Victor/Victoria

CASTING COUCH ——————————————

After Carol Channing left *Hello, Dolly!*, she was succeeded by Ginger Rogers, Eve Arden, Martha Raye, Dorothy Lamour, Mary Martin, Pearl Bailey (and an all-black cast), Phyllis Diller, and finally Ethel Merman, for whom the show was originally written.

20

March

(1952) *An American in Paris* became only the second musical to win the Oscar for Best Picture; it was also only the second film in color to win. Directed by master of the MGM musical Vincente Minnelli, the film featured some of the most unique dance sequences ever captured on film, choreographed by the film's star, Gene Kelly. While production took a break for Kelly to rehearse the ballets, Vincente Minnelli wrapped up filming *Father's Little Dividend*, his sequel to the popular *Father of the Bride*.

broadway banter

"Broadway was always breaking barriers. My first line in Kiss Me, Kate was 'You bastard!' And when I finally said it in the theater, the gasp from the audience was incredible: 'Oh no!' It's slightly different nowadays, isn't it."

–Patricia Morrison

IT TAKES A VILLAGE

Irving Caesar claimed he and George Gershwin wrote their first big hit, "Swanee," in ten minutes.

21
March

(1869) Florenz Ziegfeld Jr., self-proclaimed "Impressio Extraordinaire," was born today in Chicago. In the first third of the twentieth century, he would meld song, dance, comedy, spectacle, and the glorification of the American woman into two dozen or so editions of the *Ziegfeld Follies*. This unique entertainment paved the way for what would become American Musical Comedy, and indeed, Ziegfeld produced what is likely the first great musical to combine song and story, *Show Boat*.

Ziegfeld discovered and made stars of Fanny Brice, Will Rogers, Ray Bolger, Marilyn Miller, and countless others. The 1936 Oscar-winning *The Great Ziegfeld* immortalized his life and marriages.

broadway banter

"I planned the whole thing in a saloon, honey, I spent a lotta time in saloons in those days—I don't remember too much of anything!"

—Elaine Stritch on her first—and only—solo album

STAR POWER

In 1969, Katharine Hepburn became the first person to sing the word "shit" in a Broadway musical (*Coco*, based on the life of Coco Chanel).

March

(1948) Pop rock musicals would never have been the same. Or maybe they would never have been at all: Andrew Lloyd Webber was born. Love him or hate him, he's written some of the most enduring hits in musical history, from his early *Joseph and the Amazing Technicolor Dreamcoat* to *Evita* to *Cats* to *The Phantom of the Opera*. His spectacle-over-substance approach had a significant impact on musicals, helping to reinvigorate the flagging genre while at the same time making it more difficult to get a new musical produced because of the expense and scope audiences were now expecting.

His later work, however, has not lived up to these earlier successes: *By Jeeves* flopped on Broadway, *Woman in White* is, so far, only a semi-success, and even *Sunset Boulevard* was not the mega-hit it was expected to be.

broadway banter

"Well, thank heavens that there wasn't a song in The English Patient *is all I can say."*

—Andrew Lloyd Webber, *accepting his Oscar for*
"You Must Love Me" from Evita

CASTING COUCH

Elaine Paige took over the role of Grizabella in *Cats* from Dame Judi Dench, who left the show during rehearsals after tearing her Achilles tendon.

(2003) *Chicago* won the Best Picture Oscar today, the first time a musical won that award in thirty-four years. The film was years in the making, stretching back to the 1970s when the original stage production's director Bob Fosse wanted to make it with Goldie Hawn, Liza Minnelli, and Frank Sinatra. Later, plans fell through for a version with Goldie, Madonna, and John Travolta. Ultimately it starred Richard Gere, who started out as a singer/dancer, the musically trained Catherine Zeta-Jones, and Renee Zellweger.

March

broadway banter

"It's true. He shot the whole picture through a lady's silk stocking."

–Norman Jewison, on Fiddler on the Roof's *Oscar-winning cinematographer Oswald Morris.*

BACKSTAGE

When *Oklahoma!* played its pre-Broadway tryout, it was titled *Away We Go!*

24
March

(1994) A revival of *Carousel* opened on Broadway. More important than the show itself was the Broadway debut of the actress playing Carrie Pipperidge: Audra Ann McDonald, who went on to win the Tony for Best Featured Actress in a musical.

Audra then dropped the "Ann" and went on to dominate the next decade of Broadway, winning more Tonys for *Ragtime*, *Master Class* (a play, but her role was dominated by rehearsing an aria from Verdi's *Macbeth*), and *A Raisin in the Sun* (her first major non-singing role on Broadway).

At home, Audra can line her four Tonys up next to her three solo CDs, each of which shows off her unique voice in different ways.

broadway banter

"*I can't carry a tune, but I was determined not to have Marni Nixon sing for me.*"

—Ellen Burstyn, *on having to sing in*
Alice Doesn't Live Here Anymore

STAR POWER

Yul Brynner played 4,625 performances of *The King and I* throughout his lifetime.

25

March

(1875) *Trial by Jury* opened at the Royalty Theatre in London. Never heard of it? Neither had I. Why is it significant? It was Gilbert and Sullivan's first collaboration together. With this forty-minute comic opera, G & S brought light opera back to the British stages, which led to their more well-known endeavors, like *The Pirates of Penzance, H.M.S. Pinafore,* and *The Gondoliers.*

The trials and tribulations of the team's (conception and writing, as well as the premiere of) *The Mikado,* is chronicled—at a laborious pace—in Mike Leigh's colorful movie *Topsy Turvy.*

broadway banter

Lisa: "Kicking It: A Musical Journey Through the Betty Ford Center."

Marge: You know, when I was a girl, I always dreamed of being in a Broadway audience.

—The Simpsons

POP QUIZ

Q: For what show did David Merrick take out an ad featuring seven rave reviews from random people whose names just happened to be the same as the seven New York reviewers?

A: *Subways Are for Sleeping*

Today in

26 March

(2000) Battle of the Cartoon Musicals: The outspoken Trey Parker, co-creator of *South Park: Bigger Longer and Uncut,* went head to head with Phil Collins and *Tarzan* at the Oscars. Controversy surrounded Parker, and not only for his lambasting of Collins's schmaltzy, generic song. Parker's nominated tune, "Blame Canada," co-written by *Hairspray*'s Marc Shaiman, contained the "F" word as well as slander against Canada and Canadian singers Anne Murray and Celine Dion. Oscars' producers were at a loss as to how to handle the song until the last minute, when Robin Williams stepped up to the plate to sing it with a chorus line of leggy female Mounties. He sang the full lyrics with the exception of the "F" bomb, for which he simply turned upstage.

When all was said and done, though, *Tarzan*'s "You'll Be in My Heart" beat out "Blame Canada."

broadway banter

"You said, 'Aeschylus did not invent theater to have it end up a bunch of chorus kids in cat suits prancing around wondering which of them will go to kitty-cat heaven.'"

—Tess in Six Degrees of Separation, *by John Guare*

STAR POWER

While many singers have been dubbed in movie musicals, *South Pacific's* Juanita Hall may be the only Tony-winning actress to recreate her role on film, only to end up dubbed by Muriel Smith.

27

March

(1973) *Cabaret* won eight Oscars today, but not Best Picture, nor did it even get any nominations for its original songs. Its major players, though, came home victorious: Director Bob Fosse beat *The Godfather*'s Francis Ford Coppola, Joel Grey beat no fewer than three *Godfather* supporting actors, and Liza Minnelli trotted home with the Oscar her mother didn't win for *A Star is Born*. *The Godfather*, however, picked up the Best Picture Oscar, making *Cabaret* the winningest movie that failed to win the big prize. In the song department, some forgettable tunes like "Marmalade, Molasses and Honey" were nominated over Kander and Ebb's "Mein Herr" and "Money, Money."

broadway banter

"Being characteristically a pessimist and cynic, this and some of the other nice things that have happened to me in the last couple of days may turn me into some sort of hopefully optimist and ruin my life."

—Bob Fosse, *accepting his Oscar for directing* Cabaret, *after winning the Emmy for* Liza With a "Z" *and the Tony for* Pippin

CASTING COUCH

When Angela Lansbury was leaving the original production of *Mame*, Judy Garland was the prime candidate to be her replacement. The producers found her too risky and unstable, and she was devastated at losing the role.

28

March

(1977) Barbra Streisand won an Oscar for writing the music to "Evergreen (Love Theme from *A Star is Born*)." Not only is she one of the few women to win an Oscar for writing music, she is also one of only two women who have won Oscars for acting and something else. (Emma Thompson is the other, with an Oscar for acting in *Howards End* and for writing *Sense and Sensibility*.) The rather egregious musical, which won four other Golden Globe Awards, did not win any other Oscars.

broadway banter

"As a lighting designer I try to present the wide range of emotions that can happen on stage—dark drama and great seriousness and deeply rooted emotion. Of course, The Producers *is about none of that."*

—Peter Kaczorowski

STAR POWER

Barbra Streisand was born on the same day as her longtime friend Shirley MacLaine.

March

(1951) Rodgers and Hammerstein solidified their position as the premiere writers of musicals with the Broadway opening of *The King and I*. The show was based on the novel by Margaret Landon and the 1946 film *Anna and the King of Siam* starring Irene Dunne and (the non-bald) Rex Harrison. Fashioned as a vehicle for Gertrude Lawrence, Yul Brynner shaved his head specifically for the role of the King, stole much of Gertie's thunder, kept the bald "hairstyle" he adopted for the role for the rest of his life, and played the role until his death in 1985.

broadway banter

"Who but Rodgers and Hammerstein could come up with the idea of a British woman and the King of Siam dancing a polka?"

—Ted Chapin

ALSO ON THIS DAY

Pearl Bailey, indomitable musical and comedic presence, was born in 1918. She triumphed in everything from the film *Carmen Jones* (one of the few leads who wasn't dubbed) to *St. Louis Woman* to the voice of Big Mama in Disney's *The Fox and the Hound*.

30
March

(1992) *Beauty and the Beast* became the first animated film to receive an Oscar nomination for Best Picture and the first movie to have three Best Song nominees. Some actors feared this would be the beginning of a new trend, and that there would be more and more animated movies taking the place of live action film. But this has not proven the case, as in the ensuing fourteen years, no other animated movies have made the Best Picture fivesome.

broadway banter

"1600 Pennsylvania Avenue *had no business opening last night. It is a largely marvelous Leonard Bernstein score that drags Alan Jay Lerner's book and lyrics behind it like an unwanted relative.*"

—Martin Gottfried

ALSO ON THIS DAY

In 2000, the "non-singing, all-dancing" musical *Contact* opened, and after it won the Tony for Best Musical, people feared it would set a trend of recorded music and no singing. Thankfully, the next five Best Musical winners were all just that: musicals.

(1943) Today, Rodgers, Hammerstein, and de Mille all but gave birth to what we now know as a "musical". *Oklahoma!* combined music, lyrics, book, dance, and characterization like no musical play or film before. On its opening night, it was hailed as a masterpiece and a breakthrough, and it would achieve the greatest popular success of any musical of its time.

31

March

broadway banter

"[I] didn't know there were three steps leading to the stage. I tripped and fell flat on my face; my belt busted and my music skated out in front of me. A voice from the audience said, 'That was pretty funny. Could you do it again?'"

—Celeste Holm, *on auditioning for* Oklahoma!

ALSO ON THIS DAY

Fittingly, on this day nine years previously, Shirley Jones was born. Shirley, of course, played Laurey in the film *Oklahoma!*

APRIL

Judy Garland and Tom Drake in the 1944 film *Meet Me in St. Louis.*

(1929) Hollywood soprano Jane Powell was born today. After some small roles, Jane was launched to fame in *Royal Wedding* after both June Allyson and Judy Garland had to bow out. She played Fred Astaire's sister, despite being thirty years his junior, and sang "How Could You Believe Me When I Said I Love You When You Know I've Been a Liar All My Life," the longest song title in film history. Her most memorable role came with *Seven Brides for Seven Brothers*, but her career in films came to an abrupt halt shortly thereafter. More recently, she played JonBenet Ramsey's dance instructor in the TV film *Perfect Murder, Perfect Town*.

1
April

broadway banter

"*I'll play the great Peter Allen, a fellow Australian entertainer who actually made history as the first man ever to marry Liza Minnelli.*"

—Hugh Jackman, on his then upcoming Broadway debut,
The Boy from Oz

STAR POWER

Shelley Winters was a replacement Ado Annie on Broadway in the original *Oklahoma!*

2

April

(1966) Piggybacking off the popularity of Fox's nun-heavy hit *The Sound of Music*, MGM released *The Singing Nun* today, starring Debbie Reynolds in the title role. No Julie Andrews or Mary Martin she, Debbie tried her best with the sappy, highly fictionalized life story of the real singing nun, Soeur Sourire. At least she got to sing such memorable pop Christian tunes as "Dominique" and, umm, well there was ... no ... well, who could forget? ... hmm. Well, she got to sing "Dominique."

broadway banter

Little Sally: What kind of musical is this? The good guys finally take over, and then everything starts falling apart!

Officer Lockstock: Like I said Little Sally. This isn't a happy musical.

Little Sally: But the music's so happy!

–Urinetown, by Mark Hollmann and Greg Kotis

ALSO ON THIS DAY

The original Tin Man in *The Wizard of Oz*, Buddy Ebsen, was born in 1908. However, he had to leave the film because of a problem with the aluminum makeup used. He was replaced by Jack Haley, but would later rise to small-screen fame as Jed Clampett on *The Beverly Hillbillies*.

(1930) *Broadway Melody* was the first musical to win Best Picture; it was also the first Best Picture winner to have sound. One segment was filmed in early Technicolor. And it is probably the first movie to spawn a sequel: The subsequent *Broadway Melody of 19XX* flicks that were made every few years for the next decade.

   More important to the history of musicals, though, was its usage of prerecorded music that the performers lip-synched to while dancing. This would, of course, become the standard for nearly every movie musical made up to the present.

3

April

broadway banter

"We wanted to be good. That was more important than being successful."

—Arthur Laurents on the creation of West Side Story

IT TAKES A VILLAGE

Michael Butler got involved with the original production of *Hair* after seeing an ad that depicted beads and feathers. Thinking it was a show about Native Americans, he checked it out. When it turned out to be about hippies instead, he stayed on board and produced the show on Broadway.

4

April

(1964) *Anyone Can Whistle* opened to great consternation to most who saw it. A messy tale of insanity, conformity, and corruption, it closed a week later. None of the show's leads had ever been in a Broadway musical. Angela Lansbury's voice had been dubbed in several MGM musicals, but she proved a powerful belter. Lee Remick was charming, but her voice lacked power, tone, and color. And Harry Guardino didn't really even try. Despite its downfalls, the show was utterly unique, and Stephen Sondheim's score verged on brilliant. Destined to become a cult classic, the show's cast album reveals the hastiness in which it was made.

broadway banter

"Anyone Can Whistle *is an exasperating musical comedy. It is exasperating because it isn't very musical ... It is exasperating because it isn't very comical.*"

—Walter Kerr

ALSO ON THIS DAY

Follies, another Sondheim failure/masterpiece, opened in 1971.

5

April

(1965) In the Oscar battle between musicals *My Fair Lady* and *Mary Poppins*, one category they couldn't go head to head in even if they wanted to was original song: *MFL* didn't have any. With no competition there, Poppins won for "Chim Chim Cher-ee" today. Which is odd, considering that there were far more memorable songs in that movie alone, including "A Spoonful of Sugar," the one-of-a-kind "Supercalifragilisticexpialidocious," and the poignant "Feed the Birds," which Walt Disney claimed was his all-time favorite song.

broadway banter

"Over the past couple of decades, Broadway has gradually been creeping toward becoming a tourist industry."

–Des McAnuff

POP QUIZ

Q: What 1966 musical adaptation starring Mary Tyler Moore and Richard Chamberlain flopped before making it to Broadway?

A: *Breakfast at Tiffany's*

6

April

(1947) The theater community gathered in the Grand Ballroom of the Waldorf Astoria to pay homage to the recently deceased Antoinette Perry. The American Theatre Wing presented awards for achievement in the previous season. In recognition of Perry, they would come to be known as the Tony Awards. Among the first year's recipients were David Wayne and Michael Kidd for *Finian's Rainbow*, Agnes de Mille for *Brigadoon*, and Kurt Weill for *Street Scene*.

broadway banter

"We called ourselves 'The Revuers,' and at the beginning we were doing other people's material. No one had explained to us that you're supposed to pay royalties for that sort of thing. And that's how our writing began, really: out of necessity. We realized we couldn't afford to buy material, so we chipped in and bought a pencil."

–Betty Comden and Adolph Green

CASTING COUCH

Among the original choices for Curly and Laurey in the film of *Oklahoma!* were Paul Newman and Joanne Woodward.

(1949) Some Enchanted Evening ... *South Pacific* opened on Broadway today. The book may be creaky now and much of the score over-performed, but it was a huge hit in its day, and took musical storytelling to a new level. And while some of the songs may be "corny as Kansas in August," others like the still-searing "You've Got to Be Carefully Taught" broke barriers through its direct treatment of racism and interracial marriage. Of course, having Mary Martin at the center of it all didn't hurt either.

April

broadway banter

"She had three numbers when we opened in New Haven and the same three numbers when she withdrew from the cast to go into films. So why twenty-three years later she tells talk-show audiences that I insisted on her best number being cut I'll never know."

—Ethel Merman on Betty Hutton in Panama Hattie

BACKSTAGE

Natalie Wood recorded all of her vocals as Maria for *West Side Story.* Only later did the studio executives decide to dub her voice with Marni Nixon.

8
April

(1990) He's ba-aaaaack. Andrew Lloyd Webber opened his latest London triumph, *Aspects of Love*, on Broadway today. It was his eighth show to make it to the Great White Way in two decades, and it was the first that would not even make it a year before folding. Lloyd Webber brought in his wife Sarah Brightman as a cast replacement, but by the time the show closed, they were divorced. Aspects did launch the semi-popular hit ballad "Love Changes Everything."

broadway banter

"She made a lot of enemies because she wanted to get it right. She was a selfish old broad. Still, it's a sin that they haven't named a theater for her."

—Elaine Stritch on Ethel Merman

STAR POWER

Lena Horne's role in *Jamaica* was originally written for Harry Belafonte.

9

April

(1898) Paul Robeson—the African-American actor of Shakespeare and Eugene O'Neill who also had the most melodious bass voice this side of the Mississippi River—was born. While it's often thought that Robeson originated the role of Joe in *Show Boat*, introducing the song "Ol' Man River," he actually did not originate the role on Broadway, but played the role in the original London production, then in the 1932 Broadway revival, and finally in the 1936 film.

broadway banter

"*I have never, ever, in my life been more proud to be a member of this community—men kissing each other on stage, drag queens, children—it's a perfect world!*"

—Michele Pawk

BY THE NUMBERS

The stage versions of *Beauty and the Beast* and *The Lion King* have each grossed more than $1 billion, far more than their respective film versions.

10
April

(1952) *Singin' in the Rain* opened across America. While it's often called the perfect musical, only two of its songs were written for the film: "Moses" and Donald O'Connor's show-stopping comic dance "Make 'Em Laugh." The rest, including the title number, were all recycled hits from other Nacio Herb Brown and Arthur Freed musicals.

The film parodied the dubbing of the voice of a silent film, but ironically, Debbie Reynolds's voice is dubbed by Betty Noyes in several songs, and Gene Kelly's taps in the title number are dubbed by the then-unknown Gwen Verdon and Carol Haney.

broadway banter

"Novelty is always welcome, but talking pictures are just a fad."

—*Irving Thalberg, on* The Jazz Singer

CASTING COUCH ————————————

When Harold Prince was toying with the idea of a film version of *Follies,* his stars in mind were Bette Davis and Joan Crawford.

11

April

(1991) *Miss Saigon* opened on Broadway today, and though it went on to became a smash hit, when it transferred from London to Broadway it was in a shroud of controversy. Actors' Equity opposed the transfer of the London production's stars, Jonathan Pryce and Lea Salonga, since neither were American. Additionally, various groups protested Pryce's casting as the half-Asian, half-European "Engineer." Ultimately, the two actors were allowed to come to Broadway, but for future replacements and tours, Asian roles would need to be filled with Asian actors. Both stars won Tonys for their efforts, as did supporting actor Hinton Battle, but the show lost in every other category to *The Will Rogers Follies* or *The Secret Garden*.

broadway banter

"I don't know what the world is coming to and that's a fact, except that it is obviously not coming to Sail Away."

—Noel Coward, on his charming but only moderately attended musical

STAR POWER

Gertrude Lawrence was buried in her "Shall We Dance" ballgown, having played her last performance just three weeks before her death.

12

April

(1923) Five hundred taps a minute: Ann Miller was born today. She and her mother lied about her age so that she could appear in films and onstage: Ann was only fourteen years old when she played a would-be Broadway dancer opposite such big-time stars as Katharine Hepburn and Ginger Rogers in *Stage Door*. Miller then went to Broadway to star in the successful *George White Scandals*, but when she returned to Hollywood, she spent nearly a decade in inferior vehicles before landing a plum role in *Easter Parade*, which led to choice supporting roles in *On the Town*, *Kiss Me Kate*, and other colorful productions. In 1998, she sang "I'm Still Here" in *Follies* at the Papermill Playhouse, and made her final screen appearance in the bizarre David Lynch film *Mulholland Drive* before dying in 2004.

broadway banter

"*Hello everybody. This is Mrs. Norman Maine.*"
            —*Vicki Lester in* A Star is Born, *by Moss Hart*

POP QUIZ

Q: Who was Barbra Streisand's understudy in *Funny Girl?*

A: Lainie Kazan

13
April

(2004) *Connie and Carla,* an homage to musicals and the women and gay men who love them, premiered in Universal City, California. Nia Vardalos, of *My Big Fat Greek Wedding* fame, and Toni Collette, of *Muriel's Wedding* fame, starred in this charming but derivative campfest: The eponymous singers, playing to single-digit audiences in an airport lounge, have to flee Chicago after witnessing a mob hit (*Some Like It Hot*). The women have to pretend to be men pretending to be women (*Victor/Victoria*) and rise to unexpected fame as the only drag queens who can actually sing. Everyone winds up happy after Debbie Reynolds makes a cameo appearance, singing "There Are Worse Things I Could Do."

broadway banter

"*Oklahoma! was the bomb.*"

—*John Lahr*

BACKSTAGE

The Miklos Laszlo play *The Parfumerie,* first made into the film *The Shop Around the Corner* and then *You've Got Mail,* has been twice musicalized, first on film with *In the Good Old Summertime,* then onstage with *She Loves Me.*

14

April

(1960) *Bye, Bye Birdie*, perhaps the first stage musical to acknowledge the burgeoning "rock and roll" sound permeating American music, opened on Broadway. Because of some strange Tony rules, the show's two leads, Dick Van Dyke and Chita Rivera, were classified as supporting performers. Both were nominated as such, though only Van Dyke emerged victorious.

When *Birdie* became a film in 1963, Van Dyke got to reprise his role, thanks in part to his successful TV show, but the ever-unlucky Rivera was replaced by the unlikely Janet Leigh.

broadway banter

"You sing it. I always hated this song anyway."

—Donald O'Connor to the audience, after forgetting the lyrics to a forgettable song in the forgettable sequel Bring Back Birdie

CASTING COUCH

The London production of *Song and Dance* once starred "To Sir with Love" singer Lulu.

(1945) One quarter of ABBA was born today: songwriter Bjorn Ulvaeus. After the breakup of the '70s Swedish supergroup, Ulvaeus and fellow ABBA member Benny Andersson would provide the music for two notable Broadway musicals. First came the delectable flop *Chess*, the story of Americans versus Russians played out against a backdrop of Cold War, romantic intrigue, and soaring pop tunes like "Heaven Help My Heart" and "One Night in Bangkok."

15
April

Next came the slightly less artistic but infinitely more commercial *Mamma Mia!*, the delightfully self-aware hodgepodge of some twenty hit ABBA tunes strung together into the story of a single mother, a daughter about to be married, and the three men who might be her biological father.

broadway banter

"When they were at their peak in the British charts, I hated ABBA."

–Catherine Johnson, writer of the book to Mamma Mia!

STAR POWER

Future stars who were in the original off-Broadway production of *Godspell* included Gilda Radner, Jeremy Irons, Victor Garber, Joe Mantegna, and Andrea Martin.

16
April

(1927) Edith "Edie" Adams was born today—but 1957 was really her best year. First, she won a Tony for Best Featured Actress as Daisy Mae in *L'il Abner*. Then, she played Julie Andrews's Fairy Godmother in Rodgers and Hammerstein's television version of *Cinderella*. Unfortunately, her theatrical career did not really take off after that; she never again appeared on Broadway, though she did work occasionally in films and more frequently on television.

Her early career highlight was playing Rosalind Russell's younger sister in the original Broadway *Wonderful Town* in 1953. However, Adams claimed that when the show was redone for television, Russell had Adams replaced with Jacquelyn McKeever because Russell was jealous of the notice Adams received.

broadway banter

"People make the generalization about Americans that we're very brash and loud and in your face, and I have to say that that is ... the way a musical should be done, I think."

—Bebe Neuwirth

POP QUIZ

Q: What unlucky musical creator has been nominated for ten Tony Awards but has never won?

A: Graciela Daniele: one for directing, one for book of a musical, and eight for choreography.

17

April

(1977) Just days before the family-friendly musical *Annie* opened, another musical with slightly different themes opened today: *I Love My Wife.* Instead of orphans and New Deal optimism, *Wife* offered '70s sexual freedom and wife-swapping. The diverse Cy Coleman supplied the jazzy score, and playing one of the wives was Joanna Gleason, who would later play an adulterous wife in her Tony-winning role of the Baker's Wife in *Into the Woods* eleven years later.

broadway banter

"To be able to direct, there are two things that you need: that supreme arrogance or need to express yourself, and the right equipment."

—Harold Prince

IT TAKES A VILLAGE

Andrew Lloyd Webber wasn't the first person to try to musicalize the film *Sunset Boulevard.* The movie's original star, Gloria Swanson, attempted to have it developed into a musical in the 1950s. Swanson wanted Norma Desmond to be played by "a high-voltage opera star who is also a great actress." The show, titled *Boulevard,* never came to pass.

18

April

(1994) If it can be done on film, why not on stage? *Beauty and the Beast* opened on Broadway today. I remember after seeing the film *Beauty* that a friend of mine and I were discussing how fun it would be to do it on stage. So, I would like to personally take credit for the idea of having dancing forks and singing plates on the Broadway stage. There, I've said it, it's off my chest.

This *Beauty* wasn't the critical smash the film was, though it's been about as solid a box-office success as there can be. Moreover, it paved the way for the "Disneyfication" of Broadway, with *The Lion King, Aida, Tarzan,* and *The Hunchback of Notre Dame* all on stage or in development.

broadway banter

"Cats [was a] middlebrow cartoon come to life."

–Jeffrey Eric Jenkins

STAR POWER

Size isn't everything: Dolores Gray won the Best Actress in a Musical Tony Award in 1954 for *Carnival in Flanders,* which, at only six performances, is the shortest-running Tony-winning performance.

(2001) After decades of fans wondering if Broadway musicals were dead, or at least replaced by British mega-musicals and dance concerts, *The Producers* arrived on Broadway and proved that musical comedy can still a) be a huge hit, and b) achieve artistic and critical success. The genius of Mel Brooks, Susan Stroman, Nathan Lane, Matthew Broderick, and the rest of the cast and creative team all but swept the Tony Awards, setting a record for number of nominations (fifteen) and wins (twelve).

19
April

broadway banter

"I want to thank Stephen Sondheim for not writing a score this year."

—Mel Brooks, *winning his second of three Tonys for* The Producers

CASTING COUCH

Succeeding Lauren Bacall as Margo Channing in *Applause* was none other than Anne Baxter, who played the title role in *All About Eve*, on which *Applause* was based.

20
April

(1954) It's a lazy afternoon: *The Golden Apple* opened on Broadway today. The show retold the story of *The Iliad* and *The Odyssey*, transplanting the stories to Seattle, Washington, at the opening of the twentieth century. Despite a winning score by John La Touche and Jerome Moross, the show had only a brief run and few major revivals. Kaye Ballard starred as Helen and sang the breakout hit song "Lazy Afternoon." Musical fans may recognize her costar Portia Nelson, who later played Sister Berthe in the film *The Sound of Music*.

broadway banter

"You gotta have heart and music,
Heart and music make a song."
　　　　　　　—*Gordon in* A New Brain, *by William Finn*

BACKSTAGE

The original title of **Anyone Can Whistle** was **Side Show**; the title would be used in a rather different Broadway musical some thirty years later.

21

April

(1977) The sun'll come out ... today. Into the bleak, recession-ridden American culture came a redheaded force of nature: *Annie* opened on Broadway. Nothing could bring this plucky orphan down—not the Great Depression, not a squalid orphanage, not a kidnapping plot. Thirteen-year-old Andrea McArdle charmed Broadway with her performance, and actually went on to have an acting career as an adult, belying the old myth that all child performers wind up on a "Whatever Happened To" TV special. In *Annie*, she eventually was replaced by Sarah Jessica Parker, another child actor who went on to have something of a career as an adult.

broadway banter

"When Dorothy Loudon as the keeper of an orphanage comes in to rouse her little girls as roughly as possible with a police whistle, blows it, and nearly takes the top of her own head off because of a hangover she's forgotten she has, you know that Annie is going to be all right."

–Otis L. Guernsey Jr.

STAR POWER

Tommy Tune is the only person to win Tony Awards in four different musical categories: Best Actor (*My One and Only*), Best Featured Actor (*Seesaw*), Best Director (three shows), Best Choreography (four shows).

22
April

(1993) First it was a record album, then a movie, then, inevitably, a stage musical: *The Who's Tommy* opened on Broadway today. Despite the fact that the music was twenty-five years old, Pete Townshend won the Tony for Best Score of a Musical, tying with Kander and Ebb for their *Kiss of the Spiderwoman*. Director Des McAnuff combined the spectacle of a Lloyd Webber show with the energy of a rock concert, and beat the legendary Hal Prince for the directing Tony. *Tommy* would run for more than two years.

broadway banter

"The score consists of one of the most continuous unpleasant sounds of our time, as if the music has been incorrectly transcribed by an organized gang of imps."

    —*Brooks Atkinson, on the* Cinderella *adaptation* If the Shoe Fits

POP QUIZ

Q: What three Oscar-winners also won Tony Awards for playing the same musical role onstage?

A: Yul Brynner, Rex Harrison, Joel Grey

23

April

(1928) Shirley Temple was born today, and just six years later, she would single-handedly lift America right out of the Depression with her sunshiny personality and song-and-dance routines that leapt off the movie screens. Well, perhaps not single-handedly, but just about. Her first film role of note was Shirley Dugan in *Stand Up and Cheer!* She made eleven movies in 1934, and she went on to hoof it in films like *Curly Top*, *Dimples*, and *Little Miss Broadway*.

She was the first choice to play Dorothy in *The Wizard of Oz*, but lost the role to Judy Garland either because Twentieth Century Fox wouldn't let her work for MGM or because her singing voice was too weak, depending on whose story you believe. As an adult, Shirley Temple Black served as U.S. Ambassador to Ghana and Czechoslovakia.

broadway banter

"There was one great towering figure in the cinema game, one artiste among artistes, one giant among the troupers, whose monumental, stupendous, and elephantine work deserved special mention ... Is Shirley Temple in the house?"

—Irvin S. Cobb, *presenting Temple with her special Oscar at age six-and-a-half*

BACKSTAGE

When *The Lion King* went into its first technical rehearsals in Minneapolis, numerous problems had to be overcome, including an actor's fear of heights, set pieces and puppets being too large, and moving set pieces not moving correctly.

24
April

(1934) Shirley MacLaine was born today, named for yesterday's birthday girl, Shirley Temple. Today's Shirl started out as a Broadway chorus girl. Then, in the hit show *The Pajama Game*, she was understudying Tony-winner Carol Haney, who broke her leg. Shirley went on for her, and that night, Warner Bros. producer Hal B. Wallis just happened to be in the audience. She was discovered and whisked away to Hollywood, where she would rarely get a chance to use her musical abilities except for *Sweet Charity* and *Postcards from the Edge*.

Sadly, Carol Haney would not go on to have Shirley's good fortune (see May 10).

broadway banter

"I call it 'Lost Her Reason.' I never miss a Liv Ullman musical!"

–Bette Midler on the ill-fated film musical Lost Horizon

STAR POWER

Liza Minnelli's stage vehicle *The Act* was based in part on the real-life experiences of Shirley MacLaine.

April

(1996) *Rent* opened the door for a new era in contemporary musicals, and *Bring in 'Da Noise, Bring in 'Da Funk,* which opened on Broadway today, made it a one-two punch. Both *Rent* and *Noise/Funk* became solid hits and critical successes, and they snatched up most of the awards between them at season's end, beating out traditional, often staid shows like *Big, State Fair,* and *Victor/Victoria.*

George C. Wolfe, the prolific director of the epic *Angels in America,* conceived and directed *Noise/Funk;* Savion Glover, its whiz-kid choreographer, has not returned to Broadway in the ensuing decade.

broadway banter

"It really broke my heart. I worked on it for three years, and it was my best stuff, and it never got on."

—Mary Rodgers, on her failed adaptation of Carson McCullers's Member of the Wedding

CASTING COUCH

The original choice for the role of Fanny Brice in *Funny Girl* was Mary Martin. She passed on it, so then it was offered to Anne Bancroft. Finally, it went to Barbra Streisand, who rode the role to stardom.

26

April

(1970) *Company* opened on Broadway. As experimental and unusual as it was, it was a hit (706 performances) and was mostly well received by critics. But getting there wasn't easy: Sondheim rewrote the main song multiple times, first as the overly romantic "Marry Me a Little," then as the decidedly depressing "Happily Ever After," before finally settling on the ambiguous "Being Alive."

While writing "The Ladies Who Lunch" for Elaine Stritch, Sondheim found himself pounding away at his piano and singing the song at the top of his voice late one night. He soon found himself with an unexpected visit from his next-door neighbor, Katharine Hepburn, who had only to shoot the composer a withering look to get her point across. Sondheim soon bought an electric piano and headphones.

broadway banter

"They were so involved in this show that when there was a coffee break everyone looked sad."

—Elaine Stritch, on the creative team behind Company

IT TAKES A VILLAGE

In Sondheim's lyrics for "Company," the line "Hank and Mary get into town tomorrow" is a sly reference to his longtime friend Mary Rodgers and her husband Hank Guettel.

27

April

(**1998**) It should have been a marriage made in heaven: Cole Porter's high-society music and lyrics and Philip Barry's high-society comedy, *The Philadelphia Story*. *High Society* opened on Broadway today. But it barely worked as a movie in 1956, and it really didn't work as a revised stage musical in 1998: Despite a winning score sung by some of Broadway's best, including John McMartin, Melissa Errico, Stephen Bogardus, Randy Graff, and the darling young Anna Kendrick, the show fizzled fast and closed four months later.

broadway banter

"Cole Porter's score for Anything Goes *is one of the most glorious in the history of the American Musical Theater."*

—Thomas Cott

POP QUIZ

Q: In what musical did Angela Lansbury play a Southern widow who gets back at her dead racist husband by letting men of all minority races rape her?

A: *Prettybelle*—the show mercifully closed before reaching Broadway

28

April

(1941) Ann-Margret was born today (although it's worth noting that while I was growing up, I thought her name was "Ann Margrock," following her guest appearance on an episode of *The Flintstones*). Finally (last year), someone set me straight. Usually cast as a sexy young thing, she incongruously made her musical debut playing a R&H ingénue in the 1962 remake of *State Fair*. She also sexed it up in musicals like *Viva Las Vegas* and *Bye Bye Birdie*.

In the 1970s, she overcame a twenty-two-foot fall from a stage to win an Oscar nomination for the film version of *The Who's Tommy*. Still playing sexy in her fifties and sixties, she camped it up in the cult Disney film *Newsies* and headlined a national tour of *The Best Little Whorehouse in Texas*.

broadway banter

Princeton: Maybe my purpose is to take everything I'm learning ... and put it ...into a show!

Bryan: Are you high?

—Avenue Q, *by Jeff Whitty*

STAR POWER

Shortly after the opening of *1776*, Howard Da Silva (Ben Franklin) had a heart attack, and was replaced by his understudy, Rex Everhart, while he recovered. He missed recording the cast album, but a few years later, got to be in the film version.

April

(1919) Celeste Holm, the original girl who "cain't say no," was born. A highly versatile talent, she made her singing debut as the confused Ado Annie, then went on to play the pioneering Evelina in *Bloomer Girl*, the witty Liz Imbrie in the film *High Society*, and the no-nonsense Aunt Polly in *Tom Sawyer*. She also replaced Gertrude Lawrence in *The King and I* while the star vacationed. And I shouldn't fail to mention her trio of Oscar-nominated performances for her dramatic work; she won for *Gentleman's Agreement*.

broadway banter

"No legs, no jokes, no chance."
—Mike Todd, on Oklahoma! in previews

CASTING COUCH

When Hal Prince was casting *She Loves Me* in 1964, he couldn't decide between Barbara Cook and Dorothy Collins for his leading lady. He ultimately went with Cook. The two actresses would later be linked in the role of Sally in *Follies*: Collins played the role in 1971 on Broadway, and Cook did the concert recording in 1985.

30
April

(1908) With all the talent of a true star and a birth name like Eunice Quedens, there's only one thing to do: change your name to Eve Arden, who was born today.

Though primarily known as a film actress—playing sidekicks, secretaries, and other small but scene-stealing roles—Eve also made many stage appearances, including *Ziegfeld Follies of 1934* with Bob Hope, *Two for the Show,* and Cole Porter's *Let's Face It!* She also starred in the national tour of *Hello, Dolly!*

In the twilight of her career, Eve made herself known to a new generation of fans, playing Principal McGee in *Grease* and *Grease 2.*

broadway banter

"Miss Bacall is a sensation. She sings with all the misty beauty of an on-tune foghorn."

—Clive Barnes, on *Lauren Bacall* in Applause

POP QUIZ ———

Q: In what Woody Allen movie musical do Julia Roberts, Alan Alda, Goldie Hawn, and Edward Norton sing?

A: *Everyone Says I Love You*

MAY

Barbara Cook and Robert Preston onstage in *The Music Man* at
the Majestic on Broadway, December 19, 1957–April 15, 1961.

1

May

(1983) When all else fails, bring back Gershwin: *My One and Only* opened today, the "new Gershwin musical" developed by Tommy Tune. The six-foot-six-and-a-half-inch Tune did triple duty, as co-director, co-choreographer, and leading man, sharing the latter two duties with Thommie Walsh. Tommy and Thommie—how cute! Tune reunited with his costar from the turgid film musical *The Boyfriend*, Twiggy. Although she had improved her acting and singing somewhat since her disastrous *Boyfriend* performance, this would be the Twig's only Broadway outing.

broadway banter

"Screw the movie version! I will never accept it! And I will never do a Lloyd Webber show again."

—*"Patti Lupone"* on Evita, in Forbidden Broadway Strikes Back! *by Gerard Alessandrini*

ALSO ON THIS DAY———————————

May Day must be a favorite with Tommy Tune: In 1991, he opened his last Broadway hit to date, *The Will Rogers Follies.*

May

(1984) After the debacle that was *Merrily We Roll Along* (sixteen performances), Stephen Sondheim bounced back with *Sunday in the Park with George*, which opened on Broadway today. As he did with *Evening Primrose* after the failure of *Anyone Can Whistle*, he wrote about the struggles of the artist and the difficulty in finding acceptance therein.

With James Lapine, he brought Georges Seurat's painting *Sunday Afternoon on the Island La Grand Jatte* to life, fictionalizing Seurat's life and inventing his artist grandson who dealt with similar struggles in the 1980s. Stars Mandy Patinkin and Bernadette Peters were both at the peak of their talents. Although they lost most of the Tonys to *La Cage Aux Folles* a month later, Sondheim and book writer James Lapine received the Pulitzer Prize the following year.

broadway banter

The songs were rotten, the book was stinkin',
What he did to Shakespeare Booth did to Lincoln

—*"Opening Night" in* The Producers, *lyrics by Mel Brooks*

ALSO ON THIS DAY

Crooner Bing Crosby, star of *Holiday Inn, White Christmas,* and innumerable other musicals, was born in 1903.

3

May

(1960) A little off-Broadway musical called *The Fantasticks* opened today. Nearly forty-two years later, it would close with 17,162 performances to its credit, not only the longest-running show in New York City, but the longest-running show in the United States, ever. The little show that could outlasted the splashy *Hello, Dolly!*, the indominitable *A Chorus Line*, and set a record even *Phantom* will have difficulty outlasting. Around the world, there have been some 12,000 productions in 3,500 cities and sixty-seven nations.

Perhaps one of the most poignant recordings in musicals is that of the original *El Gallo*, Jerry Orbach, singing "Try to Remember."

broadway banter

"You can't be sad for a show that has run forty-two years."

—Tom Jones, *lyricist of* The Fantasticks

POP QUIZ ─────────────────────────────

Q: What '80s flop musical was written by Marvin Hamlisch and Howard Ashman and featured Jodi Benson, the voice of the Little Mermaid?

A: Smile

(1984) Talk about a movie that is a product of its time: *Breakin'* premiered today. If you think 1930s musicals are dated, check out the big hair, tight clothes, and dance moves in this ridiculously campy but fun 1980s cheesefest. The motion picture debut of Ice-T and a quick cameo by Jean-Claude Van Damme make this, if nothing else, a one-of-a-kind movie. Thank God.

4
May

broadway banter

"There's no plot and there's no play
Just Bert Lahr and Dolores Gray—the end!"

—*Two on the Aisle, by Betty Comden and Adolph Green*

STAR POWER

Susan Hayward played two real-life singers in film musicals: Jane Froman in *With a Song in My Heart* (Froman dubbing Hayward's singing voice) and Lillian Roth in *I'll Cry Tomorrow* (Hayward doing her own singing). Later, Hayward would again be dubbed in *Valley of the Dolls*, then did her own singing in the Las Vegas production of *Mame.*

5

May

(1915) Alice Faye was born, as was her co-star in *Alexander's Ragtime Band*, Tyrone Power, on this same day two years earlier. The two also teamed up in the classic *In Old Chicago*, which Edward Albee used to great comic effect in his *Who's Afraid of Virginia Woolf?* years later.

Faye was the darling of the 1930s musical, but after making *The Gang's All Here* in 1943, she made no more musicals and just one other film until the 1962 remake of *State Fair*. In 1974, she would make her only Broadway appearance in the revival of *Good News*, a flop that played all of sixteen performances.

broadway banter

"*Six films I made with Don Ameche, and in every one of them my voice was deeper than the plot.*"

—Alice Faye

POP QUIZ

Q: Who made her last screen appearance as the bird woman in *Mary Poppins*?

A: Jane Darwell, who played Ma Joad in *The Grapes of Wrath*.

6

May

(1933) We're in the money! *Gold Diggers of 1933* premiered today, but almost wasn't a musical. The Busby Berkley numbers were added after filming had been completed, and only after similar songs were such a huge hit in *42nd Street*. *Gold Diggers* reunited not only choreographer Berkley and songwriters Al Warren and Harry Dubin, but stars Ruby Keeler, Dick Powell, and Ginger Rogers. A few years later, Dick Powell married the newcomer to this cast, Joan Blondell.

broadway banter

"Just remember if anyone out front could do as well as you, they would be up here doing it."

—Ethel Merman, advising Betty Garrett on opening night

CASTING COUCH

Natalie Wood was an early choice for Maria in *West Side Story,* but was originally eliminated from the casting pool because the producers wanted to go with unknowns. At almost the last minute, she was given a screen test and nabbed the part.

7

May

(1937) Astaire, Rogers, Gershwin: Who could ask for anything more? *Shall We Dance* premiered today, pairing America's favorite dance team for the seventh time. Fred Astaire introduced the classic "They Can't Take That Away from Me," which was nominated for an Oscar, while Fred and Ginger danced and sang on roller skates to "Let's Call the Whole Thing Off."

broadway banter

Stan: Hey, no wonder that Barbra Streisand lady wanted it.

Barbra Streisand, in disguise: Oh, who is that?

Stan: Just this really, really old lady who wishes she was only forty-five.

—From South Park, *written by* Trey Parker, Matt Stone, *and* Pam Brady

STAR POWER

The TV show *Fame* launched the careers of future stars, semi-stars, and Broadway notables Michael Cerveris, Carrie Hamilton, Jasmine Guy, Janet Jackson, and Harold Perrineau Jr.

8

May

(1892) Italian baritone Ezio Pinza was born today. Primarily a star of opera, he gained lasting fame at the age of fifty-seven as the man Mary Martin wanted to "wash right out of her hair" in *South Pacific*. He, like everything in the show, was a huge hit. But when the film version was made, he was replaced by the non-singing Rossano Brazzi. Pinza also starred in the Broadway musical *Fanny*, which suffered an even more drastic fate: When *Fanny* was made into a movie six years later, all of the music was cut.

broadway banter

"The musical theater is totally American; and when it's good, it's like nothing else."

—Ann Reinking

BACKSTAGE

The opening dance sequence in the film *West Side Story* was shot on location in New York City, on West 61st Street and East 110th Street.

9
May

(2001) Move over Lorelei Lee: Diamonds are now Satine's best friend. Today, *Moulin Rouge* premiered at the Cannes Film Festival. Using mostly existing songs ranging from *The Sound of Music* to Madonna to The Police, Baz Luhrmann reinvigorated the musical, making it the first successful live action musical— artistically and/or financially—in nearly three decades. While some might call it a two-hour music video, it was undeniably visually stunning, and who knew Nicole Kidman or Ewan McGregor could sing?

broadway banter

"What we get at the Mark Hellinger is closer to rock bottom than rock opera: a mediocre score with less than mediocre lyrics ..."

—*John Simon*, on Jesus Christ Superstar

POP QUIZ

Q: What five actors have won Academy Awards for roles in musicals?

A: James Cagney, *Yankee Doodle Dandy*; Yul Brynner, *The King and I*; George Chakiris, *West Side Story*; Rex Harrison, *My Fair Lady*; Joel Grey, *Cabaret*

10

May

(1899) Can't sing, can't act, can dance a little: so said one Hollywood exec of the screen test of Fred Astaire, born today. With his sister Adele, he made his Broadway debut at age eighteen, later appearing in *Lady, Be Good, Funny Face,* and *Gay Divorce.* He then headed for Hollywood, where he costarred with Ginger Rogers in ten movie musicals, including *Roberta, Swing Time,* and their onscreen debut, *Flying Down to Rio.* Still a song-and-dance man throughout his fifties in movies like *Daddy Long Legs, Funny Face,* and *Silk Stockings,* Astaire played opposite increasingly younger costars like Leslie Caron, Audrey Hepburn, and Cyd Charisse. Late in his career, he lent his voice to two semi-classic Claymation holiday specials: *Santa Claus Is Comin' to Town* and the derivative *The Easter Bunny Is Comin' to Town.*

broadway banter

"I would like to thank—well, all the kids in the American Theatre would like to thank—Miss Rosie O'Donnell for the unbelievable support she continuously throws our way."

—Elaine Stritch

ALSO ON THIS DAY

Carol Haney, the Fosse dancer whose injury allowed for Shirley MacLaine to be discovered while filling in for her, died on this day in 1964 at the age of only thirty-nine. She choreographed *Flower Drum Song, She Loves Me,* and *Funny Girl.*

11

May

(1888) Israel Isidore Baline was born today, but we know him better as Irving Berlin. Berlin wrote so many show tunes in his day, and so many of them were hits, that we could have enough material to write a "Today in Irving Berlin History" book. He made his Broadway debut at the age of thirteen, and by the time he was thirty, he had contributed music and lyrics to a dozen Broadway shows. His first song for motion pictures was the title number for the animated short *When the Midnight Choo-Choo Leaves for Alabam'*.

He wrote his last Broadway score, *Mr. President*, at the age of seventy-three, and at the age of nearly eighty, he wrote a new song for *Annie Get Your Gun*. He lived to be 101 years old.

broadway banter

"The only hit that comes out of a Helen Lawson show is Helen Lawson. And that's me, baby, remember?"

—*Helen Lawson, in* Valley of the Dolls *by Jacqueline Susann, screenplay by Helen Deutch and Dorothy Kingsley*

BY THE NUMBERS

The youngest actor to win a Tony was Frankie Michaels, ten, for *Mame* (1966).

(1988) One of the most ill-fated musicals of all time opened: *Carrie*. Three days later, it closed. With music and lyrics by *Fame* songwriters Michael Gore and Dean Pitchford, this fiasco ranks among the worst ideas for musicals ever. Based on the Stephen King novel and ensuing film, the musical included such song titles as "And Eve Was Weak," "Out for Blood" (sung, of course, at the pig farm), and "I Remember How Those Boys Could Dance." It was such a huge flop that it inspired Ken Mandelbaum to write *Not Since Carrie*, a book dedicated to chronicling Broadway flop musicals, or flopsicals, as they're sometimes called.

Despite the ridiculousness of this concept, the stars Betty Buckley (Mrs. White) and Linzi Hately (Carrie) were mostly praised, though the flop clearly hurt both women's careers, as between the two, only Buckley has created another musical role on Broadway, in the (not as) short-running *Triumph of Love*.

12
May

broadway banter

"*Dreamgirls* is all style and no substance."

—*Douglas Watt*

STAR POWER

Vivian Vance, *I Love Lucy's* Ethel Mertz, spent years in Broadway musicals prior to achieving eternal fame as one of TV's funniest sidekicks.

13
May

(1923) She didn't belt out "What'll I do?" and "Hard-Hearted Hannah" for nothing. Golden Girl Bea Arthur was born on this day, probably crying for the first time with the same gravelly bass-baritone voice she put to use in the original Broadway productions of *Fiddler on the Roof* and *Mame*, for which she won a Tony.

Arthur returned to Broadway in 2002 with a one-woman show, in which she did everything from sing—her "Pirate Jenny" was one of the most amazing performances yours truly has ever seen—to tell transvestite nun jokes to give a mouthwatering recipe for lamb, eggplant, and roasted tomatoes.

broadway banter

"The man was a genius ... but he really wasn't a very nice person. Actually, he was the only director who made me cry. He was really a dreadful human being."

—Bea Arthur, on Jerome Robbins

POP QUIZ

Q: What unwieldy 1973 musical adaptation starring Lesley Ann Warren closed on the road before reaching Broadway?

A: *Gone with the Wind*

14

May

(1936) Today, Irene Dunne is best-remembered for her screwball comedy and dramatic acting skills. But in the 1930s, she was Jerome Kern's soprano of choice, and on this day, her film *Show Boat* premiered. While it was not the first version of the landmark stage musical (that came in 1929, a mostly silent version) or the splashiest (1951's color version with Ava Gardner lip-synching), Dunne and company provide the best singing and the most charm and realism.

Dunne, playing ingénue Magnolia, was accompanied by legends like torch singer Helen Morgan as Julie, Paul Robeson in his career-defining performance as Joe, future Oscar-winner Hattie McDaniel as Queenie, and a stellar supporting cast who all did their own singing.

broadway banter

"[You] know that there are any number of actresses who can do this part as well as I can ... but there is nobody who can do this better ... and further, it is my turn."

—Betty Buckley, on auditioning for Trevor Nunn for Cats

ALSO ON THIS DAY

New Girl in Town opened today, a musical version of Eugene O'Neill's *Anna Christie. Anna Christie?* You got it. It starred Gwen Verdon and Thelma Ritter. *Thelma Ritter?* You got it.

15

May

(1977) Little did I know as I was celebrating my fourth birthday in Milwaukee, Wisconsin, that two legends of the Broadway Musical were teaming up for a one-night-only event: Ethel Merman and Mary Martin appeared in *Together on Broadway*.

Audiences paid up to $150 to see them perform at the Broadway Theater, emceed by Cyril Ritchard. At one point, Merman and Martin each descended a *Hello, Dolly!* staircase wearing a *Hello, Dolly!* gown and backed up by the likes of Joel Grey, Yul Brynner, and Burgess Meredith. Walter Kerr wrote of the evening, "Ethel Merman is the bonfire and Mary Martin is the smoke. They go nicely together, if you're in the mood to burn up the town!"

broadway banter

"The hills are alive with the sound of music was the first best movie I ever saw ... All I ever wanted to be in life was the star of that show. Someone who sang like a record and ran and twirled in the mountains."

—Edna in The Good Times Are Killing Me, *by Lynda Barry*

ALSO ON THIS DAY

Sharing my birthday are Lainie Kazan, Anna Maria Alberghetti (Tony winner for *Carnival!*), Cleavant Derricks (Tony winner for *Dreamgirls*), and longtime President of the American Theater Wing, Isabelle Stevenson.

16

May

(1946) *Annie Get Your Gun* opened on Broadway today, and it became the biggest hit for composer Irving Berlin, running for nearly three years and launching such hit songs as "There's No Business Like Show Business," "You Can't Get a Man with a Gun," "Doin' What Comes Natur'lly," and "Anything You Can Do."

One of the show's most famous songs, the double-melody duet "Old Fashioned Wedding," actually wasn't added to the score until the 1966 Broadway revival, which starred the show's original Annie Oakley, Ethel Merman.

broadway banter

"Boy am I glad this wasn't a beauty contest!"

—Harvey Fierstein, *accepting his Tony for* Hairspray
over Antonio Banderas

ALSO ON THIS DAY

New Faces of 1952 opened on Broadway, launching the careers of performers Alice Ghostley, Eartha Kitt, Carol Lawrence, Charlotte Rae, and Paul Lynde, featuring sketches and songs by Sheldon Harnick and Mel Brooks.

17
May

(2000) An Icelandic songstress playing a Czech woman who's going blind and has to commit murder so that her son will be able to have an operation and avoid her fate? Only with Björk and Danish director Lars von Trier. The simultaneously moving and numbing *Dancer in the Dark* blended a gritty factory setting with fantasy musical numbers, complete with an appearance by *Cabaret*'s Emcee, Joel Grey.

The only thing that topped the film itself was Björk's legendary "swan" costume that she wore to the Oscars that year to sing her nominated song from the film, "I've Seen It All." Boy, she wasn't kidding.

broadway banter

"*Lerner, Loewe, and Hart have spent so much to mount* Camelot *that the wisecrackers have been calling it 'Costalot.*'"

—*Robert Coleman*

ALSO ON THIS DAY

Bob Merrill, lyricist to shows like *New Girl in Town, Carnival!,* and *Funny Girl,* was born in 1921.

18
May

(2003) One Day More! Well, maybe not: *Les Miserables* closed today. The long-running show—sixteen years and 6,680 performances—was another nail in the coffin of the Era of the British Musical, following the closings of *Cats* in 2000 and *Miss Saigon* in 2001.

Among the scores of replacement cast members were "Eponines" Kerry Butler, Deborah "Debbie" Gibson, and Lea Salonga; "Javerts" Anthony Crivello, Greg Edelman, Robert Cuccioli, Shuler Hensley, Chuck Wagner, and Robert Westenberg; and "Fantines" Laurie Beechman, Debbie Gravitte, Andrea McArdle, Melba Moore, Paige O'Hara, Alice Ripley, and Rachel York.

broadway banter

"He just made you go so far above what you thought was your level best."

—Rita Moreno, on Jerome Robbins

ALSO ON THIS DAY

Robert Morse, star of *How to Succeed in Business Without Really Trying* on stage and film, was born in 1931. Morse also played the Jack Lemmon role in the 1972 stage musical adaptation of *Some Like It Hot*, retitled *Sugar*.

19
May

(2003) But will it play in Cincinnati? *Boobs! The Musical (The World According to Ruth Wallis)* opened off-Broadway today. *The Village Voice*'s Michael Musto wrote, "*Boobs! The Musical* is a revue of numbers by Ruth Wallis, who in the Rock-and-Doris era devised dirty ditties like 'The Dinghy Song' and 'Johnny's Got a Yo-yo.'" The latter song featured the double-entendre-rife lyrics:

> He never lends it out to any other kids in town,
> 'Cause I'm the only one who knows
> How to get it up and down.

I hope my grandmother doesn't read this!

broadway banter

"It was called Smile, Smile, Smile. *I didn't, didn't, didn't."*

–Clive Barnes

ALSO ON THIS DAY

It's a boy, Mrs. Townshend: The Who's Peter Townshend was born in 1945. He wrote the concept albums-turned movies *Quadrophenia* and *Tommy*, the latter written at just twenty-three.

May

(1958) Almost a star is born: Judy Kuhn. Never quite a Broadway diva, Kuhn has pieced together a career of near-misses, showy roles in minor productions, and flops. Kuhn's first big break came with *Rags*, a five-performance flop. Fortunately, her next outing came later that same season: Cosette in *Les Miserables*, for which she received her first Tony nomination. She then snagged the role of her career, Florence in *Chess*. The show, despite her thrilling vocals, was another flop. Kuhn got to show off her upper register in the Roundabout revival of *She Loves Me*, but she missed taking part in the cast recording because she was off to her next venture: Betty in the American premiere *Sunset Boulevard* in Los Angeles. She didn't make the trip with *Sunset* to Broadway, though, as she was recording vocals for the title role in *Pocahontas*, reunited with her *Rags* lyricist, Stephen Schwartz. It's a crime that Kuhn hasn't found her way back into a Broadway production since.

broadway banter

"We are so excited to be here, we feel just like the Bush twins at happy hour."

—*Nathan Lane, on co-hosting the Tonys with Matthew Broderick*

IT TAKES A VILLAGE

George Gershwin was also a prolific painter.

21 May

(1959) *Gypsy* opened on Broadway. While it would ultimately become one of the greatest musicals of all time, it was only a moderate success in its first run, losing all its Tonys to the now-forgotten *Fiorello!* and the audience-pleasing but hardly superior *The Sound of Music*. Playing the title role in *Fiorello!* was Tom Bosley, who went on to lasting fame as Mr. Cunningham on *Happy Days* and the title role in *Father Dowling Mysteries*. Bosley returned to Broadway in 1994, originating the role of Maurice in *Beauty and the Beast*, and later played Herr Schultz in the revival of *Cabaret*.

broadway banter

"*I'm going to make you a star!*"

—Rose in Gypsy, *by Arthur Laurents*

BY THE NUMBERS

In 1972, *Follies* won seven Tony Awards, but lost Best Musical to *Two Gentlemen of Verona*, and *Cabaret* won eight Oscars, but lost Best Picture to *The Godfather*.

22
May

(1956) The day Gene Kelly had waited for four years finally arrived: *Invitation to the Dance* premiered. The unique film, predating *Contact* by some forty-plus years, told three different stories, all in dance/movement, with no speaking or singing. The result was, well, not that good: MGM shelved it after it tested poorly. When it was finally released, it played only in art houses.

broadway banter

"When I was thirteen years old, I was on the road with the show Gypsy *... And I played one of the Hollywood Blondes, but my bio says I played Dainty June, and that's a lie, I have to tell you. I feel really bad. I was only the understudy. My mother put it in there. She thought it sounded much better early on in a career, and I really need to apologize to that girl who played—do you remember her name? Suzy? Her name was Suzy. ... If anyone knows her please tell her. I owe her an apology and I will change that bio right away—right after this show is over."*

—Bernadette Peters

STAR POWER

West Side Story costars Richard Beymer and Natalie Wood did not like each other or speak to each other off camera.

23

May

(1921) African-American theater artists and audiences had something to cheer for today. After decades of white actors doing blackface, *Shuffle Along*, the first show written by blacks, opened on Broadway in 1921. Written by Noble Sissle and Eubie Blake, the show featured an all-black cast—the first time black actors appeared on a Broadway stage in ten years. More important, for the first time, black actors and characters were presented without stereotypes or racism. The show was a big hit, running more than a year, and Harry S. Truman later chose the show's "I'm Just Wild About Harry" for his reelection campaign song.

broadway banter

"[Moss] Hart has never hidden from the world the fact that he has been wallowing in the luxury of psychoanalysis for the past four years; and Lady in the Dark *is one way of getting back all that money."*

–Brooks Atkinson

ALSO ON THIS DAY——

The singing actress Betty Garrett was born in 1919, and the acting singer Rosemary Clooney was born in 1928.

(1966) Following his mega-hit *Hello, Dolly!*, Jerry Herman opened another hit, not quite as huge but still a substantial warhorse to be: *Mame*. Angela Lansbury, a talented but under-appreciated supporting player for more than twenty years in Hollywood, finally got the role that would launch her to stardom. She was ably supported by Bea Arthur, Jane Connell, and Frankie Michaels, but when it came time to make the movie, she was supplanted by the very miscast Lucille Ball. The leaden film was, unsurprisingly, a total flop.

May

broadway banter

"[Dahling], it looks as if you've got another hit show that's certain to run on Broadway two years. Let's see now, you've had about fifty shows that have run over two years each, haven't you."

–Tallulah Bankhead, to Ethel Merman

ALSO ON THIS DAY

Alfred Molina, star of the 2003 "British" *Fiddler on the Roof*, was born today.

25
May

(1943) At the age of twenty-three, Leslie Uggams, born today, blew the roof off the Martin Beck Theater in her Broadway debut as Georgina in *Hallelujah, Baby!* The show won a slew of Tonys, including one for Leslie. Her next trip to Broadway wasn't quite as fruitful: Cleopatra in *Her First Roman* (seventeen performances). And *The Leslie Uggams Show* on CBS was cancelled almost before it began.

In the 1980s, she belted in the national tour and then on Broadway in *Jerry's Girls* and replaced Patti LuPone in *Anything Goes*, and she more recently has experienced a career renaissance, appearing in *King Hedley II*, *Thoroughly Modern Millie*, and *On Golden Pond*.

broadway banter

"If I ever need a heart transplant I'd want David's heart because it's never been used."

—Phyllis Diller, on impresario David Merrick

POP QUIZ ——————————————————

Q: What 1930s singing sensation was also an All-American football player, a lawyer, a political activist, a classical actor, and a linguist who spoke some twelve languages?

A: Paul Robeson

May

(1955) The virginal Doris Day shed her squeaky-clean image: *Love Me or Leave Me* premiered. Day starred as Ruth Etting, a 1920s singing star with a past. Day showed the sultry side of her voice, nailing such standards as "You Made Me Love You," "It All Depends on You," "Ten Cents a Dance," and the title number. Amazingly, Day did not get an Oscar nomination for her work, but her non-singing costar James Cagney did, as did the dubbed Eleanor Parker for another musical biopic, *Interrupted Melody*.

broadway banter

"I knew her before she was a virgin."

—Oscar Levant, on Doris Day

STAR POWER

According to Elaine Stritch, in a performance of Ethel Merman's hit musical *Call Me Madam*, Merman was being hounded by a drunken heckler in the audience. As she sang the last line of her song, she stopped cold before the final word, walked off the stage and into the audience, picked up the man, led him up the aisle, tossed him out of the theater, came back onstage, and sang the final note as if nothing had happened.

May

(1908) Harold Rome isn't exactly the most famous name in musicals history, but he was one of the most prolific Broadway composers of the golden era. Born today, Rome's shows spanned some thirty years and included *Call Me Mister, Wish You Were Here, Fanny,* and *Destry Rides Again.* Young Barbra Streisand began her rise to fame in a revival of his *Pins and Needles,* then in his *I Can Get It for You Wholesale,* which was her first Broadway show.

broadway banter

"Barbra Streisand, who plays a secretary and resembles an amiable ant-eater, has her moment in the sun with 'Miss Marmelstein.'"

–John McClain on I Can Get It for You Wholesale

ALSO ON THIS DAY ————————————

Who's afraid of the big bad wolf? Not Walt Disney: The classic "Three Little Pigs" short cartoon premiered today in 1933.

28

May

(1953) *Me and Juliet* opened on Broadway today, the seventh collaboration between Oscar Hammerstein II and Richard Rodgers, the second that was only a moderate success, and the first outright comedy. Set backstage in a theater where *Romeo and Juliet* is being performed, the show featured Isabel Bigley, Ray Walston, and a young dancer named Shirley MacLaine.

broadway banter

"Opening night, I remember walking out onstage, and the next thing I knew I was taking a bow. It was like I went into a trance ... nothing like that had ever happened to me before."

—Leslie Uggams, on her Broadway debut

ALSO ON THIS DAY

An unexpected four-and-a-half-year hit, *The Magic Show* opened in 1974. Built around magician Doug Henning, the show featured the music of Stephen Schwartz and supporting performances from Robert LuPone, Cheryl Barnes, David Ogden Stiers, and Anita Morris.

29

May

(1894) The great singing comedienne Beatrice Lillie was born today—not in England, where her career would begin, but in Toronto. Early in her career as a performer in British musical revues, she became lifelong friends with Gertrude Lawrence. Bea Lillie, more of a performer than an actress, starred in numerous musical revues, but ended her career by playing two characters other than her usual self: the spiritual medium Madame Arcati in *High Spirits* on Broadway, and the white slaver Mrs. Meers in the film *Thoroughly Modern Millie*.

broadway banter

"Pearl Bailey did the show for two years and missed three years of performances."

–David Merrick, *on* Hello, Dolly!

POP QUIZ

Q: What six actresses have won Academy Awards for roles in musicals?

A: Luise Rainer, *The Great Ziegfeld*; Rita Moreno, *West Side Story*; Julie Andrews, *Mary Poppins*; Barbra Streisand, *Funny Girl*; Liza Minnelli, *Cabaret*; Catherine Zeta-Jones, *Chicago*

30

May

(1971) Idina Menzel began defying gravity today. With a powerful belt and a bod to die for, Menzel took Broadway by storm as Maureen in the original cast of *Rent*, earning her first Tony nomination. After taking over the role of Amneris in *Aida* for four months, she then ascended to the role that would take her to new heights: Elphaba in *Wicked*. Paired with Kristin Chenoweth, with whom she reportedly did not get along, Menzel all but stole the show with her Act One finale, "Defying Gravity," taking home the Tony to boot.

broadway banter

"It was lust at first sight. Then we decided we had nothing in common."

—Idina Menzel, on meeting her now-husband Taye Diggs in Rent

ALSO ON THIS DAY

Tonya Pinkins, one of the actresses Idina Menzel defeated for the 2004 Tony, was born in 1962. Pinkins, nominated that year for her astonishing work in *Caroline, or Change*, already had a Tony to her name for *Play On!*

31
May

(1979) Why are there so many songs about rainbows? *The Muppet Movie* premiered today in Great Britain, three weeks before opening in the United States. After ten years of success on television with *Sesame Street, The Muppet Show,* and various muppet specials, Jim Henson moved his muppets to the big screen for the first time. With a clever score by Paul Williams and Kenny Ascher, the film received two Oscar nominations and remains a favorite of Generation-Xers, especially the poignant opening number, "The Rainbow Connection."

Alongside the muppets, more than a dozen stars made cameos, including the likes of Orson Welles, Bob Hope, Edgar Bergen, Richard Pryor, and Madeline Kahn.

broadway banter

"Life's like a movie. Write your own ending."

—Kermit in The Muppet Movie, *by Jack Burns and Jerry Juhl*

ALSO ON THIS DAY

Brooke Shields, a replacement star for *Grease, Chicago, Cabaret,* and *Wonderful Town* who never originated a role on Broadway but who managed to get two "replacement cast" cast albums made, was born in 1965.

JUNE

Michael Crawford and Sarah Brightman in Andrew Lloyd Webber's *The Phantom of the Opera* on Broadway in 1988.

1

June

(1926) She could barely sing, but did anyone care? Marilyn Monroe was born today as Norma Jean Mortensen, and would achieve fame with her luscious lips, breathy voice, and curvaceous figure. While she sang songs in many films, she only appeared in a few true musicals: She won the role of Lorelei Lee in *Gentlemen Prefer Blondes* over Carol Channing, and she held her own against Ethel Merman and Donald O'Connor in *There's No Business Like Show Business*. In *Blondes*, her high notes had to be dubbed by the omnipresent Marni Nixon.

broadway banter

"Uncle Walt never would have permitted this, to just let some girl do it."

—Adriana Caselotti, the original voice of Snow White, on not being asked to provide the voice for the character at the 1993 Oscars telecast

ALSO ON THIS DAY

To prove that *Moulin Rouge* wasn't a fluke, Ewan McGregor took the role of Sky Masterson in *Guys and Dolls*, opening in London today in 2005 and costarring Jane Krakowski.

(1944) He's one singular sensation: Marvin Hamlisch was born today. His music for *A Chorus Line* would earn him lasting fame—and royalties. But he was never able to quite hit that level of artistic or commercial success again: *They're Playing Our Song* was his only other hit, and he suffered the disappointments of *The Goodbye Girl*, *The Sweet Smell of Success*, and his "play with music," *Imaginary Friends*.

June

Back when he was still largely unknown, Hamlisch won a whopping three Oscars in 1973. In presenting him with his Oscar for *The Way We Were*, Cher had a bit of trouble reading his name, first calling him Marmin Hamshmish, then Marvin Hammelshmish. Co-presenter Henry Mancini had to set her straight.

broadway banter

"*Once, they made musicals. Now they make music videos.*"

–Entertainment Weekly

ALSO ON THIS DAY

Another favorite not-quite-star, Joanna Gleason, was born in 1950. From her perfect performance as The Baker's Wife in *Into the Woods*, to her nearly career-killing Nora Charles in *Nick and Nora*, to her triumphant return in *Dirty Rotten Scoundrels*, Gleason is always a class act.

3

June

(1990) *City of Angels* unexpectedly triumphed over Andrew Lloyd Webber's *Aspects of Love* and Tommy Tune's *Grand Hotel: The Musical* at the Tonys, winning Best Musical, Score, and Book.

Angels tells dual stories simultaneously: 1940s crime novelist Stine is trying to get his novel turned into a movie, while his fictional detective, Stone, confronts crime, cops, and a sultry nightclub singer. Most actors played roles in both the "real" world, done in full color, and the fictional "movie" world, costumed and lit in only black and white.

broadway banter

"Always be smarter than the people who hire you."

—Lena Horne

CASTING COUCH

Debbie Boone got to light up the lives of the von Trapp children as Maria in the 1990 City Opera revival of *The Sound of Music.*

(2000) What is a musical? *Contact* won the Best Musical Tony Award today, despite having no singing or live music. It did have Susan Stroman, arguably the most powerful director/choreographer of the last twenty years. Stroman's other hit that year was a bit more conventional: the revival of *The Music Man*, starring Craig Bierko, whose biggest claim to fame was having turned down the role of Chandler in a little '90s sitcom called *Friends*.

June

broadway banter

"It was impossible not to admire Ragtime, *but difficult to love it."*

—David Lefkowitz

IT TAKES A VILLAGE

In 2000, not one but two separate new musicals based on the 1928 poem by Joseph Moncure March, *The Wild Party*, debuted in New York. Andrew Lippa's version, starring Julia Murney, Brian D'Arcy James, Idina Menzel, and Taye Diggs, played off-Broadway, while Michael John LaChiusa's (generally considered inferior) version, starring Toni Collette, Mandy Patinkin, and Eartha Kitt, played on Broadway.

5

June

(1944) The definitive Jean Valjean was born today: Colm Wilkinson. He originated the role in London, brought his performance to America, where he got a Tony nomination, and ten years later was the obvious (only?) choice to play the role in the "Dream Cast" concert.

This was his only trip to Broadway, though, and he has never really had another breakout role of this magnitude. He originated the role of Judas in *Jesus Christ Superstar*, but was eclipsed for fame by the men who would later play the role. He was the original Phantom in the pre-opening workshops, but was replaced with Michael Crawford. He also sang the lead roles on the original "concept" albums of *Evita* and *Jekyll and Hyde*.

broadway banter

"When I heard that Richard Gere was not nominated for his great performance in Chicago, I said to myself, 'Welcome to my world, Richard Gere!'"

—Steve Martin

STAR POWER ———————

Both of Nathan Lane's Tony Awards came for recreating roles first performed by Zero Mostel: Pseudolus in *A Funny Thing Happened on the Way to the Forum*, and Max in *The Producers*.

6

June

(1954) Of all the unlikely musical stars there have been, this one is perhaps the unlikeliest: Harvey Fierstein. Born today, he brought gays to the mainstream Broadway audience with his libretto for *La Cage Aux Folles* in 1984. In the film version of *Torch Song Trilogy*, he gave a hilarious if probably not definitive rendering of Cole Porter's "Love For Sale." He even was a singing warrior in the Disney cartoon *Mulan*. But it wasn't until he played the larger-than-life Edna Turnblad in *Hairspray* that he solidified his place in the pantheon of musical theater history.

Fierstein followed up his *Hairspray* success with his least gay performance ever: Tevye in the Broadway revival of *Fiddler on the Roof*. Of course, his costar was Rosie O'Donnell ...

broadway banter

"I bet you're wondering why I'm here on the night of the divas who can sing."

—*Rosie O'Donnell, at Carnegie Hall for*
My Favorite Broadway: The Leading Ladies

BACKSTAGE

Alanis Morissette donated $150,000 to the production of *Jane Eyre* that ultimately flopped on Broadway in 2000/2001.

7
June

(1924) Sassy and brassy: The larger-than-life Dolores Gray was born today. In the late 1940s, when Ethel Merman wouldn't go to London with *Annie Get Your Gun*, Gray went instead and became a star. She made only three movie musicals, but managed to steal scenes in every one of them, first in *It's Always Fair Weather*, singing the hilarious "Thanks a Lot But No Thanks," then as the exotic Lalume in *Kismet*, and finally as the bitchy Sylvia in *The Opposite Sex*, mopping the floor with costar June Allyson.

In 1960, she returned to Broadway to play the Marlene Dietrich role in *Destry Rides Again*, and in 1987 she returned to London to belt out "I'm Still Here" in *Follies*.

broadway banter

"Noble's great, but cheesy's better."

—Faith Prince

STAR POWER

Dolores Gray had a bullet lodged in her lung, left from when she was caught in gang crossfire in Chicago as a child.

8

June

(1918) He's best remembered for his definitive Broadway and film performances as Harold Hill in *The Music Man,* but Robert Preston, born today, was a prolific musical performer. An accomplished actor at the age of forty, Preston landed his first musical role in *The Music Man.* He went on to star in one big hit, *I Do! I Do!,* with Mary Martin; one small hit, *Victor/Victoria,* with Julie Andrews; one fantastic flop, *Mack and Mabel,* with Bernadette Peters; one campy flop, *Mame,* with Lucille Ball; and one forgettable flop, *Ben Franklin in Paris,* with Ulla Sallert (who?).

broadway banter

"Oh honey, I've got sheet music and gorgeous gowns and a good underwire bra—I could go on now! So chins up, boobs out, it's show time!"

—Debbie Reynolds in Connie and Carla, *written by Nia Vardalos*

ALSO ON THIS DAY—————————

Somewhere, Ethel Merman heaved a sigh of relief: Today in 2003, Bernadette Peters lost the Tony for Best Actress for playing Rose in *Gypsy;* now all those books that list Merman as the only woman not to win a Tony for Rose are wrong.

9

June

(1891) The world's most sophisticated songwriter was born today—in Peru, Indiana, of all places: Cole Porter. America's answer to Noel Coward, Porter didn't hit Broadway until the comparatively late age of twenty-five, with the unsuccessful show *See America First*. His first big hit song was the delectably naughty "Let's Do It," from the semi-successful stage show *Paris*. But it wasn't until Porter teamed up with Ethel Merman in 1934 that his career really took off with *Anything Goes*. A parade of hits followed, including *Red, Hot and Blue, DuBarry Was a Lady, Panama Hattie*, and *Something for the Boys*, all starring Merman, as well as *Let's Face It, Can-Can, Silk Stockings*, and his 1948 masterpiece, *Kiss Me, Kate*.

He was the subject of two fictionalized biopics: *Night and Day*, starring Cary Grant, and *Delovely*, starring Kevin Kline.

broadway banter

"Yentl is a movie with a great middle. The beginning is too heavy-handed ... [and] the ending, with Yentl sailing off for America, seemed like a cheat."

—Roger Ebert

BY THE NUMBERS

Broadway actually stretches more than 150 miles, from Manhattan to Albany.

10
June

(1992) Dozens of stars came together for the one-night-only benefit *Sondheim: A Celebration at Carnegie Hall.* Held at the apex of his career, this amazing evening contained definitive interpretations of his music as well as unique versions sure to either delight or grate on aficionados' nerves. Performers included Tony winners Betty Buckley, Glenn Close, Daisy Eagan, Michael Jeter, Dorothy Loudon, Patti LuPone, Liza Minnelli, James Naughton, and Bernadette Peters, as well as future Tony winners Madeline Kahn, Bill Irwin, and Karen Ziemba.

Adding to the evening's diversity were the Boys Choir of Harlem, the jazz-singing Tonics, opera stars Harolyn Blackwell and Jerry Hadley, and the bluesy/funky stylings of the trio BETTY.

broadway banter

"For those of you who have not had the pleasure of hearing my voice before, I tend to sing very loud, usually off-pitch and always write in keys that are just out of my range."

—Stephen Sondheim

POP QUIZ ————————————

Who once guest-starred on *Batman* as villainess Lola Lasagne?

A: Ethel Merman

11
June

(1982) A final nail was hammered into the coffin that was movie musicals: *Grease 2* premiered today. This retread was directed by Patricia Birch, who choreographed the first *Grease* movie as well as the original Broadway production. Other than *Grease 2* and her 1986 Broadway flop *Raggedy Ann*, Birch has pretty much stayed away from the director's chair. Michelle Pfeiffer got her first big break with this movie, and Maxwell Caulfield made his feature film debut. Sid Caesar, Dody Goodman, Didi Conn, and Eve Arden all reprised their roles from the original film.

broadway banter

"If only he had been born into a world better than this. ... If only he had been born into an all-black musical. Nobody ever dies in an all-black musical."

—Mama in "The Last Mama-on-the-Couch Play" from
The Colored Museum by George C. Wolfe

ALSO ON THIS DAY

The innocuous but charming film *The Unsinkable Molly Brown* was released in 1964. Debbie Reynolds starred as the real-life Brown, who, among other things, survived the sinking of the *Titanic*.

12

June

(1930) Golllly!

Jim Nabors was born today in Sylacauga, Alabama. He's been primarily known as a recording artist, concert performer, and Gomer Pyle, but Nabors has indeed made a few legitimate musicals—the film version of *The Best Little Whorehouse in Texas*, and *The Music Man* directed by Charles Nelson Reilly at the Burt Reynolds Dinner Theatre (well, *some* might call them "legitimate"). In the latter, he played Harold Hill opposite Florence Henderson's Marion, though both actors were in their fifties. He also was the guest star on the season premiere of *The Carol Burnett Show* every year during its twelve-year run.

broadway banter

> Grace: Mom, how's The Music Man going? Dad says it opens next week.
>
> Bobbi: Well, excuse me, it's Music Person. I'm starring as Professor Carol Hill.
>
> Will: Well, if it's as half as good as your performance as Millie Loman in Death of a Salesperson ...
>
> —Will & Grace

STAR POWER ——————————

In 1962, long before being offered the film role, Julie Andrews spoofed *The Sound of Music* with Carol Burnett in *Julie and Carol at Carnegie Hall*, doing a campy send-up of "The Pratt Family of Switzerland."

13
June

(1910) Hilarious character actress Mary Wickes, born today, made a career of playing nuns, maids, nurses, crotchety old broads, and other scene-stealing bit parts. In films, she sang with Frank Sinatra and Jack Haley in 1943's *Higher and Higher* and picked-a-little-talked-a-little in *The Music Man*. Equally at home on stage, film, and television, her final Broadway credit came as Aunt Eller in the acclaimed 1979 revival of *Oklahoma!*.

Wickes enjoyed a late-career renaissance with the *Sister Act* movies, playing Sister Mary Lazarus. She also voiced the singing gargoyle Laverne in *The Hunchback of Notre Dame*, but died before completing it, and her remaining few lines had to be completed by Jane Withers.

broadway banter

"The dance numbers are like halftime at the Super Bowl. ... The dialogue is dumbfoundedly simple-minded. The costumes would embarrass Yvonne De Carlo."

—Rex Reed, on the flop musical remake of Lost Horizon

IT TAKES A VILLAGE

The 1961 musical *The Gay Life*, written by Howard Dietz and Arthur Schwartz, has officially been renamed *The High Life*, since the original title came to mean something other than the authors originally intended.

14

June

(1956) *New Faces of 1956* opened, promising a glimpse into the future of Broadway. Some of the performers went on to prolific Broadway careers, others to sporadic stage appearances, and almost half of the cast of twenty to never appear on Broadway again. Among the notables in this edition were Jane Connell (*Mame* on stage and screen, *Crazy for You*, *The Full Monty*, and a Tony nomination for *Me and My Girl*), Virginia Martin (*How to Succeed in Business Without Really Trying* and a Tony nomination for *Little Me*), Bill McCutcheon (a Tony nomination for *Anything Goes*), John Reardon (*Do Re Mi*, introducing the standard "Make Someone Happy"), and Inga Swenson (*110 in the Shade*, *Baker Street*).

Another "new face" this year who never appeared in another Broadway musical but managed to make something of a career for herself anyway was Maggie Smith.

broadway banter

"Everything I've achieved in my life, the small things I've achieved, will come down to: 'You lost to Phil Collins.'"

—Trey Parker, on the South Park/Tarzan *Best Song battle*

ALSO ON THIS DAY

When bad things happen to good composers: The humorless film version of Sondheim's *A Little Night Music* opened in Los Angeles in 1977, featuring the vocal stylings of Elizabeth Taylor on "Send in the Clowns."

15
June

(1995) Can you paint with all the colors of the wind? Pocahontas can. Disney's latest blockbuster cartoon musical premiered in New York City today, featuring a score by Alan Menken, now paired with lyricist Stephen Schwartz. Although the film was based on real people and historic events, it didn't always portray them with 100 percent accuracy.

One of *Pocahontas*'s best songs, "If I Never Knew You," sung by Judy Kuhn and Mel Gibson, was cut from the final print, though it can now be seen interpolated into the film on DVD. The song was later recorded by Betty Buckley on her album *Much More*.

broadway banter

"I had pitched the show to John Clancy, the festival's artistic director, a few months prior, and since he hadn't tried to change the subject immediately, I felt encouraged."

—Greg Kotis, *on getting* Urinetown *produced*

POP QUIZ

Q: What versatile actor played the tiny role of Uncle Jocko in the Bette Midler TV version of Gypsy?

(1937) *The Cradle Will Rock* did not open on Broadway today. Instead, it was shut down by the WPA's Federal Theatre Project for reasons that may have been economic or, as Tim Robbins's film of the same name suggests, motivated by issues of censorship. Either way, the production was closed, but producer John Houseman and director Orson Welles moved into an empty theater and planned on having the show's composer, Marc Blitzstein, perform the show by himself at a piano. Forbidden by Actor's Equity to appear in the production, the actors performed their roles from the audience.

16

June

broadway banter

"In 1980, he decided to exhume some of my songs and re-embalmed them in the form of a revue called Tomfoolery. *And I'm not saying that I made him what he is today, although that happens to be the case, but after* Tomfoolery *came* Cats, *and the combined profits of* Cats *and* Tomfoolery *made him a wealthy man."*

—Tom Lehrer, on producer Cameron Mackintosh

BACKSTAGE

The producers of *The Producers* created "VIP" tickets that cost $480 so they could reap the benefit of the high prices the scalpers were getting for ticket sales.

17
June

(1917) That's amore: Rat-packer Dean Martin was born today. Oddly, though he gained world renown as a singer and actor, he actually made very few musicals. After splitting with his longtime comedy partner Jerry Lewis, he costarred with Anna-Maria Alberghetti in the forgettable *Ten Thousand Bedrooms*. Despite being rather miscast, he acquitted himself in *Bells Are Ringing* opposite the charming Judy Holliday. He later played Little John in the Prohibition-era gangster update of *Robin Hood*, *Robin and the 7 Hoods*, with fellow "packers" Frank Sinatra and Sammy Davis Jr.

broadway banter

"*You go to my head,*
With—and I forgot the gol-darn words ..."

—*Judy Garland, during her legendary 1961 Carnegie Hall concert*

ALSO ON THIS DAY———————

The nudie musical *Oh! Calcutta!* opened in 1969, ultimately playing Broadway for a run long on years and short on clothes. The show featured contributions from the seemingly non-musical Samuel Beckett, Jules Feiffer, John Lennon, and Sam Shepard.

18

June

(1903) I will never forget: Jeanette MacDonald was born today. She got her start on Broadway in the post–World War I years, but when the talkies came in, she went to Hollywood and made it big. MacDonald starred in some thirty screen operettas, most notably costarring with Nelson Eddy in films like *Naughty Marietta* and *Rose-Marie*, the latter of which created the iconic "Canadian Mountie" operetta image. She also teamed up with Maurice Chevalier in *Love Me Tonight* and *The Merry Widow*, as well as with both Clark Gable and Spencer Tracy in *San Francisco*.

broadway banter

"We were all kicking as high as human beings can kick all the time we made the record of that song."

—Carol Channing, *on recording the title number in* Hello, Dolly!

STAR POWER

Seinfeld star Jason Alexander won a Tony for playing Pseudolus, Tevye, Henry Longstreet, and others in *Jerome Robbins' Broadway.*

19

June

(1978) Broadway has a whorehouse in it: *The Best Little Whorehouse in Texas* opened today and ran for more than four years. Carol Hall wrote the music and lyrics, making it one of the few female-written scores ever to play on Broadway. Carlin Glinn, Henderson Forsythe, and Delores Hall starred, singing and dancing in and among chorus lines of scantily clad whores and beefy football players. When the film was made with Dolly Parton and Burt Reynolds, much of the score was dropped, while Dolly's hit "I Will Always Love You" was added in its place.

broadway banter

"Hell, I hate musicals. A bunch of candy-assed tippy-toed dancers stomping all over the dialogue."

—Larry King, who later wrote the book to
The Best Little Whorehouse in Texas

CASTING COUCH

Late in 2005, the world was spared the possibility of Britney Spears taking over for Christina Applegate in the Broadway revival of *Sweet Charity;* instead, the show just closed.

(1980) In 1979, someone had the brilliant idea of reinvigorating the flagging genre of the movie musical by casting The Village People to star in one. The result was *Can't Stop the Music*, which premiered today. I don't know what is odder—the mere fact that this movie was ever made, or the fact that it was directed by Rhoda's mother, Nancy Walker. Or perhaps the fact that it starred 1976 Olympic Decathlon champion and Wheaties coverboy Bruce Jenner. Or the fact that the songs included both "YMCA" and "Danny Boy." Or the fact that Steve Guttenberg overcame this film to go on to have a film career, albeit one highlighted by the *Police Academy* movies. Or the fact that anyone in 1980 felt the need to pay to see it ...

broadway banter

"Imagine a Saturday Night Live *with more music, more rehearsal, and less desire to get a film deal and you're halfway there."*

—The Drama Department, on As Thousands Cheer
and other similar early musical revues

CASTING COUCH

Some of the original candidates for Maria in the film *The Sound of Music* were Leslie Caron, Grace Kelly, Anne Bancroft, Angie Dickinson, and Shirley Jones.

21

June

(1921) Beautiful, hilarious, and possessing a sweet singing voice, Judy Holliday, born today, had it all. She even had an IQ of 172, despite usually being cast as a dingbat. She got her start with Comden and Green in their Greenwich Village nightclub act, *The Revuers*. Years later, they would write one of their biggest hits for her: *Bells Are Ringing*. Holliday won a Tony for her performance on Broadway, including her inimitable delivery of such songs as "Is It a Crime," "I'm Going Back," and the pop standard to-be "The Party's Over." She even got to reprise her role in the film. Sadly, her life was cut short by throat cancer in 1965, and she died at the age of just forty-three.

broadway banter

"You've got big dreams? You want fame? Well, fame costs. And right here is where you start paying. With sweat."

—Lydia on the TV show Fame

ALSO ON THIS DAY

"The Line King" Al Hirschfeld was born today in 1903. Many theater professionals have said that they knew they had "made it" when this man drew a caricature of them. For more than seventy-five years, he recorded the history of New York theater in his delightful drawings.

22

June

(1969) A star was extinguished ... Judy Garland died of an accidental overdose of barbiturates. Some 22,000 mourners in New York City waited for up to four hours to pay their respects at her wake. The death of this gay icon is considered to be a key contributing factor in sparking the Stonewall Riots, which began the gay rights movement.

Her final film role would have been Helen Lawson in *Valley of the Dolls*, a film that, ironically, was partially based on the life of Garland herself. Judy wasn't up to the task at hand, though, and she was replaced with Susan Hayward, whose singing voice had to be dubbed.

broadway banter

"She sang, and it was a religious experience for me."

—*Jerry Herman, on Judy Garland*

ALSO ON THIS DAY

Faye Dunaway was fired off the Los Angeles production of *Sunset Boulevard* in 1994.

23

June

(1927) Bowler hats, gloves, and rounded shoulders: Bob Fosse was born, and he would go on to turn the musical form on its ear with his innovative productions and movement. After doing time as a dancer, Fosse made his choreographic bow in 1954 with *The Pajama Game*, having choreographed his and Carol Haney's duet in *Kiss Me Kate* on film the year before. Next up was *Damn Yankees*, where he would team up with his muse, Gwen Verdon, for the first time.

After directing *Redhead* and *Little Me*, Fosse began to really explore more adult-oriented material with shows like *Sweet Charity*, *Pippin*, *Chicago*, and *Dancin'* on Broadway, and *Cabaret* and *All That Jazz* on film. His final works in the mid-1980s were the Broadway flop *Big Deal* and a revival of *Sweet Charity*, but his work lives on in numerous forms, including the 1999 Tony-winning revue *Fosse*, fashioned by his ex-wife, Verdon, and ex-lover Ann Reinking.

broadway banter

"Audra never seems to be singing. Rather, she is responding to a specific emotional situation and music is her natural, her only response."

—Terrence McNally, on Audra McDonald

STAR POWER

After seeing Ethel Merman in *Gypsy*, Helene Wiegel told her that she should next tackle the title role in her late husband Bertolt Brecht's searing drama with music, *Mother Courage*.

June

(1994) *The Lion King* opened wide—literally and figuratively, as the movie debuted on screens across America today. Writing his first Disney music was Elton John, who collaborated with *Aladdin*'s lyric-finisher, Tim Rice. The movie was a smash, and has become the highest-selling home video of all time. The score, however, didn't really match up to Disney's Menken/Ashman films *The Little Mermaid* or *Beauty and the Beast*. *The Lion King* had only five songs to begin with: two forgettable, "Hakuna Matata" cute but slight, and "Can You Feel the Love Tonight" beautiful but generic. Only "Circle of Life" really captured the essence of the movie's theme and tone, and ironically, it failed to win any awards.

broadway banter

"The artist must take sides. He must elect to fight for freedom or for slavery."

—Paul Robeson

ALSO ON THIS DAY

A starry film version of *Porgy and Bess* premiered today in 1959: Sidney Poitier and Dorothy Dandridge played the title roles, accompanied by Sammy Davis Jr., Diahann Carroll, and Pearl Bailey; only Davis and Bailey did their own singing.

25

June

(1887) George Abbott, the godfather of musical comedy, was born today. In 1944, he was already a thirty-some-year veteran of Broadway directing and producing when he helmed *On the Town* along with a group of Broadway newcomers: composer Leonard Bernstein, choreographer Jerome Robbins, lyricists/librettists Betty Comden and Adolph Green, and designer Oliver Smith.

Over the years, he directed the original productions of such hits as *Jumbo, On Your Toes, Pal Joey, High Button Shoes, Where's Charley?, Wonderful Town, Damn Yankees, Fiorello!,* and ... I just don't have enough room here, folks. He lived to be 107, and kept on directing musicals into his nineties, including the acclaimed 1983 Broadway revival of *On Your Toes.*

broadway banter

"I wish I was born in that era: dancing with Fred Astaire and Gene Kelly, going to work at the studio dressed in beautiful pants, head scarves, and sunglasses."

—Catherine Zeta-Jones

IT TAKES A VILLAGE —

Marvin Hamslich got his start as the rehearsal pianist for *Funny Girl.*

(1981) They're ba-aaack! At what might have been the height of muppet popularity in America, *The Great Muppet Caper* premiered today. And, as always, there was plenty of adult-oriented humor that whooshed right over kids' heads but gave parents a good chuckle. Joe "Bein' Green" Raposo's clever score paid homage to the golden age of movie musicals, including a Fred Astaire song and dance, a Busby Berkeley production number, and an Esther Williams water ballet.

June

broadway banter

"Her voice is like vinegar on sandpaper; her presence is a blessing. She growls out the most ordinary tunes as if they were pearls of great price. ..."

–*Clive Barnes, on Katharine Hepburn in* Coco

CASTING COUCH

Since *I Do! I Do!* was two-and-a-half hours long and had just two actors—Robert Preston and Mary Martin—the producers brought in Carol Lawrence and Gordon MacRae to do the two matinees each week. When Martin and Preston left the show, Lawrence and MacRae took over.

27
June

(2005) One song. Glory.

Shooting wrapped for the film version of *Rent* today. Director Christopher Columbus, who had never directed a film musical, brought the ten-years-and-running smash hit to the big screen. In doing so, he kept most of the play's original stars, including Anthony Rapp, Adam Pascal, Jesse L. Martin, Taye Diggs, Tony nominee Idina Menzel, and Tony winner Wilson Jermaine Heredia. Only Daphne Rubin-Vega (Mimi) and Fredi Walker (Joanne) were replaced, with Rosario Dawson and Tracie Thoms.

broadway banter

"This producer said to me ... 'You'll be lucky if you're playing an American mother for the rest of your life.' So I was really glad when the first show I did after Eight Is Enough, *I played—a cat. And then I played—a boy."*

—Betty Buckley on her roles in Cats *and* The Mystery of Edwin Drood

BACKSTAGE

After fifteen years of dubbing everyone from Margaret O'Brien to Natalie Wood, Marni Nixon made her onscreen debut as Sister Sophia in *The Sound of Music.*

June

(1902) How do you solve a problem like trying to capture the essence of the great Richard Rodgers in one hundred words or less? Born today, he made his Broadway debut at just eighteen with *Poor Little Ritz Girl*, co-written with the man with whom he would write for the next twenty-three years, Lorenz Hart. In 1943, as Hart's health failed, Rodgers abandoned the nightclub-style torch songs and comedy he espoused with Hart, and paired up with Oscar Hammerstein II. Together they revolutionized musicals with their integration of story, music, lyrics, dance, and theme.

Rodgers forged ahead after Hammerstein's death in 1960, but was never able to reach the same heights he had with him or Hart. He wrote his own lyrics for *No Strings* and found success, but he had a tough time working with younger lyricists after that, and his career ended with a string of flops.

broadway banter

"Thank you. That beats a nomination, doesn't it, Gloria."

—*Elaine Stritch to Tony co-presenter Gloria Foster, referring to their non-nominated performances in* Show Boat *and* Having Our Say

STAR POWER

In 1995, Tommy Tune tried to get flagging *Stage Door Charley* off the ground by changing the name to *Busker Alley*. After he broke his foot, he continued on, with a "dance double." The show failed to reach Broadway.

29
June

(1901)
"My hero must stand on a box in our love scenes
God, does he act like a lox in our love scenes
Nelson, what you're putting me through ..."

So went Jerry Herman's parody of Nelson Eddy in the revue *A Day in Hollywood/A Night in the Ukraine*. Born today, Eddy is primarily remembered for his many operetta movies with Jeanette MacDonald, but he also notably appeared in *Rosalie* with Ruby Keeler, *The Chocolate Soldier*, and *Knickerbocker Holiday*. Known as "The Singing Capon," he was often made fun of for being stiff and wooden. In 1946, though, he provided all of the voices and lots of humor and emotion for the Disney short cartoon *The Whale Who Wanted to Sing at the Met.*

broadway banter

"I've handled Indians, African natives, South Sea Islanders, rhinos, pygmies, and Eskimos, and made them act—but not Nelson Eddy."

—W. S. Van Dyke

POP QUIZ —————————

Q: What musical features a forty-five-minute span without a single musical number?

30

June

(1917) A lady and her music: Lena Horne was born today. She made her film debut in 1941 in *Panama Hattie*, singing "Just One of Those Things." The number was a showstopper, but was devised so that it could easily be cut from the movie by racist or weak-willed Southern theater owners. She went on to deliver searing ballads and delectable comedy numbers in films like *Stormy Weather* and *Cabin in the Sky*. In 1946, she played Julie in the *Show Boat* excerpt in the Jerome Kern biopic *Til the Clouds Roll By*. But when MGM remade *Show Boat* in 1951, studio execs couldn't see having a black woman play the role, and gave it to the white Ava Gardner.

Her final film performance was as Glinda in *The Wiz*, and in 1981 she returned to Broadway with a celebrated concert act, winning a Tony and a rare New York Drama Critics citation.

broadway banter

"Don't bother holding onto your hats because you won't be needing them. You'd only be throwing them into the air anyway."

—*Walter Kerr*, on Hello Dolly!

IT TAKES A VILLAGE

Jim Luigs and Scott Warrender wrote *Das Barbecu*, a Texas-set musical adaptation of Wagner's *Ring* cycle.

JULY

The Broadway cast of Jonathan Larson's *Rent*.

(1941) When I was a little kid, my sister and I would dance around our basement playing Billy Joel records. Apparently so did Twyla Tharp, born today. In 2003, she recreated her own basement dances in the "musical" *Movin' Out*. Now, this show was a big hit and highly acclaimed, but I guess I just didn't get the "We Didn't Start the Fire" ballet. If I wanted to sit through an evening of just one person singing every song Billy Joel ever wrote, I'd really rather it were Joel himself. As of this writing, Twyla has plans for a similar show based on Bob Dylan's music.

1
July

broadway banter

Joe Gideon: Oh boy, do I hate show business!

Kate Jagger: Joe, you love show business.

Joe Gideon: Oh that's right. I love show business. I'll go either way.

–All That Jazz, *by Robert Alan Aurthur and Bob Fosse*

ALSO ON THIS DAY

The elfin dancer Leslie Caron was born in 1931, making an astonishing film debut at age twenty with *An American in Paris*. Many years later, she played aging ballerina Grushinskaya in the Berlin production of *Grand Hotel: The Musical*.

2

July

(1987) But he won't regret what he did for love: Michael Bennett died today at the age of forty-four. He left behind a legacy of two decades worth of Broadway choreography, having pushed the boundaries of what both dancers and non-dancing actors can do on a stage. After five nominations, he finally won a Tony for Best Choreography for *Follies*, also winning for having co-directed the show with Hal Prince. He also directed and choreographed another "backstage" musical, *Dreamgirls*. But Bennett will best be remembered for conceiving, directing, and choreographing *A Chorus Line*, the show that defined Broadway, New York City, and theater for a generation.

broadway banter

"He showed us deep truths about ourselves. He made us more aware of being alive. ... The Greeks, I think, call this a catharsis. Michael called it a Broadway musical."

—*Frank Difilia, on his brother, Michael Bennett*

CASTING COUCH

Easter Parade was to have starred Gene Kelly and Cyd Charisse, but Kelly broke his ankle and was replaced with Fred Astaire, and Cyd Charisse, who was pregnant, was replaced with Ann Miller. Years later, Tommy Tune and Sandy Duncan tried but failed to get a stage production off the ground.

(1878) He's a Yankee Doodle Dandy, born on the Fourth of July ...

Well, almost. George M. Cohan was actually born on the third of July, a fact he tended to ignore during his prolific career that included songwriting, producing, directing, and performing in dozens of musicals. Shortly before his death in 1942, he would be portrayed on screen by typical tough guy James Cagney, and in 1969 he would be played by Joel Grey in the Broadway musical *George M!*

July

broadway banter

"The use of rollers to simulate the oncoming wildebeest harks back to eighteenth-century European theater, which often used rollers decorated with wavelike structures to create the effect of a sea."

–The Lion King *scene designer Richard Hudson*

STAR POWER

In the 1993 television version of *Gypsy*, Bette Midler insisted that all vocals be performed live on the set, instead of the almost-always-used technique of pre-recording and lip-synching.

4
July

(1898) Star and workhorse Gertrude Lawrence, born today, performed continuously on Broadway, in London, and occasionally in film for forty years. Although she wasn't a great singer, she could project emotion and connect with an audience like few others. In *Oh, Kay!*, she introduced the Gershwin standard "Someone to Watch Over Me," in Kurt Weill's *Lady in the Dark*, she captured the longing in "My Ship," and in *The King and I*, she simply embodied Mrs. Anna. She was also a frequent interpreter of the work of lifelong friend Noel Coward. At her death, the lights of Broadway were dimmed for the first time in tribute to a theater artist.

broadway banter

"One thing's for sure ... Branagh ain't no song-and-dance man."

—Max Messier, on Kenneth Branagh's laughable musical version of Love's Labours Lost

IT TAKES A VILLAGE ————

When *The Apple Tree* opened, it wasn't the first musicalization of Jules Feiffer's short story "Passionella": Stephen Sondheim had written "Truly Content" for a possible production that never got off the ground.

(1960) Douglas Sills was born today. He shot to semi-stardom playing the title role in *The Scarlet Pimpernel* (sing along: "They seek him here, they seek him there; those Frenchies seek him everywhere") in 1997. He reappeared on Broadway in the semi-successful revival of *Little Shop of Horrors*, playing numerous roles, including the sadistic dentist, Orin. He then pulled out of *Monty Python's Spamalot* before it reached Broadway, and was replaced by fellow blonde tenor Christopher Sieber.

5

July

broadway banter

"Mary Martin and Robert Preston fill the stage with their presence, brighten it with their unmatched charm, make it glow, gleam, and glitter with their skills. Together they are the equivalent of the Old Vic, Comedie Française and Moscow Art Theatre. And they can sing, too!"

—Elliot Norton, on I Do! I Do!

POP QUIZ

Q: What Broadway flop played seventy-one previews, then folded after nine regular performances?

A: Nick and Nora

6
July

(1927) Shower, anyone? Janet Leigh was born today. She made an early splash with *Two Tickets to Broadway*, costarring Ann Miller, Gloria DeHaven, and her husband, Tony Curtis. She then played the title role in *My Sister Eileen*, the second musical version of the stories of Ruth Sherwood (the far superior *Wonderful Town* being the first). In her final musical role, Leigh tried to fill the shoes of the legendary Chita Rivera as Rose in *Bye Bye Birdie*. While she wasn't terrible, she was surely the weakest lead, and she had three of her character's numbers cut. Worst of all was the dime-store black Chita wig they forced the blonde Leigh to don.

broadway banter

"When I die, it's going to read, 'Game Show Fixture Passes Away.' Nothing about the theater, or Tony Awards, or Emmys. But it doesn't bother me."

—*Charles Nelson Reilly*

BY THE NUMBERS ——————————

The youngest actress to win a Tony was Daisy Eagan, eleven, for *The Secret Garden* (1991).

July

(1915) Swiss-Mongolian Yul Brynner was born today in Siberia. Twenty-six years later, he was on Broadway. In 1946, he appeared in his first musical, *Lute Song*. His costar in that show, Mary Martin, would later recommend him to her friends Richard Rodgers and Oscar Hammerstein when they were putting together a show about the King of Siam. Brynner rode the role to stardom, despite the fact that he was billed as a supporting player and won the Best Featured Actor Tony. When he made the film version of *The King and I*—his only screen musical—he would win an Academy Award in the Leading Actor category.

broadway banter

"She hasn't worked in so long that if she does get the job, it'll practically amount to a comeback."

—Eve in Stage Door, *screenplay by Morrie Ryskind and Anthony Veiller*

STAR POWER

When *Chicago's* "I Move On" was nominated for an Oscar, Renee Zellweger was too nervous to perform it live at the show. Catherine Zeta-Jones, eight months pregnant, had no problem singing it.

8

July

(1982) If you ask me, the problem might have been that they were a couple of brides short: The stage adaptation of the movie musical *Seven Brides for Seven Brothers* opened today—starring Debby Boone, no less. It lasted just five performances, thanks in part to a scathing review by Frank Rich.

broadway banter

"My high C may sometimes shriek
Still I hit it twice last week
Which proves that I can be a musical star!"

—*Tracy in* Nick and Nora, *lyrics by Richard Maltby Jr.*

ALSO ON THIS DAY—

Walter Kerr, born today in 1913, served for thirty-two years as a theater critic, first for the *New York Herald Tribune*, then for the *New York Times*. Not limited to writing commentary on theater, he also co-wrote the failed Elaine Stritch musical *Goldilocks* with his wife, Jean.

9

July

(1989) "Little girls, little girls, everywhere I go I can—AAAAAAAAAAAAAAAAAAA!"

While rehearsing the role of Miss Hannigan in *Annie*, Eileen Brennan fell off the stage of the Starlight Theatre in Kansas City today, breaking her leg one day before the show's scheduled opening. Erstwhile soprano Brennan had gotten her start in the title role of Rick Besoyan's mock operetta *Little Mary Sunshine*, and went on to play Irene Molloy in the original *Hello, Dolly!* In the seventies, and with her voice at least an octave lower, she camped it up as Betty DeBoop in *The Cheap Detective*, and schlepped it up in the turgid Cybill Shepard musical, *At Long Last Love*.

broadway banter

"In terms of the Kazan controversy: 'Let Lainie sing!'"

—Robin Williams, *joking about the controversial Honorary Oscar awarded to Elia Kazan*

CASTING COUCH

Blood Brothers featured such starry replacements as Petula Clark, David and Shaun Cassidy, Carole King, and Helen Reddy.

10
July

(1933) There's just no tune like a show tune in two-four: Jerry Herman was born today. After a minor success off-Broadway, Herman hit the big time in 1962 with *Milk and Honey*, a vehicle for Molly Picon, Robert Weede, and Mimi Benzel about the young nation of Israel. That show looked like small potatoes next to his next shows, *Hello, Dolly!* and *Mame*.

After his success during the 1960s, Herman had a long spell of flops—including *Dear World*, *Mack and Mabel*, and *The Grand Tour*—before returning to Broadway one last time with one last hit in 1984: *La Cage Aux Folles*. Since then, he's dabbled in TV with *Mrs. Santa Claus* and on the Las Vegas stage with *Miss Spectacular*.

broadway banter

"This award forever shatters a myth about the musical theater. There has been a rumor around for a couple of years that the simple hummable show tune was no longer welcome on Broadway. Well, it's alive and well at the Palace."

—Jerry Herman, *accepting his Tony for* La Cage Aux Folles, *which beat Sondheim's semi-masterpiece* Sunday in the Park with George

IT TAKES A VILLAGE

In 1943, Irving Berlin became the first person to present oneself with an Oscar: He won for "White Christmas."

11

July

(1937) One of the most prolific songwriting careers was cut short today: George Gershwin died of a brain tumor at the age of thirty-eight. In addition to some thirty Broadway shows, Gershwin helped create an American sound in classical music with his "Rhapsody in Blue" and "An American in Paris." He also dabbled a bit in films, but held Hollywood in contempt, as evidenced by his parody of movie songwriting, "Blah Blah Blah." After his death, his music would be repurposed, recycled, and at times regurgitated into numerous movie and Broadway musicals.

broadway banter

"George Gershwin died on July 11, 1937, but I don't have to believe it if I don't want to."

–John O'Hara

ALSO ON THIS DAY

Take that, Gwen Verdon! In 2003, Melanie Griffith assumed the role of Roxie Hart in *Chicago* on Broadway for three months. All I can say is, "Oh my."

12
July

(1993) Hell hath no fury like a Patti scorned. *Sunset Boulevard* opened in London with Patti LuPone as Norma Desmond. Mixed reviews are just the beginning of this troubled, twisted production. After Glenn Close opened the show in Los Angeles, Andrew Lloyd Webber began having second thoughts about his promise to bring the tempestuous Patti LuPone to Broadway. Ultimately, he would break her contract and replace her in London with Betty Buckley, while Close opened the show on Broadway.

broadway banter

"Kid, in my day we didn't need microphones. We had voices then!"

—*"Ethel Merman"* in Forbidden Broadway Strikes Back!
by *Gerard Alessandrini*

BACKSTAGE

Heather Menzies, who played Louisa von Trapp in the film *The Sound of Music*, posed nude for *Playboy* in 1973.

(1951) Sometimes, Technicolor isn't better: MGM trotted out its remake of *Show Boat*, scarcely needed after two black-and-white versions and an extended *Show Boat* sequence in *Till the Clouds Roll By*. But that didn't stop director George Sidney from trying. The result was tepid at best: Ava Gardner acts well, but her vocal double is way off; stars Kathryn Grayson and Howard Keel ignited little chemistry as the doomed lovers; and Agnes Moorehead wastes what could have been a scene-stealing role.

13
July

broadway banter

"I remember at one point Elaine Stritch turned to Ethel Merman and said, 'Isn't it too bad that Alexis Smith has gotten so fat and ugly?' To which Merman replied, 'Christ, she looks like a microphone!'"

–Ted Chapin, on the opening night of Follies *(starring Alexis Smith)*

POP QUIZ

Q: Name the three generations of Rodgers musical theater composers.

A: Richard Rodgers, Mary Rodgers Guettel, Adam Guettel

14
July

(1918) When it comes to writers of musicals, the credit goes first to the composer, then to the lyricist, then, if at all, to the book writer. In some cases, that's not a bad thing. But for Arthur Laurents, born today, it's a downright shame. Laurents took the integrated musical form of Rodgers and Hammerstein and carried it to new heights with shows like *Gypsy*, often called the perfect book musical, and *West Side Story*. He also experimented with *Anyone Can Whistle* (what exactly was he smoking when he wrote that?) and directed such hits as *La Cage Aux Folles* and the Angela Lansbury revival of *Gypsy*.

broadway banter

"When I was thirteen, I wanted to be a professional ice skater, right? But my parents took me to see a Broadway show, and it changed my entire life! The show was Gypsy, *starring Ethel Merman."*

–Liza Minnelli

ALSO ON THIS DAY

Polly Bergen was born in 1930, and at the age of seventy-one, she was regarded as just about the only aspect of the 2001 revival of *Follies* that was not sub-par: Her husky rendition of "I'm Still Here" knocked 'em dead.

15

July

(1905) Dorothy Fields was born. (If her friends could see her now!) In a profession that was nearly impossible for women to break into, lyricist Fields carved out a name for herself like few male songwriters would. Her career spanned some forty years, outlasting nearly all of her male contemporaries, and her immense canon (more than five hundred songs) includes such diverse hits as "I Can't Give You Anything but Love, Baby," "A Fine Romance," "The Way You Look Tonight," and "Hey, Big Spender," in addition to writing the libretto to *Annie Get Your Gun*. Over the years she collaborated with several generations of music's cream of the crop, including Jimmy McHugh, Jerome Kern, Irving Berlin, Bob Fosse, and Cy Coleman.

broadway banter

Emily: Does anybody here know how many times I had to watch Funny Lady?

Howard: It was a sequel. She was under contract.

—From In and Out, *by Paul Rudnick*

STAR POWER

After he starred in *West Side Story,* Larry Kert's career was a series of disappointments: He starred in the flops *Rags, La Strada,* and *Breakfast at Tiffany's,* was a replacement for Dean Jones in *Company,* and was the standby for Peter Allen in *Legs Diamond.*

16

July

(1911) More than just half of a dance team, Virginia Katherine McMath was born today in Independence, Missouri. At the age of nineteen, she made her Broadway debut in *Girl Crazy* under the name Ginger Rogers. She then headed for Hollywood and scarcely looked back: In addition to repeatedly sharing the screen with Fred Astaire, she strutted her stuff in some seventy-five other movies, including *42nd Street*, *Gold Diggers of 1933*, and the 1965 TV remake of *Cinderella*, along the way having no fewer than five marriages ending in divorce. Late in her career, she headed back to Broadway one last time to play Dolly Levi.

broadway banter

"I'm absolutely astonished ... I can't tell you ... Best Director of a Musical that's not even a musical!"
                    —*Matthew Bourne, winning a Tony for* Swan Lake

ALSO ON THIS DAY ———————

Although his claim to fame is the non-musical *Angels in America*, Tony Kushner, born today in 1956, also wrote the book and lyrics for the semi-autobiographical *Caroline, or Change*, a story of a Southern Jewish family and their African-American maid and her children. Notably, some of the singing characters included The Washing Machine, The Radio, The Dryer, The Moon, and The Bus.

(1935) The sweetest sounds she'll ever hear are still inside her head: Diahann Carroll was born today. The versatile actress sang those (paraphrased) lyrics in Richard Rodgers's first post-Hammerstein effort, *No Strings*, and won a Tony. She also scored a huge hit in *The House of Flowers*, introducing the standard "A Sleeping Bee."

An accomplished singer, Carroll found herself dubbed in her two big Hollywood musicals: *Carmen Jones* and *Porgy and Bess*. Down the road, she would get a little bit of Hollywood revenge by playing Norma Desmond in *Sunset Boulevard* in Toronto.

17
July

broadway banter

"[We'll] just add you to the list of people going to hell. Thomas, we'll put her name right after Comden and Green."

–Sister Mary Ignatius in Sister Mary Ignatius Explains It All for You
by Christopher Durang

IT TAKES A VILLAGE

Songwriting brothers Jon and Al Kaplan wrote *Silence! Silence of the Lambs: The Musical*, which features the songs "Are You About a Size 14," "Quid Pro Quo," "Put the Fucking Lotion in the Basket," and the title number, performed by, of course, The Lambs.

18
July

(2003) The musical comedy is back! *Hairspray* played its first preview in New York. Following the success of *The Producers*, Jack O'Brien, Marc Shaiman, and Thomas Meehan converted a cult classic semi-musical movie to a blockbuster Broadway musical (Meehan co-wrote the book for *The Producers*, so he knew what it took!). The inspired casting of Marisa Jaret Winokur and Harvey Fierstein as the big-boned Tracey and Edna Turnblad sealed the "hit" fate of this infectious musical romp, and Harvey's duet with hubby Dick Latessa "Timeless to Me" was an endearing showstopper.

broadway banter

"Marisa Jaret Winokur has the voice of Lesley Gore, The Shangri-Las and Marni Nixon all rolled into one big ball of dynamite."

–John Waters

STAR POWER—————

George Rose, star of revivals of *The Pirates of Penzance* and *My Fair Lady*, was murdered by his adopted son while vacationing during the run of *The Mystery of Edwin Drood*.

(1962) When my grandfather saw *The Phantom of the Opera* on stage, his only comment on it was, "Well, it's no *Music Man*."

On this day, the film version of *The Music Man* premiered. Directed by Morton DaCosta, this was perhaps the most successful transfer of a stage musical to film (he did the same for the non-musical *Auntie Mame* in 1958). DaCosta eschewed the hyper-realism of films like *Oklahoma!* and kept nearly the entire original score intact instead of cutting or adding new numbers by other composers. He also cast actors who could sing and dance, including original cast members Robert Preston (robbed of an Oscar nomination), Pert Kelton, and the Buffalo Bills.

19
July

broadway banter

"Welcome to the Tabloid Tonys! Who knew Broadway could elbow Latoya Jackson off the cover of the New York Post*?"*

–Nathan Lane

ALSO ON THIS DAY

Helen Gallagher was born in 1926. Never a top-level star, she has churned out more than forty years of consistent performances, from *The Seven Lively Arts* to *Tallulah*, winning Tonys along the way for *Pal Joey* in 1952 and *No, No, Nanette* in 1971.

20

July

(2001) Move over, Barbra Streisand. Make room for another blonde singer/director/screenwriter/diva: John Cameron Mitchell, whose film adaptation of his smash stage success *Hedwig and the Angry Inch* opened in limited release today. This unlikely tale of a former East German punk rock singer/botched sex-change operation victim somehow resonated with just about everyone who saw it.

broadway banter

"I feel like I'm going out of my mind. I don't know whose idea this was. I can't dance, can't sing, and I can't act. I'm waiting for them to fire me."

—Ally Sheedy (see below for context)

CASTING COUCH

When *Hedwig* played its two-year-plus off-Broadway run, one of the replacements for the title role was Ally Sheedy. After weeks of erratic behavior, including skipping songs, changing the script, ad-libbing, and showing up for work only sporadically, the former Brat-Packer quit the show.

21

July

(1978) You can't keep harping on the many, many horrifically bad movie musicals between 1978 and 1982. But ... I will. Today, New York City was graced with the premiere of *Sgt. Pepper's Lonely Hearts Club Band,* giving the classic Beatles songs to the likes of Peter Frampton and the Bee Gees. I guess producer Robert Stigwood said, "We need a band with a name that sounds like Beatles. Hmm. Beatles. Bee Gees. Beatles. Bee Gees. We've got it!"

The best part of this movie (though it isn't hard to be the best part) is the finale, where the title number is sung by a bleacher full of nearly a hundred stars of every shape and size, including Alice Cooper, Gwen Verdon, Wolfman Jack, Yvonne Elliman, George Benson, Helen Reddy, Chita Rivera, Peter Allen, Robert Palmer, Dame Edna, Sha-Na-Na, and of course, Carol Channing.

broadway banter

"Susan H. Schulman's mounting at the Martin Beck starred chipmunk-cheeked Rebecca Luker as Maria, the nun who gets von Trapped in the Alps."

—*Jeffrey Eric Jenkins*

ALSO ON THIS DAY

Belter Lillias White was born in 1951. A twenty-five-year Broadway veteran, she won a Tony for her tough-talking-but-ultimately-golden-hearted hooker in *The Life.*

July

(1949) Alan Menken was born today, and the cartoon musical was given a second chance. After a few decades of forgettable Disney musicals, cartoon or otherwise, Alan Menken revived the genre with his writing partner, Howard Ashman, in the Disney animated movie *The Little Mermaid*. The golden age would last only a few more years, though, with *Beauty and the Beast* and *Aladdin* following before Ashman died in 1991 of complications following AIDS. The two also wrote the off-Broadway hit *Little Shop of Horrors*.

Menken also scored Disney cartoons *The Hunchback of Notre Dame* and *Hercules*, as well as the live-action *Newsies* and the Kelsey Grammar vehicle *A Christmas Carol*.

broadway banter

"They say the prime of life hits people all at a different age. Shirley Temple, it hit at eight years old. ... About eighty-four, I'll be entering it."

—Carol Channing

ALSO ON THIS DAY

Naked Boys Singing! opened off-Broadway in 1999. The revue, conceived by Robert Schrock, featured such tongue-in-cheek songs as "Gratuitous Nudity," "Fight the Urge," "Perky Little Porn Star," and "Nothing but the Radio On."

July

(2002) You're a good man, Clark Gesner: The composer of *You're a Good Man, Charlie Brown* died today. In 1967, he brought his charming *Peanuts* musical to off-Broadway, featuring rising talents Bob Balaban and Gary Burghoff. Gesner also wrote the revue *The Jello Is Always Red*, in addition to writing for the long-running kids show *Captain Kangaroo*. In 1999, *Charlie Brown* was revised and brought back to Broadway with the addition of new songs by Andrew Lippa; it starred Kristin Chenoweth, Roger Bart, B.D. Wong, and Anthony Rapp.

broadway banter

"[The] only theatrical achievement that you can be sure is basically American is the large, noisy, lavish, vulgar, commercial musical show, like Annie Get Your Gun, with Ethel Merman blaring undistinguished tunes by Irving Berlin. ... We ought, perhaps, to have better taste."

–Brooks Atkinson

ALSO ON THIS DAY

Trick, an independent movie about a young, struggling composer of musicals, was released today in 1999. In it, Tori Spelling, of *90210* fame, plays the main character's untalented but enthusiastic singer/actress friend. Finally, a role that fits her like a glove!

24 July

(1968) As she sang in *Wicked*, "You'll be popular; Just not as quite as popular as me!" Kristin "Glinda" Chenoweth was born today. In 1997, she made her Broadway debut in *Steel Pier*, showing off her amazing vocal range. She snagged a Tony for her role as Sally in *You're a Good Man, Charlie Brown*, thanks to the newly added "My New Philosophy" written for her by Andrew Lippa (heck, the whole character was created for her, replacing the role of Peppermint Patty). And she achieved diva status with her turn in *Wicked*, opposite her very best friend (not), Idina Menzel. She's also dabbled in television with her own short-lived sitcom, as well as playing a perky Lily St. Regis in *Annie* and a way-miscast Marion Paroo in *The Music Man*.

broadway banter

"I'm defying Chenoweth ...
I'm defying subtlety
And no one's gonna turn my volume down!"

—*"Idina Menzel"* in *"Wicked"* in Forbidden Broadway: SVU, by Gerard Alessandrini

ALSO ON THIS DAY

An acclaimed revival of *Big River* opened in 2003, presented by the Deaf West Theatre. The revival combined hearing, hard-of-hearing, and deaf actors in a unique and electrifying show.

July

(1975) "Step, kick, kick, leap, kick, touch ... Again!" *A Chorus Line* opened on Broadway. An unlikely hit—no stars, no set, no conventional storyline—it became one of the most beloved musicals of all time. Michael Bennett and team took much of the dialogue and lyrics directly from tape-recorded sessions with Broadway dancers, some of whom ended up in the final show (others did not, and weren't too happy about it). The characters were ultimately amalgams of several dancers, with a little bit of Michael Bennett in just about every one of them.

broadway banter

"I felt, 'We're not doing 42nd Street. We are doing the truth.' The truth is that these people's lives were full of people who did damage to them."

–Ed Kleban, on creating A Chorus Line

CASTING COUCH

Originally, the character Cassie in *A Chorus Line* was not picked for the job, but when Marsha Mason saw the show, she told the creative team, "You've got to give her that job." They did, and the doubtful creative team realized it was the right choice for the show, after all.

26

July

(1999) Workshops began today in Toronto for the new Lynn Ahrens/Stephen Flaherty musical, *The Seussical*. The songwriting team reunited with its *Ragtime* director, Frank Galati, and *SCTV* alum Andrea Martin played The Cat in the Hat. By the time the show reached Broadway in November of 2000, the title was changed to *Seussical the Musical*, and David Shiner had replaced Martin. The poorly received show didn't last long, but it enjoyed a healthy tour with gymnast-turned-Peter Pan Cathy Rigby. *Seussical* really found its legs, though, in countless regional and high school productions.

broadway banter

"How do you spell hit? Quite simply, really. 'The 25ᵗʰ Annual Putnam County Spelling Bee.' This ingratiating musical ... has a lot of what has been missing from many new musicals in the last several years–heart."

–Michel Kuchwara

ALSO ON THIS DAY

Ethel Mertz—I mean Vivian Vance—was born today. She got her start with a bit part in *Anything Goes*, also understudying Ethel Merman.

27

July

(2003) Thanks for the memories: At the age of one hundred, Bob Hope died today. Hope started out on Broadway in shows like *Roberta, The Ziegfeld Follies of 1936,* and *Red, Hot and Blue.* But he really leapt to fame on screen, especially in *The Big Broadcast of 1938* and *The Road to Singapore, The Road to Rio,* and *The Road to Bali,* co-starring with Bing Crosby and Dorothy Lamour. In his long career, Hope made numerous other musicals and performed on countless variety shows. He also won a special place in the hearts of many servicemen with his extensive touring with the USO during World War II and the Vietnam War.

broadway banter

"Somebody should write a musical Three Sisters *so that she can play Masha, or a musical* Streetcar Named Desire, *so she can play Blanche DuBois.*

—*Trevor Nunn, on Judy Kuhn*

POP QUIZ

Q: How many musicals have been made about the life of Buddy Holly?

A: Two: First, on screen, *The Buddy Holly Story* with Gary Busey, then in 1990 on Broadway, *Buddy: The Buddy Holly Story* starring Paul Hipp

28

July

(1969) Frank Loesser died of lung cancer today in 1969 at the age of just fifty-nine. His first show as a Broadway composer was a big one: *Where's Charley?*, starring Ray Bolger. His next one was a classic of musical comedy: *Guys and Dolls*. And his last show brought him the Pulitzer Prize: *How to Succeed in Business Without Really Trying*. In between, he also wrote the operatic *The Most Happy Fella* and the resounding flop *Greenwillow*.

In addition to his stage work, Loesser received five Oscar nominations, including the hilarious "They're Either Too Young or Too Old," introduced by the unlikely Bette Davis.

broadway banter

"Where the film had been droll and witty, though, the Broadway version was leaden and obvious."

—Barry Singer, on Victor/Victoria

CASTING COUCH

Among the original dancers cast in *Cats* were young Sarah Brightman and *All My Children*'s Finola Hughes.

29

July

(1887) *The New Moon, The Student Prince, The Desert Song* ... Sigmund Romberg was born today. In his day, he was a genius, writing some fifty-five Broadway operettas, musicals, and revues. Today, though, he is largely forgotten: The last time a show of his was revived on Broadway was a short-lived *The Student Prince* in 1973. The only other person to bring him back since then is Bob Fosse, who used Romberg's song "Stout Hearted Men" in the revue *Dancin'*.

broadway banter

"*Ever hear of* Planet of the Apes?"
"*Uhh, the movie or the planet?*"
"*The brand new, multi-million-dollar musical. And you are starring ... as the human.*"
"*It's the part I was born to play, baby!*"

—MacArthur Parker *and* Troy McClure *on* The Simpsons

BACKSTAGE

In the tree-climbing scene in the film *The Sound of Music*, stand-in Larri Thomas doubled for Julie Andrews, but all the children did their own stunts.

30
July

(1983) That's entertainment! Having spent a career in as the rare combination of lyricist and publicist, Howard Dietz died today. Usually paired with composer Arthur Schwartz, he wrote such enduring tunes as "Dancing in the Dark," and the showbiz anthem "That's Entertainment," as well as a number of comedy/novelty songs, including "Triplets" and "The Dickey Bird Song." Much of his later career was dominated by the Broadway flops *The Gay Life* and the Mary Martin vehicle *Jennie*.

broadway banter

Sophia: The man's as gay as a picnic basket!

Dorothy: Ma, that is incredible! How'd you know?

Sophia: I heard him singing in the shower the other morning. He's the only man I know who knows all the words to "Send in the Clowns."

–The Golden Girls

STAR POWER

Chita Rivera was nominated for Best Leading Actress in a Musical for the flop *Bring Back Birdie* in 1981 and the flop *Merlin* in 1983. Fortunately, she didn't have to compete against her daughter Lisa Mordente, who managed to schedule her Tony-nominated flop *Marlowe* in between. Both mother and daughter lost all three years.

31
July

(2003) *Avenue Q* opened on Broadway, in a rare transfer of an off-off-Broadway play. Even rarer, the cast mixed live actors with Muppet-like hand puppets that bear a close resemblance to *Sesame Street*'s Bert, Ernie, Cookie Monster, etc.

Stunningly, at Tony time *Avenue Q* upset the favorite *Wicked* for Best Musical and Best Score, leaving Stephen Schwartz still searching for his first Tony. But no one was more stunned than those Tony voters who were banking on making money on *Avenue Q*'s impending national tour: A few days after the Tonys, the producers announced it would not tour, but instead, play an ongoing engagement in Las Vegas. Perhaps middle America wasn't ready for muppets having sex?

broadway banter

"I'm gonna have to do the hardest thing I've ever done in my life: act humble."

—Mel Brooks, *winning his first of three Tonys for* The Producers

ALSO ON THIS DAY

The Lion King played its first public performance in 1997 in Minneapolis. Three months later it would begin previews in New York.

AUGUST

Gene Kelly's infamous title song-and-dance sequence in the 1952 film *Singin' in the Rain*.

1

August

(1996) *I Love You, You're Perfect, Now Change* opened off-Broadway. This small-scale musical revue by Joe DiPietro and Jimmy Roberts explored the worlds of dating (Act One) and marriage, parenthood, and old age (Act Two). A sort of unfocused "Sex and the City lite," it became a massive hit, running for nine years and counting, with more than three thousand performances off-Broadway, as well as hundreds of regional productions.

broadway banter

Something fiasco
Something disast-o
Something just tedious
A musical that bites!
                    —Kyle Smith, *reviewing the film version of* The Producers

POP QUIZ

Q: What flop did Stephen Sondheim call "the first really good experimental show"?

A: Rodgers and Hammerstein's *Allegro*

2

August

(1900) Helen Morgan, the original tragic torch singer, was born today. After early success on Broadway with *George White's Scandals of 1925*, her next role was the one she would be remembered for: Julie in the production of *Show Boat*, introducing both "Can't Help Lovin' Dat Man" and "Bill." She then starred in another Kern/Hammerstein musical, *Sweet Adeline*, singing "Why Was I Born?" She worked briefly in Hollywood in a few early "talkies" like *Applause* and the 1929 silent version of *Show Boat*, appearing only in the brief, musicalized prologue. After her career and first marriage tanked, she made a comeback in the classic 1936 *Show Boat* remake, where she got to reprise her role in its entirety. However, the success was short-lived, as her life mirrored the tragic songs for which she had become famous: She died at the age of forty-one of cirrhosis of the liver, just two months after her second marriage.

In 1957, she was immortalized/fictionalized with *The Helen Morgan Story*, with Ann Blyth in the title role and Gogi Grant dubbing the vocals.

broadway banter

"*Love cannot be love without 'le singing.'*"

—*Liliane La Fleur, in* Nine, *lyrics by Maury Yeston*

BY THE NUMBERS

In 2005, for the first time in twelve years, all four Tony Award-winning actors for musicals were in original productions, rather than revivals.

(1920) Maria Karnilova, the prolific actress/ singer/dancer whose career didn't really blossom until she was forty—and who made a career of playing strippers, whores, and madams—was born. Some of her most memorable roles included Tessie Tura in *Gypsy*, Madame Hortense in *Zorba*, Inez Alvarez in *Gigi*, and her Tony-winning portrayal of Golde in *Fiddler on the Roof.*

3
August

Karnilova made her Broadway debut in 1946 in *Call Me Mister*. Two years later, she married one of her fellow actors from that show, George S. Irving, a prolific Broadway actor fondly remembered by Generation X-ers as Heat Miser in *The Year Without a Santa Claus*. The two remained married until Karnilova's death in 2001.

broadway banter

"We never fully appreciated how wonderfully he directed that show until we saw what Michael Cacoyannis did to it when he staged the revival."

—John Kander, on Hal Prince's direction of the original production of Zorba

IT TAKES A VILLAGE

Composer Elton John did not see *The Lion King* until opening night on Broadway.

4

August

(1942) A bit early for Christmas, the Bing Crosby/Fred Astaire classic *Holiday Inn* had its premiere. Paired together for the first time, the two took the old songs by Irving Berlin to new heights and introduced "White Christmas," an "instant" classic if ever there was one. In the complete version of the film, Bing Crosby and Marjorie Reynolds perform Berlin's "Abraham" in blackface. This number is usually cut when aired on television, for obvious reasons.

broadway banter

"As we all should probably have learned by now, to be a Stephen Sondheim fan is to have one's heart broken at regular intervals."

–*Frank Rich, reviewing Sondheim's flop* Merrily We Roll Along, *which Rich called "a shambles"*

CASTING COUCH

When George M. Cohan sold the rights to *Yankee Doodle Dandy* to Warner Brothers, his first choice to play himself was Fred Astaire.

August

(**1957**) We love her a bushel and a peck: Faith Prince was born today. After making a small but splashy Broadway debut in *Jerome Robbins' Broadway* and surviving the disastrous *Nick and Nora,* Prince hit it big with her definitive performance of Miss Adelaide in *Guys and Dolls,* winning a Tony. Although she's been a regular fixture on the Broadway stage since, starring in *Little Me* and *Bells Are Ringing,* and as replacements for *The King and I* and *James Joyce's The Dead,* she has yet to reach her *Guys and Dolls* heights again.

broadway banter

"So picture this: On a Clear Day You Can See Forever *... Sacramento Music Circus—aptly named, I might add—summer stock, a cabana for a dressing room, a tent for a theater, in the round, with a turntable. Three hundred sixty degrees of aggravation."*

—Faith Prince

STAR POWER

While performing at the Sacramento Music Circus, Kathleen Freeman's chair collapsed while she was singing. The show came to a stop, but she just picked herself up and ad-libbed, "That's why I love the theater."

6

August

(1926) Birth of an Ovation: The sound era in motion pictures began. Not with *The Jazz Singer*, as is often touted, for sound experiments in films had met with varying degrees of success for much of the 1920s. However, on this day at the Warner Bros. Theatre on Broadway, the sound pioneer studio and Will Hays presented a "Vitaphone" program of orchestral music and opera arias. The audio quality varied, but this was a seminal step toward the "all talking, all singing" pictures of just a few years later.

broadway banter

"Thank God for film. It can capture a performance and hold it right there forever."

—Liza Minnelli

BACKSTAGE

The original title of *Seven Brides for Seven Brothers* was *Sobbin' Women*, since the script was adapted from the Roman tale of the rape of the Sabine women. The song "Sobbin' Women" remained, but the title was then changed to *A Bride for Seven Brothers*. Movie censors felt that title had a dirty connotation, so the final title was then taken.

August

(1885) Come out, come out, wherever you are ... Billie Burke was born today, and though she had a prolific career on stage and screen spanning some fifty years, she is best remembered as Glinda the Good Witch in *The Wizard of Oz* (which is ironic, since it's neither her best work, nor was she particularly well-cast, a fifty-four-year-old non-singer playing the beautiful, singing Glinda). She appeared in several other movie musicals, including *Everybody Sing* and *Irene*. After her husband, Flo Ziegfeld, died, she went on to produce a number of editions of the *Ziegfeld Follies* on Broadway.

broadway banter

"So don't give up, all you short or fat or tall girls;
Democracy says fame can come to all girls!"

–Hope Springfield *in* Fade Out—Fade In,
by Betty Comden and Adolph Green

CASTING COUCH

In the 1998 revival of *Cabaret*, after Natasha Richardson left the show, the replacement "Sally Bowles" included Jennifer Jason Leigh, Susan Egan, Katie Finneran, Joely Fisher, Gina Gershon, Deborah Gibson, Jane Leeves, Molly Ringwald, Brooke Shields, and Lea Thompson.

8
August

(1922) Take that, Sonja Henie. Equally unlikely musical star Esther Williams, born today, took Sonja's act and simply unfroze the ice. Williams's "Aqua Musicals" included *Million Dollar Mermaid*, *Bathing Beauty*, and *Neptune's Daughter*. The latter film was more noteworthy for its Oscar-winning song, "Baby It's Cold Outside." Wildly popular in her day, Esther's aqua-ballets tend to baffle modern audiences, myself included.

broadway banter

Statler: I like this movie fine so far.

Waldorf: It hasn't started yet.

Statler: That's what I like about it.

—The Muppet Movie, *by Jack Burns and Jerry Juhl*

ALSO ON THIS DAY

Liza Minnelli took over the role of Roxie Hart in *Chicago* in 1975, having had just six days to learn the role following Gwen Verdon's hospitalization.

9

August

(2003) One of dancing's biggest stars went out today: Gregory Hines died after a yearlong battle with liver cancer, at fifty-seven years young. He made his Broadway debut at the age of eight in *The Girl in Pink Tights*, and he never looked back. He would later snag Tony nominations for *Eubie!* and *Sophisticated Ladies*, winning one in 1992 for *Jelly's Last Jam*, which he also choreographed.

Hines often got to show off his versatile dance skills in films, including *White Nights* with Mikhail Baryshnikov and *Tap*. He also danced with his brother Maurice in *The Cotton Club*, and tapped his way to an Emmy nomination for *Bojangles*.

broadway banter

"A tacit in music is not a silence, it's a suspension."

—Agnes de Mille

POP QUIZ

Q: In what 1976 movie musical do young Scott Baio and Jodie Foster play a gangster and his moll?

A: Bugsy Malone

10
August

(1986) *The Lambeth Walk* came to Broadway—fifty years late. *Me and My Girl*, the 1930s British musical comedy featuring the popular song and dance "Lambeth Walk," finally made it to the Great White Way, following a London revival/revision a year earlier. It was director Michael Ockrent's first Broadway musical, and it was a huge hit, running three and a half years. In 1992, he returned with another revival he reconceived and directed: *Gershwin's Crazy for You.*

Sadly, in 1999 he died of acute leukemia at the age of fifty-three, leaving behind his widow, choreographer Susan Stroman.

broadway banter

"Jule was a madman, the most wonderful madman; writing with one hand, producing with the other."

—Sylvia Herscher, on Jule Styne

ALSO ON THIS DAY

Antonio Banderas was born in 1960, a surprisingly good singer who was nominated for a Golden Globe for *Evita* and a Tony for *Nine.*

(1965) One year after their *A Hard Day's Night* sent audiences screaming and cheering for more, the Beatles came back with their second movie musical, *Help!*, released in the United States today. The goofy spoof of James Bond movies boasted a classic Beatles score, including "She's Got a Ticket to Ride" and the title number. It even featured notable extras; one member of a crowd of screaming teenagers appearing in the film is a young Phil Collins. The movie is "respectfully dedicated to the memory of Mr. Elias Howe, who in 1846, invented the sewing machine."

11

August

broadway banter

"Once in every show
There comes a song like this
It starts off soft and low
And ends up with a kiss"

—Sir Dennis Galahad, singing "The Song That Goes Like This"
in Monty Python's Spamalot, by Eric Idle

IT TAKES A VILLAGE

"The Man I Love" was originally written for *Lady, Be Good,* but was cut before opening. It was then added to the score of *Strike up the Band,* only to be deleted again.

12

August

(1919) From soaring heights to deadly lows: Michael Kidd was born today. The innovative choreographer and sometimes director had more than a decade of huge hits, showcasing his trademark athleticism in *Finian's Rainbow*, *Love Life*, and *Can-Can* on Broadway; *Seven Brides for Seven Brothers* and *The Bandwagon* on film; and *Guys and Dolls* on both stage and screen.

The latter half of his career, though, has been marked by a string of flops and disappointments: the infamous *Wildcat*, the infamous *Subways Are for Sleeping*, the infamous attempted musical version of *Breakfast at Tiffany's*, and the (you guessed it) infamous *Star!* It's no wonder that in 1975 he played a disheartened choreographer in the film *Smile* (which later also became a flop musical, though fortunately not a Michael Kidd production).

broadway banter

"Spelling Bee *is, in essence,* A Chorus Line *with pimples.*"

—*Charles Isherwood*

ALSO ON THIS DAY——

The long-running *The Donkey Show,* a musical adaptation of *A Midsummer Night's Dream,* opened off-Broadway in 1999.

13
August

(1895) If he only had the nerve: Bert Lahr was born today. Not unlike his *Oz* costars, the talented Lahr was a prolific performer, but he will always be remembered mostly as the cowardly lion. Lahr made a dozen other movie musicals and spent nearly forty years on Broadway, showcasing his broad comic style in shows like *Seven Lively Arts*, *Two on the Aisle*, and his Tony-winning performance in *Foxy*, a musical update of Ben Johnson's *Volpone*. The versatile comic even tried his hand at Beckett, playing Estragon in the Broadway premiere of *Waiting for Godot*.

He famously paired up with Ethel Merman in *DuBarry Was a Lady*. One night, while chasing Merman around the stage, he chased her so slowly that she actually lapped him! Since it got such a huge laugh, they kept it in the show.

broadway banter

"*Do Steve Martin and Bernadette Peters really dare to put themselves in Astaire and Rogers's place? Yet they carry it off.*"

–Pauline Kael, on Pennies from Heaven

ALSO ON THIS DAY

Love Me Tonight premiered in 1932, a charming musical featuring a Rodgers and Hart score sung by the rather unlikely duo of Maurice Chevalier and Jeanette MacDonald.

14
August

(1975) Get out your rice and toilet paper: *The Rocky Horror Picture Show*, the cult classic to end all cult classics, premiered today in London. A bad movie about bad movies, it bombed in its original release, but went through the roof once the producers decided to start showing it at midnight instead of at the usual matinee and evening show times.

Proving the musical's popularity and durability, a revival of *The Rocky Horror Show* opened on Broadway in 2000. The high-energy production featured a catch-all mix of stars and has-beens, with rising stars Tom Hewitt (Frank 'N' Furter) and Raul Esparza (Riff Raff); Tony nominees Daphne Rubin-Vega (Magenta), Alice Ripley (Janet), and Jarrod Emick (Brad); eighties rocker Joan Jett (Columbia); lesbian lounge lizard Lea DeLaria (Dr. Scott and Eddie); and Dick Cavett (Narrator).

broadway banter

"*Carol Channing ... may be the only creature extant who can live up to a Hirschfeld.*"

—Walter Kerr

ALSO ON THIS DAY

Producer Lemuel Ayers died in 1954, bringing to an end to the prospect of Stephen Sondheim's first musical, *Saturday Night*, coming to Broadway. The show would have to wait until 1997 to find its first staging, at the Bridewell Theater in London.

(1946) Disney's *Make Mine Music,* a more eclectic and pop-oriented version of *Fantasia,* premiered today. *MMM* did feature classics like Prokofiev's "Peter and the Wolf," but alongside it were "Casey at the Bat," Benny Goodman, Dinah Shore, Nelson Eddy's "The Whale Who Wanted to Sing at the Met," and the Andrews Sisters singing about a love affair between two hats. Current editions of the video have cut "The Martins and the Coys" sequence, a gun-filled spoof of the feud between the Hatfields and McCoys.

15

August

broadway banter

"[Audiences] just didn't come, not even to hear [Betty] Buckley sing 'Serenity,' one of the best, and best-delivered, show tunes in years."

—David Lefkowitz, on the unfair failure of Triumph of Love

STAR POWER

In 1968, Barbra Streisand played Fanny Brice in *Funny Girl,* despite the fact that Streisand was a powerful belter and Brice was more of an interpreter of songs than a singer, and had no real belt. Similarly, that same year, Julie Andrews played Gertrude Lawrence in *Star!,* despite the fact that Andrews had a legitimate soprano voice and Lawrence was more of an interpreter of songs than a singer and had no vocal range to speak of.

16

August

(1946) Lesley Ann Warren, born today, made her Broadway debut at just seventeen playing Snookie in *110 in the Shade,* then landed the coveted role of Cinderella in the TV remake of the classic R&H musical. Most of the rest of Warren's musical career was marked by duds: her two big chances at playing leads on Broadway came with the eight-performance *Drat! the Cat!* and the never-got-there *Gone With the Wind.* In 1997, she made a brief Broadway comeback with the Johnny Mercer revue *Dream,* but it only lasted a few months. Her film career contained a few better vehicles with the Disney family musical *The Happiest Millionaire* and the more adult *Victor/Victoria.*

broadway banter

"It was everything I ever dreamed of and more."

—Jeanette MacDonald, *on being raped by Nelson Eddy (Ew!)*

ALSO ON THIS DAY —————————————

It was a big day for musical divas: Ann Blyth (*Kismet*), Eydie Gorme (*Golden Rainbow*), Julie Newmar (*Seven Brides for Seven Brothers*), Anita Gillette (*Carnival!*), Carole Shelley (*Wicked*), Dee Hoty (*Footloose*), Kathie Lee Gifford (*Putting It Together*), and Madonna (*Dick Tracy*) were all born.

17

August

(1939) *The Wizard of Oz* premiered in New York City. Fifteen thousand people lined the block around the theater to see the movie, which featured a live performance from Judy Garland and Mickey Rooney after every showing of the film. Although it was a relative hit, the expensive endeavor barely broke even in its initial release. Bu that couldn't stop Judy Garland from rocketing to the status of legend, nor the Harold Arlen/E.Y. Harburg song "Over the Rainbow" from entering the list of all-time beloved standards. Judy won a special Oscar for Best Juvenile Performance, and "Over the Rainbow" won the Oscar for Best Song—amazingly, the only one Harold Arlen would ever win.

Judy would later comment on that song: "I have sung it dozens of times and it's still the song that's closest to my heart. It is so symbolic of everybody's dream and with that I am sure that's why people sometimes get tears in their eyes when they hear it."

broadway banter

"You're Barbra Joan Streisand—you've got enough on your hands."

—Linda Richmond (the host of Saturday Night Live's "Coffee Talk" skits, as played by Mike Myers)

STAR POWER

Anges de Mille became one of the first female musical directors— and likely the first female director/choreographer— with *Allegro*.

18
August

(2001) Kathleen Freeman played her final performance of *The Full Monty* today. The veteran character actress, making her first appearance in a Broadway musical, just about stole the show from her ecdysiast male costars as a crusty old pianist hired to help the would-be strippers with their so-called act. Freeman's only song, a rousing Act Two opener about all the better piano playing gigs she's had in her lengthy career, brought the house down every night. Five days later, she died at the age of seventy-seven.

Previously, Freeman had appeared in more than a hundred movies, notably playing Lina Lamont's exasperated vocal coach in *Singin' in the Rain*, and voicing old women characters in *Hercules* and *Shrek*.

broadway banter

Jeffrey: But Darius is a dancer. He's in Cats.

Sterling: Exactly. I said you needed a boyfriend, not a person.

—Jeffrey, by *Paul Rudnick*

BACKSTAGE

Janet Jackson wrote a new song for the film *Chicago,* but it was never used.

(1956) Versatile actors Tammy Grimes and Christopher Plummer were married today. They will later become the only married couple to both have Tonys for both musicals and plays: Grimes for *The Unsinkable Molly Brown* and *Private Lives*, Plummer for *Cyrano* and *Barrymore* (though truth be told, they were divorced before either won any Tonys at all). Grimes found other musical success with *High Spirits*, *A Musical Jubilee*, and *42nd Street*, while Plummer's biggest brush with musicals was being dubbed in *The Sound of Music*.

P.S.: Seven months after the wedding, daughter Amanda was born. She would go on to win a Tony for *Agnes of God*.

19
August

broadway banter

"I thought it might be awfully saccharine. After all, what can you do with nuns, seven children, and Austria?"

—*Julie Andrews, before being offered the role in* The Sound of Music

ALSO ON THIS DAY

Alexander's Ragtime Band opened across America in 1938, giving Ethel Merman one of her best film vehicles and the chance to belt Irving Berlin's "Heat Wave," "A Pretty Girl Is Like a Melody," and "Blue Skies."

20
August

(1929) The first all-black feature film, *Hallelujah!*, premiered. Although the musical seems a mass of prejudice today, it was a major breakthrough in the early days of Hollywood. The film eschewed the usual stereotypes in favor of the most realistic portrayal of African-Americans seen on screen to date. The film's score contained a wide range of music, from traditional spirituals to Stephen Foster to Irving Berlin.

broadway banter

"You're at Urinetown!
Your ticket should say Urinetown!
No refunds, this is Urinetown!"

—Cast of Urinetown, *by Mark Hollmann and Greg Kotis*

IT TAKES A VILLAGE

The title song for the film *New York, New York* had to be titled "The Theme from *New York, New York*," because Comden, Green, and Bernstein had already written a song called "New York, New York" for *On the Town,* and Kander and Ebb didn't want to step on their toes.

(1983) The best of times is now: *La Cage Aux Folles* opened on Broadway. What *Hallelujah!* was to blacks, *La Cage* was to gays: If certain concessions had to be made to appeal to a wide audience, it was nonetheless a breakthrough moment for Broadway. Jerry Herman's glitzy score and Harvey Fierstein's book provided the frame not only for a gaggle of drag queens, but for a long-term, committed gay relationship. The show was a smash hit, snatching up six Tonys and running more than four years.

August

broadway banter

"*You know the set from 'The Harmonia Gardens' [sequence in the film] is still there. They were doing* The Love Boat *on top of it. Every time I'm there I do a dance of death on it.*"

—*Carol Channing, on the film version of* Hello, Dolly!

STAR POWER

In Minneapolis at the start of the tour of her one-woman show, Bea Arthur stepped off the stage and sprained her ankle. She kept going with the performance, turned it into an anecdote in her show, and—even after getting out of her air cast—continued to perform the show barefoot.

22

August

(1932) With more than one hundred Broadway shows and three Tonys to her credit, Theoni V. Aldredge, born today, has been one of the busiest costume designers in musicals history. She has provided the innovative and/ or definitive costume designs for shows like *Anyone Can Whistle, Two Gentlemen of Verona, A Chorus Line, 42nd Street, La Cage Aux Folles,* and *The Secret Garden.* Her film work hasn't been quite as fruitful, musicals-wise: The highlight is *Annie,* and the lowlight is *Can't Stop the Music.*

For more than fifty years, she's also been the wife of the almost equally prolific actor Tom Aldredge, most notably starring in *Into the Woods, Passion,* and the revival of *1776.*

broadway banter

"A Chorus Line *is an actor's play about actors. When that girl starts singing 'What I Did for Love,' it has nothing to do with sex. It's the love of the theater—the horror, the heartbreak, the disappointments. We've all had our share."*

—Charles Durning

CASTING COUCH

Noel Coward was an original choice for the role of Max Detweiler in the film *The Sound of Music.*

23

August

(1912) Dancer, actor, singer, choreographer, and director Gene Kelly was born today. He started out on Broadway, making a name for himself in 1941 in *Pal Joey*. He came to Hollywood shortly afterward, and there he leapt to fame in such ground-breaking dance films as *Anchors Aweigh* (the first time a human danced next to an animated character), *An American in Paris*, and one of the all-time classics, *Singin' in the Rain*.

In 1964, Gene parodied his screen persona in the comedy *What a Way to Go!*, written by *Singin' in the Rain*'s Betty Comden and Adolph Green. In this comedy, Shirley MacLaine has the bad luck of marrying poor men out of love, only to have her husband make a fortune, then die tragically. Shirley marries Dick Van Dyke in a parody of silent movies, then Paul Newman in a send-up to "arty" French films, Robert Mitchum in a take-off of "women's pictures," and Gene Kelly in a lavish movie musical spoof.

broadway banter

"*Call me Miss Bird's Eye. The show is frozen!*"

–Ethel Merman

ALSO ON THIS DAY

Oscar Hammerstein died in 1960. Traffic came to a complete stop in Times Square and the lights were turned out throughout the theater district for one minute in his memory.

24

August

(1988) From Mendel to Motel: Leonard Frey died today, just shy of his fiftieth birthday, following complications due to AIDS. Frey was the only performer to have appeared in the original production of *Fiddler on the Roof* and its film version. After playing a smallish supporting role on Broadway, he "graduated" to playing the poor tailor with a song all his own, receiving an Oscar nomination for his work. He was only three years younger than his on-screen father-in-law, Topol. He also appeared in *A Kurt Weill Cabaret* on Broadway, his only other major musical role.

broadway banter

"It was originally a very small part, no more than a cough and a 'Mazel tof' but it got bigger."

—Leonard Frey, on the role of Mendel

POP QUIZ

What pop diva has appeared on Broadway as a replacement for Chita Rivera in *Kiss of the Spiderwoman* and as the witch in the 2002 revival of *Into the Woods*?

25

August

(1980) The stage version of *42nd Street* opened on Broadway ... and fore-running *Rent* creator Jonathan Larson's death, *42nd Street* director/choreographer Gower Champion died just prior to the opening curtain. Producer David Merrick withheld this sad but choice piece of news until curtain call, when he came out on stage and announced the theater legend's death to a dismayed audience and shattered cast, including Champion's leading lady and mistress, Wanda Richert.

Interestingly, also born on this day in 1909 was the film's original fresh young star, Ruby Keeler, the dancing queen of the 1930s.

broadway banter

"You're going out there a youngster, but you've got to come back a star!"

—Julian Marsh in 42nd Street, *screenplay by*
Rian James and James Seymour

IT TAKES A VILLAGE

Actor Stephen Fry (*Wilde, Gosford Park*) revised the 1937 book to *Me and My Girl,* making it a fresh hit all over again.

26

August

(2000) Halle Berry won an Emmy for *Introducing Dorothy Dandridge*, giving a definitive portrayal of the singing screen star.

Wait a minute—no she didn't. I mean, she did win the Emmy. But definitive? Berry did not exactly capture the magnetism and vivacity of Dandridge, and she couldn't hold a candle to Dandridge's sultry dance abilities. Nor did she even do her own singing: Wendie Williams did all the vocals. Ironic, or fitting, perhaps, since Dandridge herself was dubbed in her two big films, *Porgy and Bess* and her Oscar-nominated *Carmen Jones*.

broadway banter

"It is not my fault she can only get parts in pictures that I turn down."

—Dorothy Dandridge, on Lena Horne

ALSO ON THIS DAY

Michael Jeter was born in 1952. He won a Tony for *Grand Hotel: The Musical,* and sang a memorable "Everything's Coming Up Roses" in *The Fisher King.* Sadly, the world lost this gifted and versatile entertainer at the age of fifty to AIDS.

August

(1977) In twenty years or so, it's gonna change, ya know.

The original production of *Chicago* closed today, after a healthy run of 936 performances. The dark, biting show, which satirized everything from show business to fame to violence, was underappreciated by the critics and completely overshadowed by *A Chorus Line* by the award-givers, winning zero Tonys. Despite some legendary performances by Gwen Verdon, Chita Rivera, and Jerry Orbach, the show faded into semi-obscurity until Walter Bobbie and Ann Reinking resurrected it in a concert production in 1995. In the era of the O.J. Simpson trial, the JonBenet Ramsey mystery, and reality television, audiences now responded to *Chicago* the way the creators had hoped they would back in 1975. The production transferred to Broadway in 1996, where it would run more than four times as long as the original and collect six Tonys.

broadway banter

"Hal never liked Chicago. *He hated that show even when it was a hit. He thought we ripped off* Cabaret. *He wrote us a note saying that."*

–Fred Ebb

ALSO ON THIS DAY ——————

Martha Raye, who had the unfortunate distinction of being Jerry Herman's least-favorite Dolly Levi, was born in 1916.

28
August

(1925) Impish, athletic dancer Donald O'Connor was born today. By the age of eighteen, he had already appeared in some twenty films, and by age thirty, he had made such classic musicals as *Singin' in the Rain*, *Call Me Madam*, and *There's No Business Like Show Business*. Although he rarely had the chance to play the lead, he always managed to steal the show with his effervescent dancing and backflips up the walls.

By the age of forty, though, his film career was all but over, and his Broadway career was short-lived as well, consisting only of the 1981 flop *Bring Back Birdie* and the short-lived 1983 *Show Boat* revival. O'Connor died in 2003, having made a brief return to the screen, showing off his dance abilities in *Out to Sea* and an episode of *The Nanny*.

broadway banter

"There's a miracle on Broadway—an American musical, with American jazz rhythms, American wisecracks, an original American script."

—Jack Kroll, on City of Angels

STAR POWER

For all the times actors were dubbed in movie musicals, for some reason Marlon Brando in *Guys and Dolls* wasn't.

(1964) *Mary Poppins* opened across America, and children of all ages fell in love with Julie Andrews, the ultimate nanny who could dance, fly, and clean up a messy house in no time flat. Walt Disney packed more songs by the Sherman Brothers in this two-and-a-half-hour semi-epic than he had in ten years' worth of cartoons, and still the songwriters had reams of unused sheet music, some of which turned up in later Disney movies, including *The Jungle Book* and *Bedknobs and Broomsticks*.

August

broadway banter

"[Carol] Haney looks like a tall but awkward Audrey Hepburn. She has a froggy voice, slanty eyes, and an impish grin."

–John Chapman, praising (?) Carol Haney in The Pajama Game

ALSO ON THIS DAY

The Pajama Game premiered in 1957, transplanting almost the entire Broadway cast, which made for a delightfully fun, if dated, romp through a pajama factory. Doris Day was the only major replacement, but considering that she was perfectly cast, it didn't matter.

30

August

(1935) "Heaven ... I'm in heaven ..." *Top Hat* premiered in New York City today. The fourth onscreen pairing of Fred Astaire and Ginger Rogers featured a classic Irving Berlin score, including the Oscar-nominated "Cheek to Cheek" (it lost to *Gold Diggers* of 1935's "Lullaby of Broadway"). Back for his second Fred-and-Ginger picture was comedian Edward Everett Horton, who had appeared with the duo the year before in *The Gay Divorcee* and who would also join them in *Shall We Dance* in 1937.

broadway banter

"*Rafiki is a healer, but not only in the sense of being a doctor. She is a healer spiritually, she is a guide. She is also the person who sees beyond the now in terms of time and the broad spectrum of things.*"

—Tsidii Le Loka, on her role in The Lion King

STAR POWER

In 2005, Suzanne Somers made her Broadway debut with her one-woman show, *The Blonde in the Thunderbird*. Nine performances later, Somers's debut was over. Among the songs she sang was (fittingly?) "If I Only Had a Brain."

(1918) Eight Brides for One Brother? Alan Jay Lerner, the Elizabeth Taylor of lyricists, was born. Lerner equaled Taylor's incredible eight marriages; perhaps he even outdid her as he married eight different brides. The first seven ended in divorce; the last ended with his death.

31
August

Bride #1: Ruth Boyd, 1940–1947
Bride #2: Marion Bell (the original Broadway Fiona in *Brigadoon*), 1947–1949
Bride #3: Nancy Olson (Oscar nominee for *Sunset Boulevard*), 1950–1957
Bride #4: Micheline Muselli Pozzo de Borgo, 1957–1965
Bride #5: Karen Gunderson, 1966–1974
Bride #6: Sandra Payne, 1974–1976
Bride #7: Nina Bushkin, 1977–1981
Bride #8: Liz Robertson (thirty-two years Lerner's junior), 1981–1986

broadway banter

"Now that you've given me everything I've asked for, let's see if I want it."

—*Jerome Robbins, while co-directing the film* West Side Story

BACKSTAGE

The original production of *Hedwig and the Angry Inch* was produced for just $29,000.

SEPTEMBER

Richard Beymer and Natalie Wood as star-crossed lovers Tony and Maria in the 1961 film classic *West Side Story*.

1

September

(1922) Good times and bum times, she's seen 'em all, and my dear, she's still here: Yvonne De Carlo was born today. First she was another sloe-eyed vamp—in a series of semi-trashy B movies—then she was someone's mother—as well as Moses' wife in *The Ten Commandments*—then she was camp—as Lily Munster in the classic TV series.

At the age of forty-nine, De Carlo got the best role of her career: Carlotta Campion, the follies-chorus-girl-turned-movie-star in Sondheim's *Follies*. After working the entire lengthy rehearsal period on her one solo, "Can That Boy Foxtrot," it was cut during tryouts in Boston. Fortunately for her, it was replaced with "I'm Still Here," one of several hits Sondheim wrote at the last minute.

broadway banter

"To paraphrase an actual line from this misbegotten musical: We needed this show like we needed sand up our butts."

—Entertainment Weekly, *on the 2005 flop* In My Life

ALSO ON THIS DAY

Look for the silver lining: Marilyn Miller was born today in 1898. She went on to play the title roles in *Sally* and *Sunny* on Broadway and on film, as well as a dozen other Broadway shows. She died at thirty-seven following a long battle with alcoholism.

September

(1962) Australian songstress Caroline O'Connor was born today. Although she hasn't yet gotten her big break in America—her only Broadway credit has been serving as a replacement Velma Kelly in *Chicago* in 2003—this true triple threat has taken Sydney and London by storm. On her debut solo CD *What I Did for Love*, O'Connor memorably recreates songs from many of her leading roles from shows like *A Chorus Line, Baby, Damn Yankees, Into the Woods, West Side Story,* and her Olivier-nominated turn in *Mack & Mabel*. She also holds the rare distinction of having starred in two London productions at the same time: *Hot Stuff* and *Street Scene.* On screen, she appeared in fellow Aussie Baz Luhrmann's *Moulin Rouge!* as Nini Legs in the Air, and invoked Ethel Merman in *De-Lovely*, singing and tapping "Anything Goes."

broadway banter

"Mr. Astaire is the nearest approach we are ever likely to have to a human Mickey Mouse."

–Graham Greene

ALSO ON THIS DAY —————

Marge Champion was born in 1919. She kicked up her heels with husband Gower Champion in the 1951 film version of *Show Boat,* and assisted him in many of his choreographic endeavors. Most recently, she sang and danced in the 2001 revival of *Follies.*

(1910) The eternally youthful Kitty Carlisle Hart was born today. Before she married *Camelot* and *My Fair Lady* director Moss Hart, she appeared in numerous vaudeville shows and Broadway musicals. She also starred in several 1930s musicals, including *She Loves Me Not* with Bing Crosby, *Murder at the Vanities* with Duke Ellington, and most famously, *A Night at the Opera* with The Marx Brothers.

3

September

She returned to Broadway after an absence of almost thirty years in 1983 to replace Dina Merrill in the acclaimed revival of *On Your Toes*. Still going strong, she celebrated her ninety-fourth and ninety-fifth birthdays with engagements at Feinstein's at the Regency, singing songs written by the show business legends she knew, and sometimes even dated.

broadway banter

"I'll sing all the songs of the people who played for me at parties. Gershwin, Cole Porter, Dick Rodgers, etc. So, you see, I know how the songs should go."

—Kitty Carlisle Hart, on her program for her Feinstein's cabaret

BACKSTAGE

Although it has been revised numerous times on film and stage, the complete original 1934 score of *Anything Goes* was recorded for the first time in 1990 with Kim Criswell, Frederica von Stade, and Jack Gilford.

4

September

(1931) Mitzi Gaynor was born. After a few supporting roles, her breakout role came in 1951 with the Civil War musical *Golden Girl*. She went on to short-lived stardom with high-profile roles in *There's No Business Like Show Business*, *Anything Goes*, and *Les Girls*, and was nominated for a Golden Globe for her performance as Nellie Forbush in *South Pacific*. Although her film career ended in 1963, she went on to have a successful career on stage and in nightclubs. She has never appeared on Broadway, but she did head up the 1988 National Tour of *Anything Goes*, starring as a middle-aged Reno Sweeney.

broadway banter

"[Not] to pat myself on the back, but when I do a show, the whole show revolves around me … And if I don't show up, they can just forget it!"

—Ethel Merman

ALSO ON THIS DAY

Following the success of three Broadway musical productions named *Sally, Irene, and Mary,* in 1922 a new show opened called *Sally, Irene and Mary,* running for more than three hundred performances.

(2004) The last to go shall see the first three go before: *Aida* closed today, the most recent Disney musical to open on Broadway and the first to close, preceding the still-running *Beauty and the Beast* (twelve-plus years) and *The Lion King* (eight-plus years). *Aida* enjoyed a good four-and-a-half-year run, despite receiving mixed reviews and having the unfortunate distinction of being one of the few musicals of the last twenty years that was not nominated for a Best Musical Tony Award.

September

broadway banter

"*Disney needs big elaborate sets
'Cause there's no script to get through ...*"

—*Aida and Radames in* Forbidden Broadway 2001:
A Spoof Odyssey, *by Gerard Alessandrini*

STAR POWER

During the filming of *There's No Business Like Show Business,* Donald O'Connor had separated from his wife, Gwen, who was now dating Dan Dailey, Donald's onscreen father. After shooting ended and the O'Connors divorced, Gwen and Dan were married. They ultimately divorced.

6

September

(1985) The concert version of *Follies* played for two nights only at Lincoln Center. All 5,500 tickets sold out in less than three hours. The all-star event featured performances from Barbara Cook, Lee Remick, Elaine Stritch, Carol Burnett, Mandy Patinkin, George Hearn, and Comden and Green, among others. The brief rehearsal period and highlights of the concert were videotaped and aired on PBS, now available on DVD. Though many bewail the lack of video footage of the entire event, the footage of the frantic, pressure-cooker rehearsal period is infinitely more interesting.

broadway banter

"*[Follies] is to the American musical what* Virginia Woolf *was to the American drama.*"

—Louis Botto

IT TAKES A VILLAGE

The character of Chris in *Miss Saigon* was originally named "Trevor," after the show's early director, Trevor Nunn. When the show reached production, both Trevors were gone, replaced with the name "Chris" and Nicholas Hytner.

7

September

(1946) From "Greased Lightning" to "Comedy Tonight": Jerry Zaks was born today. Zaks got his start as a replacement Kenicke in the original Broadway production of *Grease*, and later appeared in the musical revue *Tintypes*. He then turned to the world of directing, where he would direct some of Broadway's most acclaimed musicals over the next twenty-plus years. He made a splash with his first Broadway musical, the revival of *Anything Goes* starring Patti LuPone and Howard McGillan. After that, he went on to *Smokey Joe's Café* and *The Civil War*, as well as revivals of *A Funny Thing Happened on the Way to the Forum, Little Shop of Horrors, La Cage Aux Folles,* and his Tony-winning *Guys and Dolls*.

Equally at home with plays, Zaks also took home Tonys for his work on John Guare's *The House of Blue Leaves* and *Six Degrees of Separation.*

broadway banter

"Broadway, Just a Road Now; It Just Ain't the Old Street Any More."

—Variety *headline at the height of the Depression*

POP QUIZ

What MGM star chose her pseudonym from a Hoagy Carmichal song and a drama critic?

A: Judy Garland, after the song "Judy," and critic Bob Garland

8

September

(1954) The hills were alive with the sound of music. No, not those hills: the highlands of Scotland. Well, not really.

When MGM bought the rights to the stage musical *Brigadoon*, filming was to have taken place on location in the Scottish highlands. Instead, the film was shot entirely on sound stages in Hollywood, including the "outdoor" woodland set that was surrounded by a cyclorama fifty feet high and 425 feet long to create an authentic-looking panoramic outdoor view. Lyricist Alan Jay Lerner later wrote, "[It] was one of those mistakes, putting it on a sound stage instead of doing it in Scotland. I suppose, when I think about it, it takes genuinely talented people to do something really bad."

broadway banter

"There is something of Oklahoma! *in* Brigadoon—*especially in Pamela Britton's acting of 'The Love of My Life,' which is the Scottish version of the Oklahoma girl who couldn't say no."*

—Brooks Atkinson

CASTING COUCH

The 20th Anniversary tour of *Nunsense* headlined Kaye Ballard, Georgia Engel, Mimi Hines, Darlene Love, and Lee Meriwether.

(1935) Tevye was born today. I mean, Topol was born today. After Zero Mostel started things out by creating the role in *Fiddler on the Roof* on Broadway, Topol finished things off, making an entire career out of playing the poor Jewish milkman: It is his only movie musical role and just about his only major stage credit outside of Israel. After playing the role in London, Topol made the film version at the age of just thirty-five, receiving an Oscar nomination.

September

In the late 1980s, he toured the United States in the show, playing opposite Rosalind Harris— who played his daughter Tzeitel in the film—as Golde. In 1991, he took the show to Broadway opposite Marcia Lewis, receiving a Tony nomination. He has played the role thousands of times all over the world, as recently as 2005 in Sydney, Australia.

broadway banter

"As one elderly Jewish legend of the theater was heard to say, 'You want my review? No Jews, no Tevye, no heart, no show.'"

—*Jeffrey Eric Jenkins on 2004's veddy British* Fiddler on the Roof

STAR POWER

James Cagney reprised his Oscar-winning role of George M. Cohan in *The Seven Little Foys* in 1955.

10

September

(2000) *Cats'* nine lives were up today: The musical that simultaneously saved Broadway and doomed it to more than a decade of British mega-musicals closed today with 7,485 performances. The show spent its last three years as the longest-running show in Broadway history, having eclipsed *A Chorus Line* for that honor on June 19, 1997. Unlike many other long-running shows, *Cats* played its entire tenure at the same theater, The Winter Garden. Its successor, fittingly another British mega-musical, was equally as mindless but infinitely more entertaining: *Mamma Mia!*

broadway banter

"If you blink, you'll miss the plot."

—*Frank Rich, on* Cats

POP QUIZ

How many of the American Film Institute's Top 100 Movies are musicals, and what are they?

A: Eleven: *The Wizard of Oz* (#6), *Singin' in the Rain* (#10), *West Side Story*, *Snow White and the Seven Dwarfs*, *The Sound of Music*, *Fantasia*, *An American in Paris*, *Duck Soup*, *The Jazz Singer*, *My Fair Lady*, and *Yankee Doodle Dandy*

11

September

(2001) The terrorist attacks of 9/11 shut down Broadway and had a decimating effect on its box office still felt today. Perhaps even more important to the subject of this book, it pushed Broadway producers even farther into making safe, audience-appealing, and unchallenging theater, especially in the realm of musicals. With few tourists coming to New York, local theatergoers stepped up to the plate and did everything they could to help keep shows open.

broadway banter

Bart: You have such a beautiful voice.

Sideshow Bob: Guilty as charged.

Bart: Uh huh. Anyway, I was wondering if you could sing the entire score of The H.M.S. Pinafore.

Sideshow Bob: Very well, Bart. I shall send you to heaven before I send you to hell.

–The Simpsons

ALSO ON THIS DAY

Another sad event: Fred Ebb died of a heart attack in 2004. The prolific lyricist made his Broadway debut in 1960 with a little musical revue called *From A to Z*, which also marked the Broadway debuts of Jerry Herman, Woody Allen, Virginia Vestoff, and orchestrator Jonathan Tunick.

12
September

(1888) Thank heaven for Maurice Chevalier. The Frenchman, born today, had been an icon for some three decades when he made an iconic performance in *Gigi* in 1958. It was his first Hollywood musical in almost twenty years, and he received a special Honorary Oscar that year. Before that, he starred in more than a dozen musicals, including *Love Me Tonight*, *The Merry Widow*, and his Oscar-nominated *The Love Parade*, all opposite Jeanette MacDonald.

Although he never appeared in a play or musical on Broadway, he made seven trips to The Great White Way with special concerts and events, winning a special Tony Award in 1968. He died at the age of eighty-three.

broadway banter

"We shot it all in New York. We didn't go to Toronto or Yugoslavia and pretend that we were in New York. I was able to hire three hundred New York dancers, seventy-two New York musicians, a New York crew and Broadway folk."

—Susan Stroman, on bringing her stage success
The Producers *to the big screen*

ALSO ON THIS DAY

Dracula himself: Bela Lugosi made his Broadway musical debut in *Murder at the Vanities* in 1933.

13
September

(**1948**) Give her a break: Nell Carter was born today. After roles in two fantastic flops of the early seventies—*Soon* and *Dude*—in 1978, Carter won the role of a lifetime in *Ain't Misbehavin'*, winning a Tony as well as an Emmy for the television broadcast of the show. Having appeared in the stage version of *Hair*, she made a guest appearance in the 1979 film, singing "Ain't Got No" and "White Boys." She returned to Broadway two decades later to play Miss Hannigan in a revival of *Annie*. She died bankrupt in 2003 following complications due to diabetes.

broadway banter

"*I stopped believing in Santa Claus at an early age. My mother took me to see him in a department store, and he asked for my autograph.*"

—*Shirley Temple*

ALSO ON THIS DAY

Mel Torme was born in 1925. Although he appeared in several movie musicals in the 1940s, he is best remembered for having composed "The Christmas Song (Chestnuts Roasting on an Open Fire)." He also served as music director to the critically acclaimed but short-lived *Judy Garland Show*.

14
September

(2005) Robert Wise passed away today at the age of ninety-one. He worked his way up through the ranks, starting out as sound effects editor for *The Gay Divorcee* and *Top Hat*, then editing *The Story of Vernon and Irene Castle*. After a long break from musicals, he returned to the genre to co-direct *West Side Story*, famously not getting along with his fellow director, Jerome Robbins; in fact, when they co-won the Best Director Oscar for the film, neither mentioned the other in his acceptance speech. He took over directing *The Sound of Music* when William Wyler dropped out in pre-production, becoming the only person to win two Best Director Oscars for musicals. A few years later, he reteamed with Julie on the somewhat underrated flop *Star!*

A highly eclectic filmmaker, Wise directed films in every genre, and edited Orson Welles's masterpiece *Citizen Kane*.

broadway banter

"West Side Story *begins with a blast of stereophonic music that had me clutching my head.*"

—Pauline Kael, *expressing a minority dissenting opinion*

BY THE NUMBERS

A woman named Myra Franklin claims she has seen *The Sound of Music* 940 times.

15

September

(2005) *Bush Is Bad.*

Whether or not you agree with that statement, the musical began previews off-Broadway today. Written by Joshua Rosenblum, the revue featured such songs as "How Can 59 Million People Be So Dumb?," "Good Conservative Values," "The Gay Agenda," and "New Hope for the Fabulously Wealthy." *Bush Is Bad* proved to be the little show that could, extending into an open-ended run.

broadway banter

"Remember this was an all-black musical, and the theme of the story, depicting blacks as much-less-than-virtuous, bad-living folks, brought an angry reaction from the entire black community. They even picketed the show one night."

–Harold Nicholas, star of St. Louis Woman

ALSO ON THIS DAY——

A marriage made in Oz: Dorothy's daughter Liza Minnelli married the Tin Man's son Jack Haley Jr. in 1974. The marriage, Minnelli's second of four (so far) and Haley's only, lasted just five years.

16
September

(1924) She's one of the girls who sounds like one of the boys: Lauren Bacall was born today. Her twenty-five years of being a movie star had not given audiences an inkling of the musical theater star power she would unleash in the 1970 remake of *All About Eve*, retitled *Applause*. Bacall's smoky baritone voice was utterly captivating, and she truly inhabited the role of Margo Channing. A decade later, she returned—and triumphed again—in Kander and Ebb's *Woman of the Year*, a remake of the movie of the same name, which had starred her longtime friend, Katharine Hepburn.

Interestingly, in 1970, *Applause*'s Bacall defeated Hepburn (nominated for *Coco*) for the Tony, and in 1981 while Bacall was winning for *Woman*, Hepburn was nominated (and lost) in the play category for *West Side Waltz*.

broadway banter

"I am a screen star, in the tradition of Shirley Temple, Liv Ullman, and Miss Piggy."

—Bette Midler

IT TAKES A VILLAGE

Early drafts of the script of Disney's *Cinderella* contained the characters of Clarissa the turtle and Jabber the crow.

17
September

(1933) She could drive a person crazy: Dorothy Loudon was born today. Her breakout role came with the 1969 flop *The Fig Leaves are Falling*—despite its run of only four performances, she received a Tony nomination. The next decade would bring her two biggest triumphs: the boozy, frowzy Miss Hannigan in *Annie,* and the widow Bea in Michael Bennett's *Ballroom,* singing the memorable eleven o'clock number, "Fifty Percent." In the 1992 Sondheim tribute, she blended his torch song "Losing My Mind" and the Andrews Sisters' pastiche "You Could Drive a Person Crazy," bringing the house down. In 2002, she was to have returned to Broadway in *Dinner at Eight,* but had to bow out when her long battle with cancer proved too difficult to overcome. She died the following year.

Two of Loudon's biggest roles—Miss Hannigan and Dottie in *Noises Off*—were portrayed by Carol Burnett in the film versions.

broadway banter

"[The Scarlet] Pimpernel *suffered from a case of the stupids.*"

—David Lefkowitz

CASTING COUCH

Carol Channing understudied Eve Arden in *Let's Face It* in 1941.

18
September

(**1968**) Hello, Gorgeous: *Funny Girl* premiered in New York City. Barbra Streisand had already conquered Broadway, nightclubs, records, and television, but it was with this film that she truly became the legend she remains today. Overcoming a mediocre screenplay and some ridiculous attempts at "period" costumes, Babs showed her versatility as a singer, a comic ("You're gonna shoot the shvanns? These lovelies?"), and a dramatic actress. Along the way, she got to perform most of the film's score, including some of her most enduring hits like "People," "Don't Rain on My Parade," and "My Man," as well as the written-especially-for-the-movie-to-win-an-Oscar-but-now-forgotten title number. Most of the stage show's songs for the other characters were excised.

broadway banter

"You don't have to bare the whole fang to show disdain."

—Agnes de Mille

ALSO ON THIS DAY ————————————

Agnes de Mille was born in 1905. She would change the face of dance forever with her integrated work on *Oklahoma!, Carousel,* and her Tony-winning *Brigadoon.*

19

September

(**1955**) Sexy Rexy was born today (although his birth year is often listed as 1956). Not Rex Harrison, the actor who was actually given that nickname (personally, I never got that one). The other sexy singing Rex—Smith. The 1970s teen idol made a stab at Broadway, first as one of the many replacement Danny Zuko's in *Grease*, then in Joe Papp's acclaimed 1981 revival of *The Pirates of Penzance*, with costars Kevin Kline and Linda Ronstadt. Smith played the young pirate apprentice Fredric in the off-Broadway, Broadway, and film versions of the production. His next endeavor wasn't quite as successful: the thirteen-performance flop *The Human Comedy*. He bounced back several years later as a replacement cast member for *Grand Hotel* and *The Scarlet Pimpernel*, and on the road with *Sunset Boulevard*, *Annie Get Your Gun*, and *Kiss Me, Kate*.

broadway banter

Old Lady: Did you like the opera, dear?

Vivian: It was so good, I almost peed my pants!

Edward: She said she liked it better than Pirates of Penzance.

—Pretty Woman, *by J.F. Lawton*

STAR POWER

Grace Kelly did her own singing—but not much of it—in *High Society*. Her one song, "True Love," a "duet" with Bing Crosby, became a huge hit.

September

(2001) The musical with the title least likely to succeed—*Urinetown*—opened on Broadway. The meta-theatrical show, written by two men who had no prior experience writing musicals, critiqued its own title and plot, and parodied every musical from *Les Miserables* to *Fiddler on the Roof* to *Starlight Express*.

Amazingly, the decidedly dark show that examined and satirized government found an audience and won Tony Awards for Best Direction, Best Score, and Best Book of a Musical. But, tellingly, it lost the Best Musical award to *Thoroughly Modern Millie*.

broadway banter

"I've been updating my act."

—*Carol Channing, appearing with LL Cool J at the 2004 Tonys*

ALSO ON THIS DAY

One of the most curious movie musicals ever made was released in the United States in 2002: *Eight Women (Huit Femmes)*, a French murder mystery featuring eight French stars from Catherine Deneuve to Isabelle Huppert to Fanny Ardant. None of them were singers, and boy, does it show.

21

September

(1947) 'Night, Marsha: Pulitzer Prize-winning playwright Marsha Norman was born today. The author of the mother/daughter suicide drama *'Night, Mother* has also made three contributions to the world of musicals. First, she wrote the book to the all-female helmed *The Secret Garden*. She won a Tony, which I thought was odd, since in my opinion her book mangled the charming children's story, rendering it all but incoherent on the stage. A few years later, she returned to Broadway for all of five performances with the Jule Styne flop *The Red Shoes*. More recently, Norman returned to Broadway in 2005 with the book to another Pulitzer Prize-winner, *The Color Purple*. She adapted the rich, layered novel into a coherent musical story, starring LaChanze as Celie, Felicia P. Fields as Sofia, and Elisabeth Withers-Mendes as Shug Avery.

broadway banter

"This just in: Carol Channing has been arrested in a drive-by shooting."

—*Hugh Jackman, at the 2004 Tonys*

POP QUIZ

In what mindless Brendan Fraser comedy is there a brief but hilarious homage to "Don't Rain on My Parade"?

A: George of the Jungle

September

(1964) The last show of the golden era of the musical, *Fiddler on the Roof,* opened. The show featured terrific work from the ensemble of leads, including Maria Karnilova, Bea Arthur, Bert Convy, Austin Pendleton, Joanna Merlin (who became a casting director for many of the biggest hits of the '70s and '80s), Julia Migenes (who went on to an opera career), and, of course, Zero Mostel, who won his third Tony in five years for playing Tevye.

Fiddler ran for nearly eight years, becoming the longest-running musical at that time. It was also the last original show Jerome Robbins did on Broadway, culminating twenty years of imaginative work on shows as diverse as *On the Town, The King and I, Peter Pan,* and *West Side Story.*

broadway banter

"Hearing this album, I'm convinced that this Disco Diva may be taking a whole new career!"

—*Paul Jabara, on* The Ethel Merman Disco Album

IT TAKES A VILLAGE

George Gershwin's 1924 musical *Tell Me More* was originally titled *My Fair Lady.*

23

September

(1920) The male equivalent of Shirley Temple, Mickey Rooney was born today. By the age of twenty, he had appeared in some 125 movies and short films, receiving one of the first Oscar nominations for a musical performance in *Babes in Arms*. As prolific a husband as he was an actor, Rooney has been married eight times, and has joked, "My God, there's a Mickey Rooney's Former Wives Marching Band!"

His biography states that he is five-foot-three, but on an episode of *The Judy Garland Show*, as he dances (in shoes) with the four-foot-eleven-and-a-half-inch Garland (sans shoes), he appears shorter than she does. Sounds to me like somebody has fudged his résumé. After all, Mickey's first screen credit was "Midget" in the silent movie *Not to Be Trusted*.

broadway banter

"*Melanie Griffith's performance makes Broadway's Chicago reminiscent of a high school musical.*"

—*Epinions.com member "lkw617"*

ALSO ON THIS DAY

Bob Fosse died of a heart attack in 1987, leaving behind an opus of work few of his contemporaries could even begin to compare with.

24 September

(1936) It's not easy bein' green: Jim Henson was born today. His pioneering work with cheeky, singing puppets has provided some thirty-five years of entertainment for children that their parents can enjoy as well, including *Sesame Street*, three musical Muppet movies, and dozens of Muppet-related TV specials. Perhaps his greatest contribution to the world of musicals was *The Muppet Show*, the long-running variety show that introduced Generation X kids to numerous musical stars, including Ethel Merman, Joel Grey, Rita Moreno, and dozens more.

Sadly, he died of pneumonia on May 16, 1990, the same day as Sammy Davis Jr.

broadway banter

"You're a phony. You're a phony. Yes, and you know what, you can't even sing. You were dubbed."

—Miss Piggy to Charles Grodin,
The Great Muppet Caper, by Jerry Juhl, et al.

CASTING COUCH

Following Bernadette Peters in the title role in *Annie Get Your Gun* were Susan Lucci, Cheryl Ladd, and Reba McEntire.

(1969) She simply *can* do it alone: Catherine Zeta-Jones was born today. Her electrifying performance as Velma Kelly in *Chicago* is surely one of the few Best Supporting Actress Oscar winners of the last fifteen years about whom people won't look back years later and say, "What were we thinking?" Perhaps that's because she was a trained singer and dancer, having played numerous roles in stage musicals, including the London production of *42nd Street*. She was the second understudy to the lead, but when both the leading lady and the first understudy took sick, true to the show's Broadway mythology, she stepped into the role, was a huge success that night, and took over the role completely.

25
September

Zeta-Jones also shares the same birthday as her hubby, Michael Douglas, though she was born twenty-five years after him.

broadway banter

"Oh my gosh. This is too—I mean, my hormones are just too way out of control to be dealing with this."

—Catherine Zeta-Jones

ALSO ON THIS DAY

Legs, legs, L'eggs: Juliet Prowse was born in 1936. The high-kicking dancer appeared in *Can-Can* and *G.I. Blues* on film and numerous stage musicals, as well as a series of commercials for L'eggs Pantyhose, showcasing her thirty-nine-inch legs.

26
September

(1957) *West Side Story* opened on Broadway. While this revolutionary musical would later be hailed as groundbreaking, and the film version would win ten Oscars, including Best Picture in 1961, the stage version was received with less enthusiasm. Leonard Bernstein's beautiful yet dissonant music, the tragic love story, and the integration of Jerome Robbins's dances into the plot met with only moderate critical and box office success. At the Tonys, *WSS* was overshadowed by the more mainstream and crowd-pleasing *The Music Man*.

broadway banter

"I can't do this show ... I've never been that poor and I've never even known a Puerto Rican!"

—Stephen Sondheim, on being asked to write lyrics for West Side Story

IT TAKES A VILLAGE

In 1955, the sappy song "Three Coins in the Fountain," by Jule Styne and Sammy Cahn, somehow beat out one of the all-time greats, "The Man That Got Away," by Harold Arlen and Ira Gershwin, for the Oscar.

(2005) *The Great American Trailer Park Musical* opened off-Broadway. The comic romp, set in Armadillo Acres, was written by David Nehls and Betsy Kelso and contained such tongue-in-cheek song titles as "Road Kill," "That's Why I Love My Man," and "Flushed Down the Pipes," as well as a trio of women named Betty, Linoleum, and Pickles. Unfortunately, the title seemed to be the most clever thing about the show, as it didn't quite catch on with audiences or critics as intended, and it folded just two months later.

September

broadway banter

"If you've been married three times and still have the same in-laws, you might just identify with The Great American Trailer Park Musical.*"*

–*Eric Beckson*

STAR POWER

In *Red, Hot, and Blue,* Ethel Merman and Jimmy Durante shared top billing with their names in an "X" since neither would cede first billing to the other.

28
September

(1902) He couldn't sing, dance, or act, but he did more to promote musicals across America than just about anyone: Ed Sullivan was born today. For twenty-three years, he interspersed his animal acts, juggling acrobats, and The Beatles with the crème de la crème of musical theater on his "real big show." Thanks to Sullivan, live performances of the original casts of shows ranging from *Oklahoma!* to *West Side Story* to *Hair* have been preserved.

He was also immortalized in *Bye Bye Birdie* with the song "Hymn for a Sunday Evening," in which the simple McAfee family sings about their impending appearance on *The Ed Sullivan Show*. The Broadway cast performed it live on Sullivan's show, and Ed Sullivan played himself in that scene in the film version.

broadway banter

"I was definitely a fan of Michael's work, but I'm not sure that Michael was a fan of anybody else's."

—*Tommy Tune, on Michael Bennett*

POP QUIZ

Q: What 1966 television musical starring Anthony Perkins and Charmian Carr did Stephen Sondheim write?

A: Evening Primrose

29

September

(1954) Judy Garland, fired off the set of *Annie Get Your Gun* a few years earlier, made one of show business's greatest comebacks with the epic musical *A Star Is Born*, which opened on this day. The opening was a smash success, with Lucille Ball, then the hottest star on television, predicting Oscars for everyone involved.

But middle America didn't respond as strongly, and Warner Brothers hacked nearly thirty minutes out of the film, greatly reducing the coherence of the plot and the film's emotional impact. Much of the cut footage was lost forever. But in 1983, the film was restored to nearly its original state, with still photographs and audio outtakes.

broadway banter

"Dear Judy, this is the biggest robbery since Brink's."

—Groucho Marx, in a telegram to Judy Garland after she lost the Best Actress Oscar for A Star Is Born *to* Grace Kelly in The Country Girl

ALSO ON THIS DAY ————

In 1983, *A Chorus Line* became the longest-running show in Broadway history with 3,389 performances. To celebrate the event, Michael Bennett staged a special one-night-only production that utilized 332 members of the Broadway, touring, and international companies.

30

September

(**1954**) Julie Andrews made her Broadway debut in *The Boyfriend*, a hit spoof of 1920s-era Charleston musicals. It was Cy Feuer's first Broadway directorial effort after having produced a few hits, including *Guys and Dolls*. Sandy Wilson wrote the book, lyrics, and music; it would be his first and only Broadway musical. Also making their Broadway debuts were most of the young cast, including Mickey Calin (later Riff in the original *West Side Story*), Millicent Martin (later a Tony-nominee for *Side By Side by Sondheim*).

broadway banter

"I've always wanted to perform on the Broadway stage. The wigs, the makeup, the costumes ... and then I'd walk to the theater."

–Jack McFarland, on Will & Grace

ALSO ON THIS DAY

Moss Hart and Irving Berlin's *As Thousands Cheer* opened on Broadway in 1933. The entire show was a smash hit, especially Ethel Waters, who introduced the red-hot "Heat Wave" and the devastating "Supper Time."

OCTOBER

Alfred Drake, Joan Roberts, and the original Broadway cast of
Oklahoma!

1

October

(1935) We've grown accustomed to her face: Julie Andrews was born today. Make that Dame Julie Andrews. Although she started out as an English Music Hall entertainer, she gained her greatest fame with musicals, bringing some forty years of classic performances to life. Having played a goodie-two-shoes in almost all of the first twenty or so of those years, she spoofed her screen image in *S.O.B.*, playing an actress trying to overcome a similar casting stigma—in order to do so, she (Julie and the character she played) bared her breasts on film.

Onstage, she went down in history as the Broadway Diva Who Never Won a Tony, despite her winning work in *The Boyfriend*, *My Fair Lady*, *Camelot*, and *Victor/Victoria*. In 1992, she played Anna in a studio recording of *The King and I*, with Ben Kingsley, Marilyn Horne, and Lea Salonga.

broadway banter

"I can write a song cue for anything."

–George Abbott

ALSO ON THIS DAY

Lyricist Lynn Ahrens was born in 1948. With her songwriting partner Stephen Flaherty, she would write the scores to Broadway hits *Ragtime* and *Once on This Island*, the cartoon *Anastasia*, and off-Broadway's touching *A Man of No Importance*.

October

(1994) Like Ol' Man River, it just keeps going: A new revival of *Show Boat* opened on Broadway today. This was the fifth production of the landmark musical to reach the Great White Way. Hal Prince directed and adapted this version from the various stage and film incarnations. This production featured a stellar cast that included Broadway veterans John McMartin and Elaine Stritch; rising stars Rebecca Luker, Mark Jacoby, Gretha Boston, Joel Blum, and Michel Bell; and a reprise performance from the 1983 Julie, Lonette McKee. The show won five Tonys and ran for more than two years.

broadway banter

"That's why Judy Garland was great. She acted her songs. If you can tell the truth with a monologue, you can tell the truth with 'I Like New York in June.'"

—*Elaine Stritch*

ALSO ON THIS DAY

Sting was born in 1951; in 1989, he played Macheath in a new translation of the short-lived and critically drubbed *3 Penny Opera*.

3

October

(1963) Stop the world—Anthony Newley wants to do a musical. On this day, his show—and I mean *his* show—*Stop the World—I Want to Get Off!* opened on Broadway. Newley co-wrote the book, lyrics, and music with Leslie Bricusse, as well as directed and starred in the production. The show, which played only one preview before opening, ran well over a year. In 1965, Newley and Bricusse were back with another musical, *The Road of the Greasepaint—The Smell of the Crowd.* Newley wore the same five creative hats this time around, receiving a total of six Tony nominations between these two long-titled shows.

broadway banter

"Andrew Lloyd Webber, the composer who is second to none when writing musicals about cats, roller-skating trains, and chandeliers, has made an earnest but bizarre career decision in Aspects of Love. ... He has written a musical about people."

—*Frank Rich*

CASTING COUCH

Among the original candidates for the Mother Abbess in the film *The Sound of Music* were former 1930s singing stars Irene Dunne and Jeanette MacDonald.

(1945) Singer, actor, Baptist minister: Clifton Davis was born today. On Broadway he appeared in *Hello, Dolly!* And struck it big with *Two Gentlemen of Verona* in 1971. His explosive performance of the lovesick Valentine received a Tony nomination, but this would also be his last Broadway outing. He did, however, go on to play Absalom in the American Film Theater production of Kurt Weill's *Lost in the Stars*, and ragtime composer Louis Chauvin in the TV biopic *Scott Joplin*.

October

broadway banter

"The glory of the theater is also its bane; you have to be there to experience it. When a production closes, it is gone forever."

—Terrence McNally

IT TAKES A VILLAGE

South Park creator Trey Parker's first movie musical, *Alferd Packer: The Musical*, inspired by Colorado's only convicted cannibal, was filmed in 1993, then turned into an off-Broadway musical in 2000, retitled *Cannibal! The Musical*.

5

October

(1923) Well done, Sister Suffragette: Glynis Johns was born today. The versatile comedienne wasn't really a singer, but hey, when did that stop anyone from becoming a musical comedy star? Her musical appearances were few but unforgettable. In 1956, she starred opposite Danny Kaye in the *Robin Hood* spoof *The Court Jester*, sending up Maid Marian with her role as Maid Jean. In 1964, she played Mrs. Banks in *Mary Poppins*, though she almost didn't take the role because she had wanted to play the title character. In 1973, she won the role of Desiree Armfeldt in *A Little Night Music*, winning a Tony for her heart-breaking rendition of "Send in the Clowns." Her final film appearance to date was *Superstar*, in which she played the grandmother of main character Mary Katherine Gallagher (played by Molly Shannon).

broadway banter

"I'd rather be Mark Wahlberg than Stephen Sondheim. I'd rather be adored for what I look like than what I think."

—Composer Andrew Lippa

ALSO ON THIS DAY

Carmen Jones was released in 1954; the all-black musical received two Oscar nominations, including one for its leading lady Dorothy Dandridge, the first African-American actress to be so honored.

6

October

(1927) You ain't heard nothin' yet: *The Jazz Singer* premiered in Los Angeles, revolutionizing movies forever with the introduction of spoken dialogue to feature-length films. The film represented such a breakthrough in sound that it was deemed ineligible to compete against silent films for the Best Picture awards at the inaugural Academy Awards; instead, the film was given a special, non-competitive award.

Al Jolson is strongly identified with the title role, but he wasn't the first choice for it—that was George Jessel, who originated the role on stage. Jolson wasn't even the second choice—that was another song-and-dance man who often did blackface, Eddie Cantor. But the part was ultimately Jolson's (his first screen role of note), and he made it his own, singing "Toot Toot, Tootsie, Goodbye," "Blue Skies," and "My Mammy."

broadway banter

"The writing was so clear that I wanted to come home and be Andrew Lippa."

—Fred Ebb, on Lippa's The Wild Party

STAR POWER

Vera-Ellen was dubbed by no fewer than seven different actresses in her career, but never by infamous off-screen voice Marni Nixon.

October

(1982) Now and Forever. Or at least for eighteen years. Eighteen looooong years. On this day, *Cats* opened on Broadway. If nothing else, the show gave us two things. First, the quotable *Saturday Night Live* joke, "I loved it. It was better than *Cats*. I'm going to see it again and again." Second, Betty Buckley's definitive (sorry Elaine Paige) performance of the show's haunting eleven o'clock number, "Memory," for which she won a Tony.

broadway banter

"Griffith is no more singer and dancer than she is stage actress, but, all things considered, she acquits herself tolerably, if not dazzlingly ... She sings in a somewhat amateurish but heartfelt manner ... She does execute the dances, but without the full Fossean élan, and with some facial unease, as of someone silently counting, although this could improve with time. Only her cartwheel fell conspicuously short—or, more precisely, sideways."

—John Simon, on Melanie Griffith in Chicago

POP QUIZ

What is the highest-grossing movie musical ever?

October

(1979) "Is that Hortense?"

"She looks pretty relaxed to me."

So went one of the corny jokes in the burlesque review *Sugarbabies*, which opened on Broadway today. The show paired Hollywood legends Mickey Rooney and Ann Miller, the former making his Broadway debut at age fifty-nine. Both performers revitalized their careers with this show, and both took it on the road after it closed on Broadway. *Sugarbabies* received eight Tony nods, but got lost in the wake of that year's blockbuster, *Evita*. Astonishingly, the hokey but lovable show ran nearly three years.

broadway banter

"Now, the key to great dancing is one word: tappa-tappa-tappa."

—Little Vicki, on The Simpsons

CASTING COUCH —————

When understudy Laura Benanti took over the role of Maria from Rebecca Luker in the revival of *The Sound of Music* on Broadway, she was just nineteen; her leading man, Richard Chamberlain, was sixty-three.

9
October

(1968) *Finian's Rainbow* was released in the United States. The film, made some twenty years after the original stage production, felt dated and creaky, despite charming performances from Fred Astaire (in his last musical role) and pop singer-turned-actress Petula Clark. Known for her peppy rendition of "Downtown," she chose her acting projects carefully, turning down a lead role in *Valley of the Dolls.* Clark went on to star in the musical remake of *Goodbye, Mr. Chips,* as well as London productions of *The Sound of Music* and *Someone Like You,* which she also wrote.

In her sixties, she was a replacement star in *Blood Brothers* on Broadway and in *Sunset Boulevard* in London, touring both shows throughout the United States. Now in her seventies, she continues to perform concerts and record albums, mixing her pop hits and movie and stage songs with an ever-expanding repertoire that includes everything from Sondheim to *Tommy.*

broadway banter

"... a jeep among limousines."

—*Ethel Merman, on her semi-flop* Happy Hunting

ALSO ON THIS DAY —————

Jacques Brel died in 1978. But he had lived to see his music and lyrics turned into an off-Broadway revue that ran from 1968 to 1972 before transferring for a short stint on Broadway.

10

October

(1935) At its New York premiere today, *Porgy and Bess* received a fifteen-minute standing ovation. But critics didn't know what to do with the show, which straddled the worlds of musical theater and opera. Thanks to the mixed reviews, it ended up a moderate flop by musical standards, running only 124 performances. It was not until it was revived in 1942—with original stars Todd Duncan and Anne Brown returning in the title roles—that it began to achieve masterpiece status. It has been revived on Broadway four more times since then, and produced countless times in opera houses and theaters alike.

broadway banter

"The question we constantly asked each other, as we discussed possible themes, was: What is so special about this subject that it simply has to be sung?"

–Alain Boublil, on writing Miss Saigon

ALSO ON THIS DAY

Two song-and-dance men were born: Ben Vereen (1946), Tony winner for *Pippin* and star of *Jesus Christ Superstar, All That Jazz,* and *Wicked;* and Daniel Massey (1933), who starred in *She Loves Me* on stage and received an Oscar nod for his portrayal of his godfather, Noel Coward, in *Star!*

11
October

(1918) Gotta dance: Jerome Robbins was born today. He started out as a ballet dancer on Broadway in *Stars in Your Eyes*, starring Ethel Merman and Jimmy Durante, then appeared in *The Straw Hat Revue* alongside other young talent like Alfred Drake, Danny Kaye, and Imogene Coca. In 1944, he teamed up with Leonard Bernstein for the one-act ballet *Fancy Free*. This served as the basis/inspiration for the full-length musical *On the Town*, which the two collaborated on later that year.

In 1953, he appeared before the House Un-American Activities Committee, where he got Jerome and Edward Chodorov and six other colleagues blacklisted when he named them as communists.

broadway banter

"I owe a lot to Jerry Robbins. For one thing: as far as I'm concerned, he invented reading a musical before rehearsals."

–Harold Prince

STAR POWER

Emma Thompson starred in the 1985 London production of *Me and My Girl*.

(1971) *Jesus Christ Superstar* opened on Broadway, marking the composer's Broadway debut. The rock opera, already a hit concept album, starred Ben Vereen as Judas, Jeff Fenholt as Jesus, and Yvonne Elliman as Mary Magdalene. The Broadway version couldn't quite match the power of the original recording, featuring Murray Head as Judas and Ian Gillan as Jesus, nor the subsequent film version, with Ted Neeley as Jesus and Carl Anderson as Judas. Yvonne Elliman, however, got to play Mary Magdalene all three times.

12
October

Serving as the assistant to the director on Broadway was Harvey Milk, who would later achieve fame and notoriety as the first openly gay elected official of any large city in the United States. While serving in that position, as city supervisor of San Francisco, Milk was brutally murdered in 1978.

broadway banter

"*The title page of the program for* Jesus Christ Superstar *as done in New York in 1971 stressed that Tom O'Horgan had not only directed the production but had 'conceived' it. It was not an immaculate conception.*"

—Walter Kerr

ALSO ON THIS DAY

Hugh Jackman was born in 1968. He has starred in the Australian production of *Sunset Boulevard*, the London revival of *Oklahoma!*, and *The Boy from Oz* in Australia, then on Broadway, winning a Tony for his energetic portrayal of singer/songwriter Peter Allen.

13

October

(1939) A franchise was born: The screen version of *Babes in Arms* premiered. Few people cared that the filmmakers all but tossed out the plot and score and replaced it with other songs and storylines. What they cared about was the pairing of Mickey Rooney and Judy Garland for their first big-time musical together. Mickey copped an Oscar nomination, and the two went on to make five more films together. And, true to the times, Mickey and Judy don blackface for one scene.

Over the years, everyone from Carol Burnett to Tom Cruise (in *A Few Good Men*) would poke fun at the "let's put a show on in the barn" schmaltz.

broadway banter

"Yes, I've heard how difficult it is to work with Judy Garland. Do you know how difficult it is to be Judy Garland? I've been trying to be Judy Garland all my life!"

–Judy Davis as Judy Garland, in
Life with Judy Garland: Me and My Shadows

POP QUIZ

Q: While *Babes in Arms* was the first big Mickey and Judy musical, what was their first movie together?

14

October

(1930) It was written as a star vehicle for Ginger Rogers, but the star was left in the dust the moment her costar opened her mouth. *Girl Crazy* opened on Broadway today, marking the Broadway debut of Ethel Merman. Ethel stepped out on stage and sang "Sam and Delilah" and just about stole the show, but when she came back to deliver "I Got Rhythm," she brought the audience to its feet and stopped the show cold. Legend has it she belted a high C for sixteen full measures while the orchestra played the chorus underneath her.

broadway banter

"She is the most thoroughly professional star I've ever done business with. She's out there every single performance, dedicated, making a show really work."

—David Merrick, on Ethel Merman

ALSO ON THIS DAY

How to Succeed in Business Without Really Trying opened on Broadway in 1961. The show would win the Tony, Pulitzer, and New York Drama Critics awards. The 1967 film version retained the show's original stars, Robert Morse and Rudy Vallee.

15
October

(1937) There's a new girl in town, and she's feelin' good: Linda Lavin was born today. Best known for her title role in the long-running '70s sitcom *Alice*—and her belting of the show's opening number—Lavin started out in musical theater, with a featured role in *It's a Bird ... It's a Plane ... It's Superman*. She then replaced Barbara Harris as the star of *On a Clear Day You Can See Forever* and belted out "Shoeless Joe" in the 1967 TV remake of *Damn Yankees*, alongside a miscast Lee Remick as Lola. She returned to musicals in 1990, replacing fellow TV legend Tyne Daly as Mama Rose in *Gypsy*.

One of her *Alice* costars was also a musical theater vet: Beth Howland, who played the dimwitted Vera on *Alice* and starred as Amy in the original production of *Company*.

broadway banter

"A musical is only as good as its director. The same can also be said for the CIA."

—Martin Short

CASTING COUCH

During the run of *Panama Hattie,* understudy June Allyson got her big break when Betty Hutton couldn't go on.

(1925) She's played everything from Mame to Mama Rose, Mrs. Lovett to Mrs. Santa Claus ... Angela Lansbury was born today. Ironically, she began her career in MGM musicals, in which her voice was dubbed. But Angie showed them she was a force of nature in the fantastic flop *Anyone Can Whistle* in 1964. Two years later, performing in the star vehicle *Mame*, she won the highly coveted Best Actress in a Musical Tony Award—her first of an unprecedented four in that category. She would later win for *Dear World*, *Gypsy*, and *Sweeney Todd*. She also stepped into the role of Anna in the 1977 Broadway revival of *The King and I* during Yul Brynner's vacation, and sang a touching "Send in the Clowns" in 1981's *A Stephen Sondheim Evening*.

16
October

broadway banter

"What Titanic *lacked was any depth at all.*"

—*Barry Singer*

POP QUIZ

Q: What is the name of Marc Blitzstein's musical adaptation of Lillian Hellman's *The Little Foxes?*

A: Regina

17

October

(1967) *Hair* opened at the Public Theatre for a brief off-Broadway run of just fifty performances. A few months later, it would transfer to Broadway and play for 1,742 more. In addition to bringing rock music to Broadway, *Hair* launched the careers of numerous future stars of Broadway, television, and film: Diane Keaton, Melba Moore, Paul Jabara, Nell Carter, Ben Vereen, Philip Michael Thomas, Meat Loaf, Andre de Shields, Elaine Paige, and Donna Summer, to name just a few. The 1979 film version kept most of the songs but added greatly to the musical's tissue-paper-thin plot.

broadway banter

"*George Berger (Gerome Ragni) [in* Hair *is] a fury with a fringe on top.*"

—Nat Shapiro

ALSO ON THIS DAY

Rita Hayworth was born in 1918. Although her singing voice was almost always dubbed, she was a fabulous dancer, which she showed off in *You Were Never Lovelier* with Fred Astaire, *Cover Girl* with Gene Kelly, and the non-musical *Gilda*, in which she set the screen on fire with her performance of "Put the Blame on Mame."

18

October

(2001) A musical for gay men and middle-aged women opened on Broadway today. *Lifetime Television: The Musical?* No, *Mamma Mia!* Dancing queens Louise Pitre (in a stunning, Tony-nominated Broadway debut), Judy Kaye, and Karen Mason camped it up in this cheesy but delightfully infectious show. The creative team managed to string nearly two dozen ABBA hits into some semblance of a storyline, revolving around the impending marriage of a twenty-year-old woman and her search to find her biological father. Thank you for the music!

broadway banter

"Mamma Mia! *is actually quite Brechtian in calling attention to form and the relationship the audience develops with the characters onstage.*"

—*Phyllida Lloyd* (director *of* Mamma Mia!)

POP QUIZ

Q: What is *Shock Treatment?*

A: The 1981 "sequel" to *The Rocky Horror Picture Show*, featuring returning performances from Richard O'Brien, Patricia Quinn, and Nell Campbell, as well as an appearance from Barry "Dame Edna" Humphries.

19

October

(1960) She is changing: Jennifer Holliday was born today. At just twenty-one, she became a Broadway legend with her gutsy performance in *Dreamgirls*. Her role of Effie was originally written for Nell "Gimme a Break" Carter, based on her show-stopping performance of "Can Your See?" in *The Dirtiest Musical*. Carter did an early workshop, then the role was played by Holliday. Later workshops were done by Jenifer "Jackie's Back" Lewis, then Cheryl "Hair" Barnes, then Alaina "Sesame Street" Reed. As the show headed to Broadway, it once again starred Holliday, and she's owned the role ever since.

Since then, she toured in *Sing, Mahalia, Sing* and co-wrote and starred in *Downhearted Blues: The Life and Songs of Bessie Smith*. She also served as a novelty replacement on Broadway in *Chicago* as the Matron and in *Grease* as Teen Angel; guest starred on a number of *Ally McBeal* episodes, singing Randy Newman's "Short People"; and perhaps most famously, lost two hundred pounds in 1990.

broadway banter

"[Jennifer] Holliday's violent protest when she is both professionally and emotionally jilted at end of Act I in the number 'And I Am Telling You I'm Not Going' was a powerful outburst on a scale seldom realized outside grand opera."

—Otis L. Guernsey Jr., on Dreamgirls

STAR POWER

Agnes de Mille was the niece of Cecil B. DeMille.

(1935) Jerry Orbach was born today. This versatile actor, remembered by non-musical fans for his roles in *Law and Order* and *Dirty Dancing*, enjoyed a lengthy career on the stage as well. The 1960s were a golden decade for Orbach, beginning with his portrayal of El Gallo in *The Fantasticks*. He went on to star in *Carnival!*, the revival of *Guys and Dolls* with Anita Gillette and Sheila MacRae, and the 1966 revival of *Annie Get Your Gun* with Ethel Merman. He finished the decade with his Tony-winning performance in *Promises, Promises*, the musical adaptation of the film *The Apartment*.

In 1975, he originated the role of Billy Flynn in *Chicago*, and closed out his Broadway career as Julian Marsh in *42nd Street*. He also voiced the role of Lumiere in the animated *Beauty and the Beast*. On December 28, 2004, he died at the age of sixty-nine, following a battle with prostate cancer.

20
October

broadway banter

"It's showtime, folks."

—*Joe Gideon, in* All That Jazz, *by Robert Alan Aurthur and Bob Fosse*

ALSO ON THIS DAY

Peter Pan flew onto Broadway in 1954, having had a troubled time getting there: Jule Styne, Betty Comden, and Adolph Green had to be called in to beef up Moose Charlap and Carolyn Leigh's score. The show ran only 152 performances, but it later found its audiences on television and in numerous revivals and tours.

21

October

(1933) It's a fine life: Georgia Brown was born today. She originated the role of Nancy in *Oliver!* in London, then reprised her performance on Broadway, receiving a Tony nomination for her blending of comedy, pathos, and belting as the doomed battered cockney girlfriend. She lost out on the movie role, however, to an inferior Shani Wallis.

Like so many stars who struck gold with their debuts, she never again hit those same heights, though not for a lack of trying. In the '70s, she starred in the Lerner and Lane flop *Carmelina*, and in the '80s, she starred in Hal Prince's flop *Roza*. Her final Broadway role was Mrs. Peachum in yet another flop, *3 Penny Opera*, playing Maureen McGovern's mother. Brown died in 1992 of complications following surgery.

broadway banter

"Probably it is a mistake ever to produce a musical show without Bert Lahr."

—*Brooks Atkinson*

ALSO ON THIS DAY

Probably it is a mistake ever to do *Saturday Night Fever* without John Travolta, but Robert Stigwood did anyway, opening the new stage musical on Broadway today in 1999. Thud!

(**1942**) Choosy moms choose Annette Funicello. Born today, the bustiest Mouseketeer came of age on *The Mickey Mouse Club* and other Disney television shows. In 1961, she made her first movie musical, *Babes in Toyland*, opposite Ray Bolger. She went on to do a series of Beach musicals with Frankie Avalon: *Bikini Beach, Beach Party, Muscle Beach Party, Beach Blanket Bingo*, and other equally uniquely titled films. In 1987, she reteamed with Frankie to spoof their many beach outings with *Back to the Beach.*

October

broadway banter

"Just because the whole thing is crazy doesn't mean it won't make it on Broadway!"

—Bernard Crawford, in The Muppets Take Manhattan, by Frank Oz, et al.

ALSO ON THIS DAY——————

If you were holding out for a hero, you had better keep on looking: *Footloose* opened on Broadway in 1998, steamrolling over any of the charm of the original movie, in part because it was done sans Kevin Bacon.

23

October

(1972) Stephen Schwartz's *Pippin* opened on Broadway today. Or rather, Bob Fosse's *Pippin* opened. Once the maniacal auteur took over, relative newbies Schwartz and book writer Roger O. Hirson relinquished control of their simple little show about the son of Charlemagne finding his way. Legend has it that Fosse ultimately had to lock the writers out of rehearsals, though Schwartz tells a different story (see below). Fosse won two Tonys, though, and turned *Pippin* into a hit that ran for nearly five years. Irene "Granny Clampett" Ryan died during the Broadway run, just a few weeks after receiving a Tony nomination for her performance as Pippin's wise and wisecracking grandmother.

broadway banter

"Bob and I had some clashes. But some of the working relationship was very good, and ultimately I think we were both pretty happy with the show … I'm sorry to ruin a good story."

—Stephen Schwartz, *on working with Bob Fosse during* Pippin *rehearsals*

IT TAKES A VILLAGE

Dan Goggin based his musical *Nunsense* on his eponymous line of greeting cards.

24

October

(1947) Before *The Big Chill*, before *A Fish Called Wanda*, Julliard graduate Kevin Kline, born today, won two Tony Awards for performing in musicals. First, he stole the show with the small but choice role of Madeline Kahn's boyfriend in *On the Twentieth Century* in 1978. Then, in 1981, he snagged the role of the Pirate King in the Public Theater's production of *The Pirates of Penzance*. He played the role off-Broadway, on Broadway, and finally on film. He returned to his musical roots in the 2004 Cole Porter biopic film *De-Lovely*, in which he did all his own piano playing and singing live on the set.

broadway banter

"It does seem strange to me, however, that changes in my lyrics are often made, and even changes in the music, without anyone ever asking my permission."

–Cole Porter

POP QUIZ

Q: Who was often mistaken for Cole Porter's mother?

A: Linda Porter, his wife

25

October

(1927) Glitter and be gay—no, not that gay: Barbara Cook was born today. In her early years, she played every ingénue in the book, from her debut in *Flahooley*, to her definitive Cunegonde in *Candide*, to her Tony-winning Marian the Librarian in *The Music Man*. She tackled a more adult role in *She Loves Me*, giving indelible performances of future standards like "Will He Like Me" and "Vanilla Ice Cream." Her final role in a Broadway musical was Dolly Talbo in the seven-performance flop *The Grass Harp*. Since then, she has stuck mainly to concerts, cabarets, and recordings, as well as lending her talents to the 1985 *Follies* concert, putting her stamp on the Sondheim classics "In Buddy's Eyes" and "Losing My Mind."

broadway banter

"The beautiful part of the musical theater is, however—and this is unique among all other arts—its collaborative nature. It doesn't function well if it's not collaborative."

—Jerry Bock

CASTING COUCH

Henry "Fonzie" Winkler was the original choice to play Danny in the film *Grease.*

(1971) Anthony Rapp was born today. He is best known for originating the role of Mark in *Rent*, though his other musical work has been in slightly less gritty shows. At the age of eleven, he played the Little Prince in *The Little Prince and the Aviator*; after sixteen previews, the show folded without ever officially opening. Following his *Rent* success, he played the title role in *You're a Good Man, Charlie Brown* in 1999. In 2005, he reprised his *Rent* role on film.

26
October

broadway banter

"I wish I could do justice with my words to the resounding things happening in my body tonight."

—Anthony Rapp, at the premiere of the film Rent

ALSO ON THIS DAY

Robert Westenberg was born in 1953. He received a Tony nomination for his delectably sleazy portrayals of the Wolf and Cinderella's Prince in *Into the Woods*, but this fairy tale had a happy ending: He married his Cinderella, Kim Crosby.

27
October

(1925) Jane Connell was born today. Her breakout role came in 1966 as Agnes Gooch, the ultimate candidate for a makeover, in the smash hit *Mame*. She would reprise her role in the leaden film, and again in the 1983 revival, reuniting with the original Mame, Angela Lansbury. In 1986, she copped her only Tony nomination for *Me and My Girl*, and she teamed up again with that show's director, Mike Ockrent, in *Crazy for You* in 1992. Still acting well into her seventies, she played the Widow Douglas in *The Adventures of Tom Sawyer* on Broadway in 2001, and she appeared in a brief off-Broadway revival of *70, Girls, 70* in 2000, co-starring other musical veterans Helen Gallagher, Mimi Hines, George S. Irving, Jane Powell, and Charlotte Rae.

broadway banter

"Frankly, having experienced Tommy *in various forms—as an album, a movie, and now a stage show—I have yet to see in it the profound meanings much of my generation has."*

—*Jeffrey Sweet*

ALSO ON THIS DAY ——

Nanette Fabray, darling of the 40s/'50s musical comedy, was born in 1920. The versatile actress is best remembered for holding her own opposite Fred Astaire and Jack Buchanan in *The Band Wagon* on screen, and for her Tony-winning performance in Kurt Weill and Alan Lerner's early experimental musical take on marriage, *Love Life.*

(1897) She couldn't sing, but she clothed those who did (and some who couldn't sing either). Edith Head, born today, designed costumes for nearly five hundred movies in a career spanning some fifty-five years. Her range and versatility can be seen in the more than seventy musicals she designed, including *Love Me Tonight*, *Lady in the Dark*, *White Christmas*, *Anything Goes*, *Funny Face*, Elvis's *Girls! Girls! Girls!*, *Sweet Charity*, and the ill-fated Mae West self-indulgence-fest, *Sextette*. Head was the queen of the Oscars, winning an unprecedented eight times for her designs.

October

broadway banter

"I was a clown in high school. I said, 'What's the most ridiculous instrument I could pick up? The tuba.'"

—Patti LuPone, on how her early tuba-playing days helped her play Mrs. Lovett *in* Sweeney Todd

STAR POWER

Fred Astaire and Ginger Rogers would have made just nine films together, but when Judy Garland had to be replaced on *The Barkleys of Broadway*, Ginger was called in, and the two danced together once more.

29

October

(1891) If a girl isn't pretty ... well, it doesn't matter—if she's Fanny Brice. The star of a dozen editions of the *Ziegfeld Follies* was born today. While in France, Flo Ziegfeld heard the song "Mon Homme," which he brought back to America for Fanny to perform, translated into "My Man." The comedienne wanted to perform it as a spoof, but Ziegfeld asked her to sing it straight, wearing just a simple black dress. It became her signature song. Although she made cameos in *The Great Zeigfeld* and *Ziegfeld Follies*, her one major film, *My Man*, is not known to exist today in any complete form.

broadway banter

"You think beautiful girls are going to stay stars forever? I should say not! Any minute now they're going to be out! Finished! Then it'll be my turn!"

—Fanny Brice in Funny Girl, *by Isobel Lennart*

ALSO ON THIS DAY

Here comes Sandy Claws: Tim Burton's *The Nightmare Before Christmas* opened across America.

30

October

(2003) Just in time for Halloween, two witches landed on Broadway in the musical *Wicked*. Based on the novel *Wicked: The Life and Times of the Wicked Witch of the West* by Gregory Maguire, the show featured a tuneful score by Stephen Schwartz, who tailored it to showcase the endless lungpower of Kristin Chenoweth and Idina Menzel. Taking colorful supporting roles were old pros Joel Grey and Carole Shelley as The Wizard and Madame Morrible, who have been succeeded by George Hearn and Ben Vereen, and Carol Kane and Rue McClanahan, respectively.

broadway banter

"I am so proud to be in a musical that celebrates women, that celebrates their strengths and their differences."

–Idina Menzel, *accepting her Tony for* Wicked

ALSO ON THIS DAY————————————

While rehearsing a number for the 2005 musical *The Drowsy Chaperone*, Sutton Foster fell down and broke her wrist. The song she was singing at the time? "Accident Waiting to Happen."

31
October

(1896) Stormy Weather: Ethel Waters, the nightclub singer for whom Harold Arlen wrote his famous torch ballad, was born today. The soulful African American tore up Broadway in shows like *As Thousands Cheer*, *At Home Abroad*, and *Cabin in the Sky*. On film, she reprised her role in *Cabin in the Sky*, famously not getting along with her younger costar, the scene-stealing Lena Horne. Still, she turned in great performances of Vernon Duke's "Taking a Chance on Love" and Arlen's "Happiness Is a Thing Called Joe." A strong dramatic actress as well, Waters turned in a poignant performance in *The Member of the Wedding* on stage and screen.

broadway banter

"*I've been offstage for far too long*
It's ages since I had a song"

—*The Lady of the Lake, in* Monty Python's Spamalot, *by Eric Idle*

POP QUIZ

Q: Who received his 1999 Honorary Oscar by singing "Cheek to Cheek" and tap dancing?

A: Stanley Donen

NOVEMBER

Audrey Hepburn as Eliza Doolittle in the classic 1964 film *My Fair Lady.*

1
November

(1987) A musical based on a Roger Corman horror movie about a man-eating plant named Audrey? *Little Shop of Horrors* closed today, playing its 2,209th performance. Given its origins, the show had been a surprise hit, starring Lee Wilkof as Seymour and Ellen Greene, who turned the stereotypical role of a dumb-blonde-abused-by-her-boyfriend on its ear, as Audrey. The show ran more than five years, at the time the fourth-longest off-Broadway production in history, and spawned a somewhat sunnier movie starring Greene, Rick Moranis as Seymour, Steve Martin as the dentist, and Vincent Gardenia as Mr. Mushnik.

broadway banter

Fozzie: You don't go to Bombay to become a movie star. You go where we're going, Hollywood.

Gonzo: Well, sure, if you want to do it the easy way.

—The Muppet Movie, *by Jack Burns and Jerry Juhl*

ALSO ON THIS DAY

Character actress Beth Fowler was born in 1940. She has appeared in a dozen Broadway musicals, most notably playing Mrs. Lovett in *Sweeney Todd*, Mrs. Potts in *Beauty and the Beast*, and Mrs. Woolnough (Hugh Jackman's mother) in *The Boy from Oz*.

November

(1961) Into every life, some rain must fall. For Alfred Drake, the skies opened up with rain today, in the form of _Kean_, a disappointing flop musicalization of the life of nineteenth-century British actor Edmund Kean. Despite the show's pedigree—music and lyrics by Robert Wright and George Forrest, and a book by Peter Stone based on the writings of Jean-Paul Sartre and Alexandre Dumas, père—the creators just couldn't get it right, and folded a few months later.

Drake had plenty of hits to fall back on, though: He created the leading males roles in _Oklahoma!_, _Kiss Me, Kate_, and _Kismet_, and recreated Maurice Chevalier's role in the stage premiere of _Gigi_.

broadway banter

"As [Sweeney] Todd, Michael Cerveris, smoothly short and maggot-pale, emits a ghastly sensuality. ... And Patti LuPone, wielding a tuba with a proficiency that's downright erotic, has relieved Mrs. Lovett of her pop-eyed frumpiness. ..."

–Entertainment Weekly

ALSO ON THIS DAY

I'd Rather Be Right opened on Broadway in 1937. Kaufman and Hart wrote the book, and Rodgers and Hart supplied the lyrics (the Harts being both Moss and Lorenz). George M. Cohan came out of semi-retirement to star as Franklin Roosevelt, whom he'd campaigned for. The show featured the ever-relevant song "We're Going to Balance the Budget."

3
November

(1990) Cockeyed optimist Mary Martin died today. She got her start in Cole Porter's *Leave It to Me!*, singing what would be her signature song, "My Heart Belongs to Daddy"; also making his Broadway debut in that show was Gene Kelly. She cemented her place in musical history when she introduced "Speak Low," "That's Him," and other Weill standards-to-be in *One Touch of Venus*. She also starred in *Lute Song, I Do! I Do!*, and the flop *Jennie*, which told the fictionalized life story of stage legend Laurette Taylor.

Martin won three Tonys for her work in *South Pacific, Peter Pan*, and *The Sound of Music*. Although she made few film appearances, she recorded extensively, toured in *Annie Get Your Gun* and *Hello, Dolly!*, and appeared in television versions of *Peter Pan* and *Annie Get Your Gun*.

broadway banter

"I don't know what all the fuss is about. I always knew Mary Martin could fly."

–Walter Kerr, on Peter Pan

ALSO ON THIS DAY

The Wizard of Oz was broadcast on television for the first time in 1956; it was one of the first big Hollywood movies to play on the small screen.

November 4

(1879) He never met a man he didn't like: Will Rogers was born today. Though not really a musical performer per se, he starred in many editions of the *Ziegfeld Follies* and other vaudeville entertainments. In 1991, some fifty-five years after Rogers died in an airplane crash, his life story was turned into a musical by Tommy Tune, Cy Coleman, Betty Comden, and Adolph Green: *The Will Rogers Follies*. The show won six Tonys, including Best Musical. Keith Carradine played the rope-twirling humorist, Dee Hoty played his wife, Betty Blake, and Gregory Peck recorded the voiceovers for the role of Flo Ziegfeld.

broadway banter

"I arrived in Hollywood twenty pounds overweight and as strong as an ox. But if I put on white tails and a tux like Astaire, I still looked like a truck driver."

—Gene Kelly

ALSO ON THIS DAY

Doris Day and Howard Keel paired up for their only musical together: *Calamity Jane*, which opened today. Keel played Wild Bill Hickok and Day the title role, singing Sammy Fain's Oscar-winning "Secret Love."

5
November

(1987) *Rapunzel and the Beanstalk?* No. *Cinderella Meets the Big Bad Wolf?* No. *Little Red Riding Hood and the Harlem Globetrotters?* Stephen Sondheim and James Lapine's adaptation of familiar folk tales, *Into the Woods*, opened today on Broadway. A near-perfect cast of Bernadette Peters (sinfully not nominated for a Tony!), Joanna Gleason, Chip Zien, Tom Aldredge, Barbara Bryne, and more than a dozen others performed as a seamless ensemble in what would become one of Sondheim's longest-running shows. Of course, its 765 performances pale in comparison to the big show it was up against that season: *The Phantom of the Opera.*

broadway banter

"Oscar really believed that there was 'A bright golden haze on the meadow.' I never have."

—Stephen Sondheim, on mentor Oscar Hammerstein II

POP QUIZ

Q: What was the first Broadway musical to be shown live on pay-per-view television?

A: Sophisticated Ladies

6

November

(1989) Most composing teams would give their eyeteeth to have kept some of the songs Richard Maltby Jr. and David Shire tossed out. The songwriting duo of *Baby*, *Big*, and *Starting Here, Starting Now* selected some two dozen of their "trunk" songs from the past thirty years and fashioned them into a revue called *Closer Than Ever*, which opened off-Broadway today. The simply staged show featured four versatile singers—Brent Barrett, Sally Mayes, Richard Muenz, and Lynne Wintersteller—accompanied by just piano and bass.

broadway banter

"The thing about Gary [Beach], Roger [Bart], Nathan [Lane], and Matthew [Broderick] is that they are one of a kind. They understand comedy, they sing, they dance, they have perfect diction. They have it."

—Susan Stroman, on her four principals making the leap from stage to screen in The Producers

ALSO ON THIS DAY

Bali Ha'i will call you ... Juanita Hall was born in 1901. She performed on Broadway in *St. Louis Woman*, *House of Flowers*, *Flower Drum Song*, and, most notably, as Bloody Mary in *South Pacific*, winning a Tony award. She reprised the latter two roles on film.

7

November

(1979) Bette Midler, already a gay icon and recording star, made her motion picture debut with *The Rose*, which opened today. Based loosely on the life of Janis Joplin, Bette played the booze-drinking Mary Rose Foster, known as "The Rose," compared to heroin-addict Joplin's nickname of "The Pearl." Fiction aside, Bette certainly evoked Joplin-like qualities in her throaty renditions of "When a Man Loves a Woman" and "Stay with Me." The title number, written by Amanda McBroom, was nominated for a Golden Globe, but was shunned by the Academy. The song later turned up in McBroom's musical *Heartbeats*.

broadway banter
broadway banter
broadway banter

"...? You're right, I have never been on Broadway. I was asked to present the award for Best Revival of a Musical because people think that I saw the original productions of all the shows nominated."

–Barbara Walters

ALSO ON THIS DAY

Earrrrrrrrrrtha Kitt made her Broadway debut in 1946 in the revue *Bal Negre*. She would achieve greater fame in shows like *New Faces of 1952* (singing the hilarious "Monotonous"), *Shinbone Alley*, *Timbuktu!*, and *The Wild Party*.

(1954) My way or the highway: Chuck Cooper was born today. The deep-voiced actor won a Tony for playing a sleazy, abusive pimp who gets knifed by his mistress/ho' in *The Life*. Showing his versatility, his next Broadway roles were as The Dryer and The Bus in *Caroline, or Change*. Unfortunately, his next assignment was in Yoko Ono's troubled John Lennon tribute, *Lennon*, which barely made it to Broadway and flopped upon arrival.

8 November

broadway banter

"One of the featurettes is a visit with the seven actors who portrayed the von Trapp children back in 1965. The septet was trotted out for a recent press event in New York, complete with the original Bil Baird Marionettes, and they made quite a sight. They all seemed to belong to the same friendly clan, more or less; this despite the fact that the average age, forty years later, seemed to be about fifty-eight. Also in attendance was Ms. Andrews, who after forty years looked about sixty. Go figure. The marionettes looked the same as in the film."

—Steven Suskin, on the 40th Anniversary The Sound of Music DVD

BACKSTAGE

In *Sparkle*, the 1976 movie musical about a Supremes-like girl group, the mother of the three singing sisters was named Effie. In *Dreamgirls*, the 1982 stage musical about a Supremes-like girl group, one of the singers was named Effie. Coincidence?

9

November

(1908) Think Pink: Kay Thompson was born today. A true renaissance woman, Thompson did it all, though she was most often cast as a music arranger and vocal coach on some of MGM's biggest musicals. On her only Broadway show, 1937's *Hooray for What!*, she worked with director Vincente Minnelli. The two would pair up again in his film *Ziegfeld Follies*, for which she wrote the lyrics for Judy Garland's number, with longtime pal Roger Edens writing the music. Judy would later ask Kay to be the godmother of her first child: Liza Minnelli. Kay, Judy, and Roger enjoyed a long friendship (chronicled in the TV movie *Life with Judy Garland*). An accomplished singer, she made only a few movies, but put a stamp all her own on *Funny Face*, playing the Eve Arden-esque fashion editor Maggie Prescott.

broadway banter

"*I could do* Dolly! *every day of my life until I die.*"

—*Carol Channing*

STAR POWER

When Florence Henderson guest starred on *Roseanne* as a mother with a son named Elijah who sings under his breath, Roseanne nicknamed him "Elijah Minnelli."

10

November

(1949) We've got Annie: Ann Reinking was born today. After dancing in the ensembles of *Coco* and *Pippin*, she won a featured role in *Over Here!* alongside fellow youngsters John Travolta, Treat Williams, Marilu Henner, and Janie Sell, as well as oldsters Maxene and Patty Andrews (of Andrews Sisters fame). She often worked with her off-stage lover Bob Fosse in musicals, including *Dancin'*, *All That Jazz*, and *Chicago* (as a replacement Roxie in the original production). In the 1990s, she helped start a Fosse renaissance, choreographing the concert version and Broadway revival of *Chicago* "in the style of Bob Fosse" and co-directing the Tony-winning dance revue *Fosse*.

broadway banter

"Broadway theatergoers love to see elderly folks in romantic affairs. But on the screen, it's embarrassing."

—Producer Cy Feuer on how Cabaret *changed from stage to screen*

IT TAKES A VILLAGE

Although *Les Miserables* originally premiered in French, almost all of the songs were written for the London production, and thus were written directly in English, rather than in translation.

11
November

(1955) The film version of *Oklahoma!* premiered, and it was heralded as the first film shot in Todd-AO widescreen. This corn really was as high as an elephant's eye! Getting her due was Charlotte Greenwood, for whom the role of Aunt Eller had been written back in 1943. Greenwood couldn't play the role at that time because of other commitments, but she got to play it on film.

Greenwood, a.k.a. Lady Longlegs, was six feet tall and double-jointed, and she could kick her lanky legs higher than any petite chorus girl. She had a prolific stage career, singing in Broadway choruses beginning at the age of just thirteen. Her character "Letty" provided the basis of several shows written just for her: *So Long, Letty; Linger Longer, Letty;* and Irving Berlin's *Music Box Revue.* After taking a long stage absence to do film work, she returned in Cole Porter's intriguing flop *Out of This World* in 1950.

broadway banter

"Night by night and inch by inch, the specific character of the theater will be eroded—until, one miserable day, it will have no distinguishable identity at all."

—Walter Kerr, on the use of microphones in Broadway shows

STAR POWER

Al Jolson made his Broadway debut in 1911 in Jerome Kern's *La Belle Paree* singing the beyond politically incorrect "Paris Is a Paradise for Coons" in blackface.

12

November

(1989) *Grand Hotel: The Musical*, the brainchild of Tommy Tune, bowed on Broadway today. Tune had taken an existing musical by Wright and Forrest, jettisoned much of the music, and brought in his *Nine* collaborator Maury Yeston to round out the score. Eerily, the fates of several of the lead characters were mapped out by the actors who originated them: David Carroll, who played the Baron who died near the end of the show, died of AIDS during the run of the show. Michael Jeter, who played the accountant who was about to die, also died of AIDS at the age of fifty. Jane Krakowski, who played the secretary who wanted to become a movie star, became a TV star playing a secretary on *Ally McBeal*.

broadway banter

"[His] idea of a good time is sitting around listening to Angela Lansbury shrieking about 'The Worst Pies in London.'"

—Mendy in Terrence McNally's The Lisbon Traviata

ALSO ON THIS DAY

Bert Williams was born in 1874. The black entertainer broke new ground, appearing alongside white cast members in numerous editions of the *Ziegfeld Follies* before his early death in 1922. A songwriter as well, his music would turn up later in *Bubbling Brown Sugar* and *Tintypes*.

13

November

(**1940**) Masterpiece, travesty, or throbbing bore? *Fantasia*, one of Walt Disney's most beloved film projects, premiered in New York and laid an egg. Audiences didn't know what to make of the film's animated interpretations of classic works of music. Some music aficionados were appalled at some of the choices in animation— and the changes made to Stravinsky's ground-breaking *Rite of Spring* score. Only Mickey Mouse, in one of his most enduring roles as the Sorcerer's Apprentice, emerged unscathed. Disney planned to have periodic updates made to the film, each of which would call for a re-released edition, but it took sixty years for the next edition to come out: *Fantasia 2000.*

broadway banter

"There is no single correct way to interpret Dolly any more than there is to play, say, Lady Macbeth. And that, by the way, is a role I've always hankered to play."

—Ethel Merman

ALSO ON THIS DAY

Taboo opened on Broadway in 2003: The messy tale of London's gay and transgendered club scene in the 1980s, featuring music and lyrics by Boy George, a book by Charles Busch, and Rosie O'Donnell as its producer, is quite possibly the gayest thing to ever play Broadway.

(1996) It was just a matter of time before the world discovered the masterpiece that is *Chicago*. Twenty years after it played on Broadway, Walter Bobbie and Ann Reinking brought it back in concert form, and on this day, its revival opened on Broadway. It would enjoy a run more than four times longer than the original. The creative team ditched the sets, costumes, and any semblance of period, focusing on Kander and Ebb's score, Reinking's choreography, and Fosse's vision. Bobbie and Reinking won their first Tonys, and stars James Naughton and Bebe Neuwirth each won their second.

broadway banter

"There's something to this day that I love about being tight through the middle—it keeps me straight, it keeps the boobs up, it keeps the stomach in, and it worked beautifully then and it works now and I wish they'd bring them back, honey."

—*Ruta Lee, on singing and dancing in a corset in* Seven Brides for Seven Brothers

POP QUIZ

Q: What Gilligan's Island star played a small role in the 1963 flop *Fade Out—Fade In*?

A: Tina Louise, playing a beautiful but untalented actress

15

November

(1989) A franchise was reborn: the Disney animated musical. *The Little Mermaid* had its premiere, and after decades of mostly lackluster cartoons, Disney revitalized itself with the tuneful songs and catchy lyrics of Alan Menken and Howard Ashman, the team that brought *Little Shop of Horrors* to the stage. *Mermaid* launched the second "golden era" of the Disney musical. It was also the last animated Disney film to use hand-painted cels. A bevy of musical talent provided the voices, including Jodi Benson (Ariel), Rene Auberjonois (Louis the cook), Samuel E. Wright (Sebastian), Buddy Hackett (Scuttle), and Pat Carroll (Ursula).

broadway banter

"I expected to see something more than a bland reworking of old Disney fairy tales, featuring a teenage tootsie in a flirty seashell bra."

—*Pauline Kael*, on The Little Mermaid

STAR POWER ————

Xanadu wasn't the first time Gene Kelly sang and danced in roller skates (though it was certainly the least memorable): He did the same in *It's Always Fair Weather* to the song "I Like Myself."

16

November

(1968) Life is what you do while you're waiting to die: *Zorba* opened on Broadway today. An unlikely and underrated musical from the creators of *Cabaret*, *Zorba* paired *Fiddler on the Roof* vets Herschel Bernardi and Maria Karnilova. Highlights included Lorraine Serabian's dazzling vocals and Carmen Alvarez's touching inner dialogue, "Why Can't I Speak?" A 1984 revival starred the 1964 film's stars Anthony Quinn and Lila Kedrova, the latter becoming the only person to win an Oscar, then a Tony, for the same role.

broadway banter

"I have been invited to say something about how dancers feel about Fred Astaire. It's no secret that we hate him. He gives us complexes because he's too perfect. His perfection is absurdity."

—*Mikhail Baryshnikov*

IT TAKES A VILLAGE

If you thought *Boobs! The Musical* was gross, or *Urinetown: The Musical* was tasteless, turn the page now—or get ready for *Poop: The Musical*. Written by Joe Major and Catherine Serbousek and subtitled *The Life and Times of Thomas Crapper*, the show features songs like "I'm Regular!" "The Hard One That Hurts," and "I Can't Hold It In."

17

November

(1942) Martin Scorsese was born today. Wait a minute—what's he doing in a book about musicals? Well, in between *Taxi Driver* and *Raging Bull*, Marty went through an inexplicable "Liza Minnelli Musical" phase. First, he directed her and his leading man of choice, Robert DeNiro, in the expensive film flop *New York, New York*. A glutton for punishment, he came back for a second time, directing Liza in a stage vehicle about a nightclub singer. The show had a rocky tryout, changing names and ultimately directors—Gower Champion was brought in to help out. *The Act* was all but forgettable except for Liza's practically one-woman-show of a performance. She won her third Tony, even though it had been revealed that in some numbers, she lip-synched to a recording of her own voice.

broadway banter

"I'm gonna do a scene from the movie Raging Bull."

–*Auditioner in* Waiting for Guffman,
by Christopher Guest and Eugene Levy

CASTING COUCH

Nathan Lane's replacement as Pseudolus in *A Funny Thing Happened on the Way to the Forum* was Whoopi Goldberg.

(1909) You've got to acc-en-tu-ate the positive: Johnny Mercer was born today. Primarily a lyricist, he wrote with some of Hollywood's top composers, including Harold Arlen, Henry Mancini, Harry Warren, Artie Shaw, Jimmy McHugh, Jerome Kern, Marvin Hamlisch, and sometimes even himself. He received eighteen Oscar nominations, winning four times, including for *The Harvey Girls'* "On the Atchison, Topeka and Santa Fe" and *Here Comes the Groom's* "In the Cool, Cool, Cool of the Evening." He also wrote the lyrics for Broadway's *L'il Abner, St. Louis Woman,* and *Top Banana.*

18
November

broadway banter

"*A show about a doll? Why not write a musical about the common cat, or the king of Siam? Give it up, Smithers.*"

—Mr. Burns in The Simpsons

ALSO ON THIS DAY

Papa, can you hear her? Barbra Streisand's opus *Yentl* opened in limited release today. Streisand won a Golden Globe for Best Director, but the Academy shunned her completely, and she picked up a Razzie Award for Worst Actress of the Year.

19
November

(1912) Eleanor Powell, the tap-dance champion of the world, was born today. After nearly a decade of dancing on Broadway, she brought her talents to Hollywood, where she enjoyed a short-lived stardom as the Queen of Ra-Ta-Taps. She couldn't sing or act, but she lit up the screen with her dancing, hoofing with Buddy Ebsen in *Broadway Melody of 1936*, with George Murphy in *Broadway Melody of 1938*, and with Fred Astaire in *Broadway Melody of 1940*.

broadway banter

"Hugh ... oh, Huey, Huey, Huey, Huey, Huey, I am one of your biggest fans. I saw you in Oklahoma! *in London and* Sunset Boulevard *in Sydney and I'm wishing you the best of luck on winning Best Leading Actor in a Musical."*

—Rod *from* Avenue Q, *to Hugh Jackman*

ALSO ON THIS DAY

Savion Glover was born in 1973. In 1996, he became perhaps the youngest person ever to win a Best Choreographer Tony for his work on *Bring in Da Noise, Bring in Da Funk.* He also danced his way through Broadway's *The Tap Dance Kid, Jelly's Last Jam,* and the film *Tap.*

(1926) She was born Catherine Gloria Ballotta, but when you're from Cleveland, you have to do something. Kaye Ballard was born today. She would grow up to make her Broadway debut with one of her most memorable roles: Helen in *The Golden Apple*, introducing the now-classic "Lazy Afternoon." She found further success on Broadway in *Carnival!* and on television as one of the stepsisters in the original Rodgers and Hammerstein *Cinderella*. She also survived the disappointment of the failure of her star vehicle, *Molly*. In 2004, she published a memoir of her life and career titled *How I Lost 10 Pounds in 53 Years*.

November

broadway banter

"South African singer Tsidii Le Loka, in white makeup and looking cowerie-shell chic as a baboon, tore the lid off the newly constructed New Amsterdam Theater with her chanting."

—David Lefkowitz, *on the opening scene of* The Lion King

CASTING COUCH

When she left *DuBarry Was a Lady*, Ethel Merman was replaced by Gypsy Rose Lee, whose mother she would later play in *Gypsy*.

21
November

(1952) This is my daughter Liza. And this is my other daughter, Liza's Sister. Lorna Luft, Judy Garland's other daughter, was born today. A singer/actress/recovering drug addict like her mother and sister, Lorna hasn't quite managed to hit the same heights as her more legendary family members. She has made a numerous stage appearances, though, including playing Miss Adelaide in the national tour of *Guys and Dolls* (incidentally, she also shares her birthday with the role's creator, Vivian Blaine). On film, her biggest "hit" was as the #2 Pink Lady in *Grease 2*.

broadway banter

"He was a big awkward hunk of a man, very shy. He made me feel uncomfortable because all he did was look at me."

—Jeanette MacDonald, on meeting her future costar and lover, Nelson Eddy

POP QUIZ

Q: In what 1953 Technicolor bomb did forty-five-year-old Joan Crawford dance and lip-synch her way through "Two-Faced Woman" in blackface?

A: *Torch Song*

November

(1943) He'll take Manhattan, the Bronx, and Staten Island, too: Lorenz "Larry" Hart died today at just forty-eight years old, following battles with alcohol, depression, and his sexual identity. Along with composer Richard Rodgers, he wrote some of the wittiest and most sophisticated songs of the '20s and '30s. Able to dash off peppy numbers like "Johnny One-Note," "Zip," and "The Lady Is a Tramp," in a single bound, he was equally comfortable writing torch songs like "My Funny Valentine" and "Bewitched, Bothered and Bewildered." Ironically, his biggest hit, "Blue Moon," was written as a satire of the generic love songs coming out of Hollywood at the time.

broadway banter

"The first time I met Elaine [Stritch], she came to see me in a little show called Nick and Nora. *That musical hit."*

—Faith Prince

ALSO ON THIS DAY

Man of La Mancha began dreaming the impossible dream in 1965, ultimately running nearly six years, spawning numerous revivals, and inspiring a dreary film version starring Peter O'Toole and Sophia Loren.

23
November

(1959) Pop quiz: Which musical became only the third to win the Pulitzer Prize in 1960? *Gypsy*, often called the perfect musical? *The Sound of Music*, perhaps the most beloved musical of all time? Nope and nope. The answer is *Fiorello!*, which opened today. It was the first musical to win the Tony, Pulitzer, and New York Drama Critics Awards.

Fiorello! chronicled the life of New York Mayor Fiorello LaGuardia. The show was penned by the future *Fiddler on the Roof* team, Jerry Bock and Sheldon Harnick, and starred Tom Bosley, who later achieved fame as Mr. Cunningham on *Happy Days*.

broadway banter

"If anyone wonders why Gower Champion's death is a bitter loss for the American theater, I suggest that he head immediately to the Winter Garden, where 42nd Street opened last night."

—Frank Rich

ALSO ON THIS DAY

Two Weeks with Love was released in 1950, launching the career of Debbie Reynolds, who sang the film's big hit, "Abba Dabba Honeymoon."

(1950) *Guys and Dolls* opened on Broadway, claiming a rare seven rave reviews from the leading New York critics and winning eight Tonys. The show was also selected by the Pulitzer Prize jury for that award, but the judges overruled the nomination because the show's co-author, Abe Burrows, had ties to the communist party. Ultimately, no Pulitzer was awarded that year. But that didn't stop the show from becoming a smash hit, running for 1,200 performances and becoming a semi-successful movie, despite the notable handicap of having three severely miscast leads.

November

broadway banter

"How was the matinee?"

"Very intimate. We had a hundred people on the stage and fifty in the audience."

"Well, you had 'em outnumbered."

—Three chorus girls in Stage Door, *screenplay by Morrie Ryskind and Anthony Veiller*

IT TAKES A VILLAGE

Maury Yeston and Arthur Kopit wrote a version of *The Phantom of the Opera* before Andrew Lloyd Webber. Their musical, simply titled *Phantom,* has never made it to Broadway.

25

November

(1920) Singer, actor, and Latin heartthrob Ricardo Montalban was born today. Before he rose to pop culture fame playing Mr. Roarke on *Fantasy Island*, he starred in a number of movie musicals. Notably, he played a character named Jose O'Rourke in *Neptune's Daughter*, singing "Baby It's Cold Outside" with Esther Williams. He also starred in *Sombrero* and, in non-singing roles, *Two Weeks with Love* and *Sweet Charity*. On Broadway, he starred with Gloria DeHaven and Bea Arthur in *Seventh Heaven* and with Lena Horne in *Jamaica*, receiving a Tony nomination for the latter.

broadway banter

"The lights come up on a party at Abby's swank penthouse apartment. Abby appears at the top of a staircase. The audience applauds wildly, even though she hasn't done anything yet."

—The stage manager setting the scene for the Jerry Herman parody in The Musical of Musicals, The Musical! by Eric Rockwell and Joanne Bogart

STAR POWER

During the filming of *The Sound of Music*, Julie Andrews helped costar Marni Nixon prepare for an audition for a production of *My Fair Lady*.

(1933) From Lancelot to Lance-a-Lounge: Robert Goulet was born today. The cheeseball baritone who has parodied his image in films, commercials and cartoons leapt to fame in 1960 in the original production of *Camelot*, playing opposite Julie Andrews and Richard Burton. In the late 1960s, he won a Tony for his role in Kander and Ebb's *The Happy Time*, and he also starred in television versions of *Brigadoon*, *Carousel*, and *Kiss Me Kate*. In 2005, he returned to Broadway as a replacement star in *La Cage Aux Folles*, having recently done a national tour of *South Pacific*. You can check out his Web site, www.robertgoulet.com, for his latest news and original poetry.

November

broadway banter

"Sometimes I'll watch an old movie on television, and once in a while one of mine—such as April Showers*—will come on and I'll watch it. And you know something? I'm always amazed at what a lousy actress I was. I guess in the old days we just got by on glamour."*

—Ann Sothern

CASTING COUCH

Company and **Merrily We Roll Along** librettist George Furth played Van Johnson in **Blazing Saddles**.

27

November

(1911) Impressario Extraordinaire David Merrick was born today. Merrick may have been respected, feared, and sometimes hated, but no one could deny that he knew how to produce and market a show. His first Broadway musical was *Fanny* in 1954, and for forty-two more years he churned out a string of hits sporadically interrupted by some notable flops, including the failed musical version of *Breakfast at Tiffany's*. He won Tonys for what were by far his biggest hits, *Hello, Dolly!* and *42ⁿᵈ Street*, as well as five Best Play Tonys and two special Tony Awards for his career achievements. He produced his last show, *State Fair*, at the age of eighty-five.

broadway banter

"*I wanna be a producer
and say, 'you, you, you, not you.*'"

—*Leo Bloom in* The Producers, *lyrics by Mel Brooks*

ALSO ON THIS DAY

Fifty Million Frenchmen, one of Cole Porter's earliest musicals, opened on Broadway. The seldom-revived show featured his hit ballad "You Do Something to Me" as well as the witty "The Tale of the Oyster," "Find Me a Primitive Man," and "I'm Unlucky at Gambling."

(1944) Clang, clang, clang went the trolley: *Meet Me in St. Louis* rolled into New York City today. The film showcased its major players at the top of their game: director Vincente Minnelli, in his first big MGM project; star Judy Garland, at her most beautiful and before her addictions began impeding her work; songwriters Hugh Martin and Ralph Blaine, composing songs like "Skip to my Lou" and "Have Yourself a Merry Little Christmas" that fit brilliantly into feel of the film's 1903–04 time period. At the early peak of her career was seven-year-old Margaret O'Brien, who won an Oscar for Best Juvenile Performance in her role as Tootie.

In 1989, the film was turned into a lackluster Broadway musical, featuring Betty Garrett as Katie.

28
November

broadway banter

"I was born at the age of twelve on a Metro-Goldwyn-Mayer lot."

–Judy Garland

POP QUIZ

Q: Who did Jeanette MacDonald replace in her first big MGM musical *The Merry Widow*?

A: Grace Moore

29

November

(1895) Listen to the lullaby of Broadway: Busby Berkeley was born. In the 1920s, he choreographed a dozen Broadway shows, but when sound came to Hollywood, he headed out west. Amazingly, in the three short years that a Best Dance Direction Oscar was presented (1936–1938), Berkeley lost each year. Some of Berkeley's best-known work came before an Oscar in that category was given: _42nd Street_ and _Gold Diggers of 1933_ both arrived three years too early.

broadway banter

"In an era of breadlines, depressions, and wars, I tried to help people get away from all the misery ... to turn their minds to something else. I wanted to make people happy, if only for an hour."

—_Busby Berkeley_

ALSO ON THIS DAY

Natalie Wood died in 1981, having already entered movie musical immortality with her performances in _West Side Story_ and _Gypsy_. Her vocals in _WSS_ were dubbed by the ubiquitous Marni Nixon, though Wood can be heard in outtakes on the DVD.

30

November

(1952) I loved Antonio Banderas in *Evita*, but there will never be another Che as good as Mandy Patinkin. Born today, Patinkin won his only Tony for Best Featured Actor for *Evita* in 1980. He went on to create leading roles in *Sunday in the Park with George*, *The Secret Garden*, and *The Wild Party*. He also has toured extensively with his one-man shows, bringing them to Broadway several times. Known as one of the premiere interpreters of Sondheim, his one misstep in that arena was his uber-energetic performance as Buddy in the 1985 concert version of *Follies*.

broadway banter

"If I had my life to live over I would do everything the exact same way— with the possible exception of seeing the movie remake of Lost Horizon.*"*

—Woody Allen

STAR POWER

Liv Ullman wasn't the first person to taste disaster in a musical version of *Lost Horizon*. In 1956, a stage version called *Shangri-La* starred Jack Cassidy and Alice Ghostley. Walter Kerr called it "rather deadly," and it lasted just twenty-one performances.

DECEMBER

Carol Channing in her iconic title role in the 1964 Broadway production of *Hello, Dolly!*

(1945) "Ol' Red Hair Is Back": Bette Midler was born. After she got her start playing Tzeitel in the Broadway production of *Fiddler on the Roof*, she gained a cult following with her gay bathhouse cabaret acts. She won acclaim for her musical films *The Rose* and *For the Boys*, the latter also attracting a lawsuit from Martha Raye, who claimed Midler stole her life story. She has also playfully mocked her affinity for show tunes with her recurring nightclub character Vicki Eydie. In what was quite possibly the highlight of her career, she tackled the role of Mama Rose in the 1993 television version of *Gypsy*, rectifying everything that had been wrong with the 1962 movie and almost making you forget about Ethel Merman.

1
December

broadway banter

*"Just tell me what could be better than shakin' your buns
In front of a chorus of thirty-five nuns!"*

—*Bette Midler in her show* Mud Will Be Flung Tonight!

ALSO ON THIS DAY

Candide opened today, and the overture stopped the show. But just seventy-three performances later, the show stopped entirely.

December

(1914) Ray Walston, better known as *My Favorite Martian*, was born today. He appeared in *Me and Juliet* and *House of Flowers* before taking on the role of a lifetime as Applegate in *Damn Yankees* in 1956. He won a Tony and, two years later, went on to play the role in the film. That same year, he brought comic relief to the rather static film version of *South Pacific* playing Luther Billis. His last musical role was in the Clint Eastwood-Lee Marvin monstrosity *Paint Your Wagon*. Walston died in 2001 at the age of eight-six.

broadway banter

"If the American musical didn't already exist, it would have to be invented for Audra McDonald."

–Frank Rich

ALSO ON THIS DAY

Medea: The Musical! Well, almost. Michael John LaChiusa gave Audra McDonald her first leading role with *Marie Christine,* a retelling of the ancient Greek tale set in turn-of-the-century New Orleans.

(1999) Madeline Kahn died today at fifty-seven, ending a yearlong battle with ovarian cancer. The versatile comedienne started out in the final edition of Leonard Silliman's *New Faces of 1968*, then performed alongside Danny Kaye in the Noah's Ark musical, *Two by Two*. After copping a pair of Oscar nominations, deliciously sending up both Marlene Dietrich and Jeanette MacDonald along the way, she returned to Broadway to star in *On the Twentieth Century*, the perfect vehicle for her light comedy, operatic soprano voice, and distinctive good looks. She ended up leaving the show early, but still received a Tony nomination.

In the 1990s, she delivered a couple of memorable Sondheim performances at Carnegie Hall, pattering out "Getting Married Today" in the 1992 Tribute and playing Mayoress Cora Hoover Hooper in the concert version of *Anyone Can Whistle*.

3

December

broadway banter

"*I never got that show—Les Miz. It's about this French guy, right, who steals a loaf of bread, and then he suffers for the rest of his life. For toast.*"

—*Darius* in Jeffrey, *by Paul Rudnick*

ALSO ON THIS DAY

Clue: The Musical opened off-Broadway in 1997. Mrs. White's number, "Life Is a Bowl of Pits," spoke volumes about the show itself, and it shuttered on December 28.

4
December

(1921) Little Edna Mae Durbin was born. By the age of fourteen, she was no longer Edna Mae but Deanna, one of the world's highest paid singing actresses. She appeared in relatively few movies in her career, but no one played a squeaky-clean teen who bursts into song better. After taking Hollywood by storm for a decade with films like *Three Smart Girls* and *One Hundred Men and a Girl*, she more or less retired at the age of twenty-seven.

broadway banter

*"Every time I start to feel defensive
I remember vinyl is expensive!"*

*—Barbra Streisand, "Putting It Together," revised lyrics just for her by
Stephen Sondheim*

STAR POWER

Chita Rivera, the original Velma in *Chicago*, made a cameo appearance in the 2002 film version as inmate Nickie. She played another character named Nickie in the film version of *Sweet Charity*.

5

December

(1901) A dream is a wish your heart makes: Walt Disney was born today. Few people have done more to promote music in movies than Walt did, and few people have touched those they've worked with quite like Walt has. After several years of making musical short films and cartoons, he helmed the first full-length animated musical, *Snow White and the Seven Dwarfs*. All in all, he oversaw production of nearly eight hundred films, shorts, and television shows, receiving more Oscars than anyone else in history—twenty-six, including special awards—as well as the most nominations ever—fifty-nine. His death at the age of sixty-five was felt by children of all ages.

broadway banter

"Now, I can't explain to you exactly why I didn't want to see Nunsense *so much, but I think it just has to do with my fear of Catholic vaudeville."*

–Julia Sweeney

ALSO ON THIS DAY

The long-running off-Broadway hit *Nunsense* closed in 1993. The show spawned such sequels as *Nuncrackers, Meshuggah Nuns,* and *Nunsense A-Men.*

6

December

(1896) When you hear the name Gershwin, you most likely think of George. But the other half of that songwriting partnership was a key factor in their success: Lyricist Ira Gershwin was born today. On Broadway, he worked almost exclusively with his brother George on shows like *Lady Be Good, Funny Face, Oh Kay!,* and *Rosalie.* After George's premature death, he also collaborated with Kurt Weill on *Lady in the Dark* and *The Firebrand of Florence.* In Hollywood, he worked with many other composers as well, including Jerome Kern on *Cover Girl* and Harold Arlen on *A Star Is Born.*

broadway banter

"Look, they drummed you right out of Hollywood. So, you come crawling back to Broadway. Well Broadway doesn't go for booze and dope."

—Helen Lawson, in Valley of the Dolls *by Jacqueline Susann, screenplay by Helen Deutsch and Dorothy Kingsley*

ALSO ON THIS DAY

James Naughton was born in 1945. The uber-masculine baritone made his Broadway debut in *I Love My Wife* and later won Tonys for *City of Angels* and the revival of *Chicago.*

(1967) I never miss a Brenda Vaccaro musical: *How Now, Dow Jones* opened on Broadway today. The show, produced by David Merrick and with a score by prominent film composer Elmer Bernstein, was expected to be a huge hit, but after a troubled out-of-town tryout, it ran just seven months, prompting theater historian Ken Mandelbaum to ask, "Was there a dumber plot in postwar musicals than that of *How Now, Dow Jones?*" For that matter, was there ever a dumber title?

December

broadway banter

"[Tonight], you will all be transformed from dead-eyed suburbanites into white-hot grease fires of pure entertainment! Except you, you're not working out, I'll be playing your part."

–Llewellyn Sinclair, director of Marge's musical
Oh Streetcar! *on* The Simpsons

BACKSTAGE

A film version of the rarely revived *St. Louis Woman* was planned with Lena Horne, but it never got off the ground. A cast recording was planned in 1988 with Pearl Bailey, Sammy Davis Jr., Ben Vereen, Leslie Uggams, Della Reese, and Phylicia Rashad, but that never happened either. In 1998, City Center Encores! did a concert version starring Vanessa Williams and Charles S. Dutton, and it was also recorded on CD.

8

December

(1925) Rat-packer Sammy Davis Jr. was born today. Dancing since the age of five, he made numerous movie musicals, including *Sweet Charity* (in which he memorably sang "Rhythm of Life") and his final film, *Tap*. Perhaps most notable was his performance as Sportin' Life in *Porgy and Bess*, in which he stole the movie from the film's dubbed leads. On Broadway, he starred in *Mr. Wonderful*, a revival of *Stop the World—I Want to Get Off*, and *Golden Boy*, for which he received a Tony nomination.

broadway banter

"You just don't succeed on Broadway if you don't have any Jews."

—*Sir Robin, in* Monty Python's Spamalot, *by Eric Idle*

IT TAKES A VILLAGE

Marvin Hamlisch and Christopher Adler, son of Richard "*Pajama Game/Damn Yankees*" Adler, wrote a musical about the tragic life of actress Jean Seberg called *Jean* that never made it to Broadway.

(2004) *The Phantom of the Opera* had its world premiere in Spain. Not the show—the major motion picture. After Internet gossip had cast Antonio Banderas, John Travolta, or Michael Crawford in the film's title role, the part went to Gerard Butler, with newcomer Emmy Rossum playing Christine and Broadway vet Patrick Wilson playing Raoul. During the past few years, Wilson had picked up two Tony nominations for his leading roles in *The Full Monty* and *Oklahoma!*

9
December

broadway banter

"To get right down to it, do you realize that C. C. may be the only entertainer left who can carry a whole show by herself, portal to portal? Or even compete with her own lobby photos? Or stand there with her hands clasped and make you believe she's surprised you like her?"

—Walter Kerr, on Carol Channing

ALSO ON THIS DAY

Husky-voiced, rubber-faced British comedienne Hermione Gingold was born in 1897. In addition to her scene-stealing roles in *Gigi* and *The Music Man* on film, she also received a Tony nod at the age of seventy-five for *A Little Night Music*.

10
December

(1985) The worst film musical ever opened: *A Chorus Line.* How anyone could take one of the most successful and acclaimed stage musicals and turn it into a turgid, lifeless, banal film ... only Richard Attenborough knows. And how Richard Attenborough managed to get nominated for a Golden Globe Award for his direction, only the Hollywood Foreign Press knows. But if you're ever dating someone that you're not sure how to break up with, tell him you want to show him your favorite musical of all time, and haul out this DVD. He'll head for the hills, and you'll be free!

broadway banter

"[By] the end of the evening, we were saying, 'Murderers! Baby killers!'"

—James Kirkwood, on seeing the lamentable film version of his masterpiece, A Chorus Line

BY THE NUMBERS

Judy Garland's live concert album *Judy at Carnegie Hall* won five Grammy Awards in 1961, including Album of the Year.

11

December

(2005) *Chita Rivera: The Dancer's Life* opened on Broadway today, culminating fifty years of ups and downs in the career of the legendary singer/dancer/actress. After a series of small roles and dance assignments in the 1950s, she won the role of Anita in *West Side Story*, cementing her status as a true triple-threat performer. After snagging a Tony nomination for *Bye Bye Birdie* and starring in *Bajour*, it would be another ten years before she returned to Broadway, in 1975's *Chicago*, originating the role of Velma Kelly. She opened the eighties with a string of flops, but also was nominated for three more Tonys, finally winning for *The Rink* in 1984. She won another in 1993 for her magnetic portrayal in *Kiss of the Spider Woman*, and at the age of seventy, received her eighth nomination for her supporting role in *Nine*.

broadway banter

"*I wanted to kill myself. When Rita got the Oscar for it, I wanted to kill Rita.*"

—Chita Rivera, on losing the role of Anita in the film West Side Story

ALSO ON THIS DAY

Chita's nemesis, Rita Moreno, was born in 1931. Despite her more prolific film career, including *Singin' in the Rain* and *The King and I*, Rita has made only one appearance in a Broadway musical—*Gantry*, which had just one performance.

12

December

(*1915*) Frank Sinatra was born today, or as my mom's friend's dad called him, Frank "Not-so-Hot-ra." I don't know if he made that one up, but to me, it works—we must be the only two Americans who don't quite get his appeal. My opinion withstanding, Frankie made some two dozen musicals in the golden era, though after becoming a "serious" actor, he sort of disavowed his musical work: "If I hadn't copped that Oscar [for *From Here to Eternity*], I'd still be working with Gene Kelly in sailor suits." Truth be told, he only sailed away with Gene twice, in *Anchors Aweigh* and *On the Town*, and played his baseball teammate in a third film, *Take Me Out to the Ball Game*.

broadway banter

"There's nothing like a PBS tribute to proclaim the death of an art form."

—*"Julie Andrews"* in Forbidden Broadway: SVU,
by *Gerard Alessandrini*

ALSO ON THIS DAY

The Actor's Fund of America held a benefit concert of *A Wonderful Life*, based on the classic holiday film, in 2005. The nontraditionally cast show starred Brian Stokes Mitchell and Judy Kuhn as George and Mary Bailey and David Hyde Pierce as Clarence.

13

December

(1972) Hell, Upside Down: *The Poseidon Adventure* opened across America. Unmusical as it may have seemed then, thirty years later it would spawn not one but two musical versions. *POSEIDON! An Upside-Down Musical*, by David Cerda, featured the delicious "Just Panties" for Linda Rogo (Stella Stevens) and "In the Water, I'm a Very Skinny Lady" for Belle Rosen (Shelley Winters). *The Poseidon Adventure: The Musical!*, by Bill Robens and Genemichael Barrera, which incorrectly billed itself as "The only ocean-liner-themed action-adventure movie told through interpretive song and dance!", also featured the same song title for Mrs. Rosen.

broadway banter

"*There Are Absolutely No Tickets for* Elaine Stritch: At Liberty—*Not Even One*"

—*A sign at the Public Theater*

STAR POWER

At the age of eight, Sammy Davis Jr. sang and danced his way through the title role in *Rufus Jones for President*. Ethel Waters played his mother in this short musical film about a young black dancer who is elected president of the United States. Their performances were spectacular, but the film's racial stereotypes make it all but unwatchable today.

14
December

(1963) Alice Ripley, one half of the onstage Siamese twins Daisy and Violet Hilton, was born today. Her cohort, Emily Skinner, was born June 20, 1970. The two rocketed to fame as the best things in the short-lived musical *Side Show*, and shared a Tony nomination for Best Actress. The two went on to do a number of other projects together, including *James Joyce's The Dead* and two duo CDs. Alice, who originated the role of Betty Schaefer in the Broadway *Sunset Boulevard,* also starred in *The Rocky Horror Show*, while Emily has appeared in *The Full Monty.*

broadway banter

"The movie is for the five-to-seven set and their mommies who think their kids aren't up to the stinging sophistication and biting wit of Mary Poppins.*"*

–Judith Crist, on The Sound of Music

IT TAKES A VILLAGE

Stewart Lee and Richard Thomas wrote *Jerry Springer: The Opera,* which debuted in London in 2004.

15
December

(1943) Ain't misbehavin' anymore: Thomas "Fats" Waller died today at just thirty-nine years old. His music was featured in several early all-black shows and movies, including *Hot Chocolates* on Broadway and *Stormy Weather* on screen, where he sang Nat "King" Cole's "That Ain't Right" and his own "Ain't Misbehavin'."

After the 1976 revue *Bubbling Brown Sugar* featured some of his songs, Richard Maltby Jr. fashioned his music into the hit revue *Ain't Misbehavin'*, showcasing his diverse range of hits like "Black and Blue," "Honeysuckle Rose," "Keepin' out of Mischief Now," and "The Joint Is Jumpin'."

broadway banter

"People ask me, 'Jimmy, how'd you get here tonight?' Let's just say it involved a two-hour make-out session with Elaine Stritch. It got pretty heavy actually, I almost had to host."

—Jimmy Fallon, on presenting at the Tonys

ALSO ON THIS DAY

A stage production of Disney's *Mary Poppins* opened in London in 2004.

16
December

(1899) Sir Noel Coward did it all: He served as actor, singer, playwright, songwriter, artist. Born today, he's best remembered for his urbane, sophisticated plays like *Private Lives*. But he also wrote a number of musicals and revues, as well as hundreds of songs that have made their way into revues, shows, and concerts. His *Words and Music* featured the wit of "Mad Dogs and Englishmen" and the torch song "Mad About the Boy," and *Bitter Sweet* introduced the eloquent "If Love Were All." He wrote the second female lead in *Sail Away* for Elaine Stritch, but in out-of-town tryouts, cut the leading lady from the show and combined the two roles together for Stritchie. He also directed his longtime friend Beatrice Lillie in *High Spirits*, a musical adaptation of his otherworldly comedy *Blithe Spirit*.

broadway banter

"You see, I never considered myself a singer. I was always an actress who told a story to the most beautiful music and the most beautiful words I could find."

—Liza Minnelli

POP QUIZ

Q: What is the highest-ranked quotation from a movie musical on the American Film Institute's "Top 100 Movie Quotes" list?

A: "Toto, I've got a feeling we're not in Kansas anymore," from *The Wizard of Oz*

17

December

(1980) Neil Diamond's film career began: *The Jazz Singer* premiered. Two hours later, it came to an end. To add insult to injury, Diamond later won the Golden Raspberry Award for Worst Leading Actor in a field that included fellow failed musical stars Bruce Jenner for *Can't Stop the Music* and Michael Beck for *Xanadu*. Meanwhile, his costar, greatest actor of the twentieth century Laurence Olivier, picked up his own Razzie for Worst Supporting Actor as Diamond's Jewish papa.

The infectious score, much of which Diamond wrote, received a Grammy nomination, and "Love on the Rocks" received a Golden Globe nomination, but the blackface number "You Baby" was given a Razzie nomination for Worst Song.

broadway banter

"Once upon a time, musical theater was the class of American pop culture, a source of democratic delight and artistic ingenuity. Now, many big musicals represent the lowest common denominator: theme park attractions for tourists."

–A.O. Scott

ALSO ON THIS DAY

Composer Jason Robert Brown made his Broadway debut at just twenty-nine with *Parade* in 1999, later winning the Tony for Best Score.

18
December

(1916) World War II pinup girl Betty Grable was born today. After a decade of minor film roles, mostly in musicals, she headed to Broadway, where audiences took more notice: In *DuBarry Was a Lady*, she scored a hit when she introduced the naughty Cole Porter ditty "Well, Did You Evah?" After that, it was back to Hollywood, where she was launched to fame with *Down Argentine Way* (a part she landed only after Alice Faye had to turn down the role because she needed an appendectomy). After a slew of musical roles, including *Moon Over Miami* and *Tin Pan Alley*, she retired from movies in 1955. In her fifties, she returned to Broadway as a replacement star in *Hello, Dolly!* She died a few years later of lung cancer.

broadway banter

"A director can't just say, 'Take it out.' Even Jerry Robbins couldn't take 'Little Lamb' out of Gypsy."

—Jule Styne

ALSO ON THIS DAY

Carol Burnett returned to the show that made her a star: *Once Upon a Mattress*, a new version of which aired on TV today in 2005. Burnett had originated the role of Princess Winnifred the Woebegone on Broadway in 1959. This time around, she took on the role of the worst potential mother-in-law in history, Queen Aggravain, while Tracey Ullman essayed the part of Winnifred.

(1957) *The Music Man* opened on Broadway. The show—practically perfect but utterly traditional—defeated the practically perfect and utterly groundbreaking *West Side Story* for the Tony award.

Robert Preston had never sung on Broadway prior to playing Professor Harold Hill, but he made the role his own with his unique speak-singing and infectious personality. The performer/role combination was so strong that fans of the show have never quite been able to erase the memory of Preston in the part. In 1980, the show came back to Broadway with Dick Van Dyke, surprisingly miscast, and the show's original Marcellus, Iggie Wolfington, now playing Mayor Shinn. A 2000 Broadway revival starred Craig Bierko, later succeeded by Robert Sean Leonard, and a 2003 TV version starred Matthew Broderick.

19
December

broadway banter

"Wet, she's a star. Dry, she ain't."

—Fanny Brice on Esther Williams

POP QUIZ

Q: Who sang the title role in the first concept album of *Evita*?

A: Julie Covington

20

December

(1979) Bob Fosse's thinly veiled autobiographical musical movie *All That Jazz* premiered today. Roy Scheider stood in for the egomaniacal director/choreographer/Casanova. Fosse dancer Leland Palmer stood in for Fosse dancer/estranged-wife Gwen Verdon. Ann Reinking stood in for Fosse dancer/girlfriend Ann Reinking (yes, she basically played herself, and had to audition to get the part). Jessica Lange, whose career had nowhere to go but up after making *King Kong*, stood in for the Angel of Death.

broadway banter

"It was like being shot out of a cannon."

—*Carol Burnett, on the concert version of* Follies

ALSO ON THIS DAY

Prolific movie director George Roy Hill was born today in 1921. One of my earliest film memories is watching a suspense/thriller of his when I was four years old. It scared the crap out of me! Years later, I realized that this "thriller" was actually the vanilla ice cream of movie musicals, *Thoroughly Modern Millie*, starring Julie Andrews, Mary Tyler Moore, Carol Channing, and Bea Lillie.

(**1937**) The animated musical is born: *Snow White and the Seven Dwarfs* premiered in Los Angeles. Three years and $1.5 million in the making, it was known at the time as "Disney's Folly." But from the minute it opened, the film was a surprise hit, grossing more than $8 million in its first release, the highest since D.W. Griffith's *The Birth of a Nation* in 1915.

21
December

broadway banter

Statler: *Well, how do you like the film?*

Waldorf: *I've seen detergents leave a better film than this.*

–The Muppet Movie, *by Jack Burns and Jerry Juhl*

STAR POWER

Chita Rivera did not get to reprise her role of Anita in the film *West Side Story*, but her then-husband, Tony Mordente, played Action, having originated the role of A-rab on stage.

December

(1976) *Your Arms Too Short to Box with God* opened on Broadway, the second musical based on the Gospel According to Matthew to open on Broadway in six months; the first was *Godspell*, a transfer from off-Broadway. *Arms* was conceived and directed by Vinnette Carroll, who had done the same with *Don't Bother Me, I Can't Cope* earlier in the decade. In doing so, Carroll became the first African-American woman to direct a Broadway show. Both shows featured music and lyrics by Micki Grant, who also contributed three songs to the 1978 production of *Working*.

broadway banter

"The lump in my throat was so big when I sang that I sounded more like Flip the Frog than the most excited girl in Hollywood."

–Judy Garland, on singing *"Over the Rainbow"* at the Oscars

POP QUIZ

Q: In the *Ziegfeld Follies* number "A Great Lady Has an Interview," what famous actress is Judy Garland parodying?

(1958) You're invited to a party: *A Party with Comden and Green,* which began a limited-engagement run on Broadway today. The writing team of Betty Comden and Adolph Green performed the musical material they had written over the last fifteen-plus years together, ranging from the skits they did in nightclubs as *The Revuers;* to their hit stage musicals *On the Town, Wonderful Town, Peter Pan,* and *Bells Are Ringing;* to their movie musicals *Bonanza Bound, Good News,* and *It's Always Fair Weather.*

December

After this party, they returned with another installment in 1977, including newer material from *Do, Re, Mi; Subways Are for Sleeping;* and *Straws in the Wind.* They went on to write several more shows together and continued performing together until Green's death in 2002.

broadway banter

"I think that Chris really captured something special about each of us, and I think it's completely faithful to the show. ..."

—Idina Menzel, on the film version of Rent

ALSO ON THIS DAY

In 2005, Broadway theater going more-or-less returned to normal following a rather scary two-day New York City Transit Workers Union strike. It was the first transit strike in that city in twenty-five years.

24

December

(1893) I Only Have Eyes for You: Harry Warren was born today. Along with lyricist Al Dubin, he wrote songs for most of the iconic movie musicals of the 1930s, including *42nd Street, Gold Diggers of 1933, 1935,* and *1937,* and *Go Into Your Dance.* He later paired up with Johnny Mercer ("Jeepers Creepers"), Mack Gordon ("Down Argentine Way," "Chattanooga Choo-Choo," and "You'll Never Know"), and Leo Robin ("Zing a Little Zong"). He also wrote the music for the ill-fated Broadway musical *Shangri-La.* Warren died in 1981, a year after his music was re-immortalized on Broadway in *42nd Street.*

broadway banter

"She is singing in a three-octave range and is stronger vocally than anyone could have imagined."

—David Gest, on his now-estranged wife, Liza Minnelli

CASTING COUCH

Replacing Alan Cumming in the 1998 revival of *Cabaret* were Neil Patrick Harris, Adam Pascal, Jon Secada, and John Stamos.

(1996) Don't cry for Madonna, Argentina. Her film vehicle *Evita* opened on Christmas Day, but it wasn't exactly a love-fest for this Madonna and her child. Reviews ranged from positive—"It's stunning, impressive cinema" (Liz Smith)—to tongue-in-cheek—"A $60 million Karaoke session" (Peter Travers)—to downright nasty—"this suffocatingly monotonous movie" (John Hartl). Madonna got luckier with the Hollywood Foreign Press, as *Evita* won three Golden Globe Awards, including Best Musical or Comedy and Best Actress in a Musical or Comedy for Madonna herself.

December

broadway banter

"Trunk songs mean nothing to me; they are songs written but used for one show that are stored and perhaps later dropped into another show, often with the aid of a shoehorn. I don't do that."

—Stephen Sondheim

POP QUIZ

Q: What MGM singing star was known as "The Iron Butterfly" and "The Lingerie Queen?

A: Jeanette MacDonald

26
December

(1931) *Alice in Wonderland* has been musicalized more often than just about any other work of literature. Today in 1985, another version emerged, adapted for television by Paul Zindel. The two-part mini-series was less memorable for its songs than its all-star lineup of stars, including Steve Lawrence and Eydie Gorme as Tweedledee and Tweedledum, Carol Channing as the White Queen, and Ringo Starr as the Mock Turtle; Oscar winners Ernest Borgnine, Red Buttons, Karl Malden, and Shelley Winters; as well as Sid Caesar, Imogene Coca, Sammy Davis Jr. Sherman Helmsley, Roddy McDowall, Jayne Meadows, Anthony Newley, Donald O'Connor, Martha Raye, Sally Struthers, Jonathan Winters, and many others.

broadway banter

"I think I saw him in Rent, *or* Stomp, *or* Clomp, *or some piece of crap."*

–*Homer Simpson in* The Simpsons

ALSO ON THIS DAY

Of Thee I Sing, a depression-era musical satire of American politics, opened on Broadway to rave reviews and terrific box office numbers. Penned by Moss Hart and George and Ira Gershwin, it also became the first musical to win the Pulitzer Prize for Drama.

27

December

(1901) The sexy but genderless Marlene Dietrich was born today. She never appeared in what was strictly a musical, but she managed to sing a number or two in nearly every film she made, starting with her breakout role in *The Blue Angel* in 1930. Equally at home in a revealing evening gown or a tuxedo, she introduced songs written for her by many great composers of the day, including Friedrich Hollaender, Frank Loesser, Cole Porter, and Jack Brooks. In her recordings, she leant her unique interpretation to dozens of standards and show tunes.

A naturalized American citizen, she won legions of fans for her USO performances during World War II, taking great risk to perform on the front lines in Europe after having refused to return to Germany and make movies for the Third Reich. In her fifties, sixties, and seventies, she toured extensively with nightclub acts and concerts, winning a special Tony in 1968.

broadway banter

"Dietrich singing 'The Boys in the Backroom' is a greater work of art than the Mona Lisa."

–Max Aitken

POP QUIZ

Q: What popular sitcom star played Harold Hill in *The Music Man* on Broadway in 2001?

A: Eric McCormack, of *Will & Grace*

December

(1944) Today, their names read like a "who's who" of musical theater, but at the time, the creators of *On the Town* were all newbies. The show, which opened on Broadway today, picked up where *Oklahoma!* left off in terms of integrating story, song, dance, and character, but this show added another key element to musical theater: sex. And who would have guessed it would come in the form of Nancy Walker, who lasciviously belted out "Come up to My Place" and "I Can Cook Too," and the show's co-authors, Comden and Green, who waxed operatic with "Carried Away."

broadway banter

"Having made the decision not to hide the performers within animal suits or behind masks, the challenge was to convey the animal's essence while maintaining the presence of the human."

—*Julie Taymor, on designing puppets/costumes for* The Lion King

POP QUIZ

Q: Who gave Sonja Henie a run for her money for the title of reigning queen of skating musicals in *The Ice Follies of 1939*?

(1933) At the height of his career, Eddie Cantor starred in *Roman Scandals*, released nationwide today. The vaudeville star of numerous editions of the *Ziegfeld Follies* and the stage and screen versions of *Whoopee* played a contemporary Oklahoman who dreams he is a slave back in ancient Rome. The comedy also starred nightclub singer Ruth Etting, future *Titanic* star Gloria Stuart, and, in her motion picture debut, Lucille Ball.

In 1992, Annie Lennox parodied the inherent misogyny of Al Dubin and Harry Warren's song from *Roman Scandals* "Keep Young and Beautiful" with a tongue-in-cheek recording on her *Diva* album.

29
December

broadway banter

"Puppet shows replace what we used to call content. ..."

–*"The Lion King,"* Forbidden Broadway Cleans Up Its Act,
by Gerard Alessandrini

IT TAKES A VILLAGE

Carol Reed won an Oscar for directing *Oliver!*, his first musical, having directed more adult-oriented films such as *The Fallen Idol*, *The Third Man*, and *The Agony and the Ecstasy*.

30
December

(2005) The woman who finally grew up: Fifty-three-year-old Cathy Rigby played her final New York performance as the boy who wouldn't grow up in her final farewell tour of *Peter Pan*. The two-time Olympic gymnast first played the role in 1990, receiving a Tony nomination. She brought it back in 1998, having toured with the show throughout the decade. Rigby also toured in the title role of *Annie Get Your Gun* and starred on Broadway and on tour as The Cat in The Hat in *Seussical*.

broadway banter

"The end of the movie, in a long single take, is a bravura stroke, brilliantly aware of the star as a performer and of the star's pride in herself as a performer. The pride is justified."

—*Pauline Kael*, on Funny Girl

POP QUIZ

Q: Who played Sally Bowles in the original London production of Cabaret?

A: Judi Dench

(1958) Almost the first baby of 1959, Bebe Neuwirth was born today. Before she played Frasier's icy wife Lilith on TV, she hoofed it in *A Chorus Line, Dancin', Little Me,* and *Xanadu,* then snagged the featured role of Nickie in the 1986 revival of *Sweet Charity,* winning a Tony. She was back on Broadway as Lola in *Damn Yankees* in 1994, then Fosse-ed her way to a second Tony playing Velma in the 1996 revival of *Chicago.*

Since then, she's become an interpreter of the work of Kurt Weill, starring as Jenny in the American Conservatory Theater production of *The Threepenny Opera* opposite Philip Casnoff, and singing in the Lincoln Center's *An Evening of Kurt Weill* and the off-Broadway revue *Here Lies Jenny.*

31
December

broadway banter

"The cast and audience had become one, united in the at least momentary conviction that A Chorus Line *was the best thing that had ever happened to any of us."*

−Frank Rich, on the special 3,389th performance

BY THE NUMBERS

In 2005, for possibly the first time in history, all four Best Musical nominees were still running more than six months after the Tony Awards.

ABOUT THE AUTHOR

JOE STOLLENWERK is the Artistic Director of Ovation Theatre Company in Cincinnati, Ohio. He is an actor, singer, director, writer, editor, teacher, and long-time musical theater fan. He holds a BA in Drama from Kenyon College, as well as a Master of Arts in English and a Master of Education, both from Xavier University.